ENDORSEMENTS

What would it be like to meet Jesus? This important question is probably considered by all Christians at some time. In *Revelations from Heaven*: *A True Account of Death, the Afterlife, and 31 Supernatural Discoveries* author Randy Kay provides important insights into this question as he dramatically describes encountering Jesus during his near-death experience (NDE). Consistent with what I found in my NDE research, this book describes the powerful love of Jesus and how important we all are to Jesus. With each turn of the page, you will find insights about Jesus that are profoundly inspirational. As an example, in a message of hope and reassurance Jesus tells Randy Kay "I am with you my beloved, always." You won't want to miss this outstanding book that is well written and enthusiastically recommended.

Jeffrey Long, MD
Author of the *New York Times* bestselling *Evidence of the Afterlife: The Science of Near-Death Experiences*, and *God and the Afterlife: The Groundbreaking New Evidence for God and Near-Death Experience*

"God's Spirit was drawing me to open my heart and unpack all of the treasures I had carefully locked away." Randy Kay is a remarkable man and a wonderful author. Best described as a skeptic in life, he was transformed by his meeting with Jesus. The quote above says it all. His heart was opened by the Lord. Randy's account of his amazing experience after death brings me to tears.

HEIDI TELPNER BARR, R.N.
Author of *One Foot in Heaven, Journey of a Hospice Nurse*

If reading and interviewing Randy Kay about his first book *Dying to Meet Jesus* was not awe inspiring enough, then prepare to enter a new dimension as you embrace his new book *Revelations from Heaven*. This biblically sound account of Randy's NDE takes you right into the heart of God so vividly that it is as if you are there by Randy's side as he describes more than we can ever hope for in the presence of God. If the encounter described is not enough, the truths revealed will profoundly change how you perceive and receive God's grace, wisdom, mercy, and love. We cannot live unless we die and through Randy Kay's experience those words carry more weight than we can even imagine. This is a life-changing read that will challenge you and bless you on multiple levels.

RABBI ERIC E. WALKER
Executive Director/On-Air Host
Revealing the Truth

Randy Kay's *Revelations from Heaven* is by far more than a book. My spirit was immediately awakened to the presence of Jesus in my room as I read. Each chapter invokes the person of Jesus. One of my many favorite quotes from Randy is "God lives on the other side of death." If you have lost a loved one or are now walking through loss, this book will release comfort and love to your soul. Randy shares heavenly experiences I never would have imagined could exist but now believe there is so much to look forward to in Heaven. Randy's love for Jesus will invoke in every reader a childlike sense of "I want that too."

BEATRIZ ZALDANA
Convergence Ministry
Winnetka, CA
bea@convergenceministry.org

In *Revelations from Heaven*, Randy Kay has given us a powerful and insightful gift! He says: "Before writing this, I prayed that God's wisdom would illuminate my ability to interpret a spiritual language into this world's dialect, so that I could help you understand, primarily, the love of God." That is what, more than anything else, these 31 revelations will reveal: The Love of God! In addition, you will find some of the best teaching on purpose that I have seen, as well as comfort and encouragement about the future, Heaven! You will find that Randy is not just a gifted writer, he is an excellent student of and teacher of the Bible. Don't be tempted to skip pages, or hurry to the end; there is too much enlightening information on every page and within each of the revelations. Take your time, ask God to show you what you need most—and what you need to share with others.

And Randy, thank you!

RICH MARSHALL
Author *God@Work* and *God@Work II*
Host of God@*Work* on GodTV

Author Randy Kay expertly unfolds the wonders of Heaven, which are far superior and more real than anything one can experience on earth. Randy's story is credible and his storytelling and choice of descriptive words are compelling. This book is a powerful testimony to what Heaven is really like and what is eternally true.

I recommend *Revelations from Heaven* to anyone seeking a reliable NDE account, but readers should be prepared. The reader will likely receive clearer meaning about their own life on earth, as well as deeper understandings about the One True God who rules and reigns in Heaven.

CAPT. DALE BLACK
Bible Teacher
Author *Flight to Heaven* and *Visiting Heaven*

Revelations from Heaven is a book that brilliantly combines sound theological and scientific research with the sublimely glorious spiritual journey the author experienced through an agonizing death and subsequent return to life. I can attest to the truth of this supernatural event because I was one of the friends at Randy Kay's bedside praying for his life as he lay dying. In the writing of this riveting book he weaves his miraculous half hour in Heaven with stories of his life, Bible teaching and best of all, the wisdom and thrilling words in 31 revelations from Jesus. This intensely moving book is to be savored and shared.

MARIE CHAPIAN
New York Times Bestselling author of *Angels in Our Lives,* and *Quiet Prayer, the Hidden Purpose and Power of Christian Meditation*

I, Dean Braxton, with great pleasure, endorse my friend Randy's book on his death experience. I also had a death experience that put me in Heaven, and I can tell you Randy's story of his time in that glorious place will build people's outlook on the good things in life in Heaven, as well as here on earth. I believe this book will bring hope and love to many that read it, and thoroughly believe that upon finishing this book you will have experienced happiness and love from your heavenly Father. So, with a big smile, enjoy this story of Heaven.

DEAN BRAXTON
Author of *In Heaven*

The testimonies and experiences of brother Kay are moving in such a way that many will find life changing. As someone who has been blessed to have Randy join our podcast, I have firsthand, interactive experience with the sense of reality he brings to his experience in Heaven, such that Jesus becomes His true self and fills you with a love for Him that could not be expressed in any other way. There is a spiritual "knowing" and a sense of intimacy that is communicated supernaturally through the words Randy shares.

We all need to know the Lord as our "First Love" (Revelation 2:4). For me this has been a struggle over the years because those of us who truly immerse ourselves in the scripture also know that Jesus spends much of His ministry correcting and warning people of their unrighteous behaviors. Sometimes it's challenging to realize how deep the Lord's love is for those He has chosen. The devil spends much of his time trying to convince us of how unworthy we are so we struggle to "fall in love" with God. This is our first commandment. Through Randy's anointed way of sharing what He experienced with Jesus, we are able to see Him for who He truly is and understand the depth of the blessing associated with Jesus' love for us, so we feel the same for Him. It changes you and empowers you to overcome the struggles of daily life in hope of the promise that awaits us all. God bless you Randy for your work in this book and I pray it touches the hearts of as many of God's chosen as possible.

JOHNNY BAPTIST
Tribulation Now podcast

"It was the most freeing experience of my life." Wow! Dying was the most freeing experience for Randy Kay. I have never met someone with a near-death experience before. Randy is the real deal. He is so full of life because he understands what God has given him in this world. This book, *Revelations from Heaven,* will transform you into a better version of yourself. You will see the world differently. You will love people more. You will love life more. Why? Because Randy has a supernatural gift from God to walk us through His personal experience as if we were there ourselves. Prepare to be transformed. Prepare to be elevated to the next level in your walk as a human being. I'm blown away and you will be too.

Brae Wyckoff,
President of Kingdom Creativity International,
Director of Kingdom Writers Association,
and award-winning author
www.BraeWyckoff.com

Revelations From Heaven by Randy Kay needs to be read by anyone interested in Christianity and the intersection with near death experiences. For some on both sides of these subjects, there are differences of opinion about correctness and suspicion. If one reads Randy Kay's book they will find wonderful mutual compatibility and harmony from both perspectives. This book is much more than an academic exercise because Randy has also made his life vividly transparent, which is honest beyond doubt. If you want a really good read and to learn more than you ever knew about how the faith in Jesus Christ is revealed in the personal experience of an articulate man, this is the testimony for you. Congratulations, Randy, on your contribution to our salvation.

Reverend Howard Storm
Author of *My Descent Into Death* and *Befriend God: Life with Jesus*

In his book, *Revelations From Heaven,* Kay gives insight and answers to theological questions that have puzzled believers for centuries. His recall of his visitation to Heaven and his descriptions of Hell and all curiosities of the afterlife, are especially fascinating. He delves into subjects that most would never venture, but that all would want to have clarity and answers. And in his easy style, through his great storytelling gift, Kay paints pictures that bring God's truths to light.

Needless to say, Kay's book, *Revelations From Heaven*, is one of the most captivating and interesting reads that I have picked up in a long time. It is revealing, compelling, captivating and an overall, wonderful read.

TOMMY BARNETT
Global Pastor, Dream City Phoenix
Co-Pastor, Los Angeles Dream Center

After reading Randy Kay's book I could only think of this great verse: *"Teach us to number our days and recognize how few they are; help us to spend them as we should"* (Psalm 90:12 The Living Bible). We need to be about the business of Heaven during our few minutes on earth.

Somehow, his 30-minute tourist stop in Heaven inspired me to work harder to live "God's will on earth as it is in Heaven." As I read Randy's account, I felt myself wanting to share the experience with him. *"For indeed in this house we groan. longing to be clothed with our dwelling from heaven"* (2 Corinthians 5:2). *Revelations of Heaven* is a page-turner that left me wanting to know more, read more, and learn more from this gifted author.

DR. STEVE GREENE
Executive Vice President
Publisher, Charisma Media Group
Executive Producer of the Charisma Podcast Network

It is said that a man with a testimony is never at the mercy of an argument. The sharing of these life changing experiences challenges each of us to elevate our perspective of God and eternity. Your view on eternal things will change not only how you think about this life but indeed how you live it. May the reading of this book challenge you to cultivate an eternal biblical perspective on the life you live.

JURIE KRIEL
Senior Pastor at 5twelve City Church
Austin, Texas

In Randy Kay's book, *Revelations From Heaven*, he shares his intriguing encounter with Jesus Christ in Heaven from a NDE, near death encounter. Being a former agnostic qualified Randy in a unique way for this supernatural encounter. If you have ever wondered what it was like to die, read this book. It is intriguing. Very few people can share their story of death. Randy's descriptive account of his physical struggle to breathe and his awareness of his impending death is unforgettable.

Randy shares amazing stories of his life with miracles that will restart your heart faith in places where you have succumbed to doubt. Randy's medical field analytical approach of comparing Christianity and other religions when he was an agnostic in college is brilliant with clarifying insights that even many Christians may not know. Beyond these facts is Randy's heavenly encounter. As I was reading his book, the presence and the love Jesus Christ that touched him was touching me. His encounter with Jesus was filled with unyielding intimacy and extraordinary love.

Randy had more attitudes towards God than expectations, but he was very honest in midst of his doubts concerning God. I found his story to be refreshing to my spirit, and mentally challenging to my deep faith in Jesus Christ. This book should be read by believers to gain a greater understanding of Him, Jesus Christ. This book is a treasure gift to given to others that doubt God's existence and His love for humanity. I have never read another book like it. Randy's book, *Revelations From Heaven*, is beyond fascinating, it is heart changing. Take a journey to Heaven with Randy and meet an amazing Jesus.

Dr. Dale L Mast
International Speaker and Senior Pastor
Author of *And David Perceived He Was King,*
Two Sons and A Father, The Throne of David,
and *Shattering The Limitations of Pain*

I am a hope fanatic. I love accounts of signs, miracles, and wonders because I have personally experienced the supernatural side of God. There is so much hope in Randy's testimony of his time in Heaven. This is not just another book on near death experience. It is a contemplative, Scripture-fulfilling witness to the majesty and love of our heavenly Father, and His amazing Kingdom. If you need hope and a future, read this next-level revelation of King Jesus and His plan for your destiny. It's good, I promise you that. It will transform your thinking and activate that piece of eternity God Almighty placed in your heart (Ecclesiastes 3:11). It sure did mine!

Troy Brewer
Senior Pastor, OpenDoor Church, Burleson, Texas
Author of *Redeeming Your Timeline: Supernatural*
Skillsets for Healing Past Wounds, Calming Future
Anxieties, and *Discovering Rest in the Now*

OTHER BOOKS BY RANDY KAY

Dying to Meet Jesus

The Power to Thrive!

The 22 Most Important Things

Daily Keys to Success

REVELATIONS
—— *from* ——
HEAVEN

A True Account of
Death, the Afterlife, &
31 Supernatural Discoveries

RANDY KAY

DESTINY IMAGE® PUBLISHERS, INC.

P.O. Box 310, Shippensburg, PA 17257-0310

"Promoting Inspired Lives."

This book and all other Destiny Image and Destiny Image Fiction books are available at Christian bookstores and distributors worldwide.

Cover design by Eileen Rockwell

Interior design by Terry Clifton

For more information on foreign distributors, call 717-532-3040.

Reach us on the Internet: www.destinyimage.com.

ISBN 13 TP: 978-0-7684-5937-1

ISBN 13 eBook: 978-0-7684-5938-8

ISBN 13 HC: 978-0-7684-5940-1

ISBN 13 LP: 978-0-7684-5939-5

For Worldwide Distribution.

1 2 3 4 5 6 7 8 / 25 24 23 22 21

DEDICATION

This book is dedicated to my best Friend and my revered God, Jesus Christ. Thank You for allowing me stay at Your place for a while.

ACKNOWLEDGMENTS

Writing a book about Heaven and what I learned during this period took me to places I previously thought defied description, and to my family in Heaven that I will always remember. None of this would have been possible without the driving influence of God's Spirit. Jesus hugged me as my body slowly died and as we journeyed through Heaven. I am nothing without Jesus, and everything of value with Him.

I'm eternally grateful to my wife, Renee, who supported me through the many hours, days, and nights I labored trying to put thoughts to words. She knew that the consuming process of authoring this book would require sacrifices, and yet she felt my message important enough for me to spend countless hours and efforts in completing this work.

This might appear obvious, but I must thank the Holy Spirit and all of those who have spoken into my life with His leading for giving me the inspiration to write of things that are clearly beyond my limited capacity to express them. I read back over some of what I typed with my own hands thinking, *Did this really come from me?* In those cases, I think the correct answer is: No, they only came through me.

A warm appreciation for John Burke, who spent decades of his life researching near-death experience stories to substantiate the validity of those true accounts of the afterlife. Largely because of his book, *Imagine Heaven,* I felt liberated to share my own story.

Thank you to my publisher, Destiny Image, and specifically Shaun Tabatt, who enabled me to get this book to as many who might be blessed by it.

A very special thanks to my children, Ryan and Annie, who blessed me with their childhood and youth, and who now honor me with their character. And to my extended family members, Jonathan and Florencio, who blessed me with their lives while I adopted them into my heart.

Finally, to all those who have been part of my spiritual journey: Rich Marshall, John Burke, Joe Irwin, Sheila Harden, Ted Lloyd Jones, Sheri Briggs, Kenny Crews, Judy Bay, Vic Hisaw (in Heaven), and Wayne Miller (in Heaven). And finally, to that little boy dying of cancer in the hospital who prayed for me and I met again in Heaven—thank you.

CONTENTS

FOREWORD

WHEN I FIRST met Randy, I was impressed by several qualities. First, Randy is a CEO with a past career in the medical profession, which got him featured in an article in Time magazine. He's had fame and fortune. Randy has nothing to gain and everything to lose by making up stories of visiting Heaven. Randy fits the exact profile I looked for as I studied over 1000 cases of Near Death Experiences (NDEs), where people clinically died, yet modern medicine resuscitated them.

As a former engineer, I have a skeptical bent. I wrote *Imagine Heaven* to show how the commonalities reported by thousands of NDEs around the world align spectacularly with the Bible. And I looked for those stories where there could be no ulterior motives. So, when Randy contacted me after reading *Imagine Heaven* and having a story of his own to share, I was eager to meet with him.

As my son and I enjoyed a meal with Randy at a harborside restaurant in San Diego, I was struck by the second quality you should know about Randy—his humble posture and overwhelming, sincere love for God. When you sit across the table from a person who has clinically died, and you hear the person tell of their experience in God's presence, there's an authenticity and emotion to their retelling that leaves you realizing, "This person has been deeply changed by this experience." There is no doubt about Randy's integrity or sincerity.

Since that first meeting, I've become friends with Randy, and I've heard Randy tell of his encounter with Jesus four or five times. He's never been able to talk about Jesus embracing him without becoming overwhelmed with emotion—as if his mortal body cannot contain the depth or breadth of Jesus's love, and that he's once again experiencing that love in the retelling. In my study, many NDErs say their memory of Heaven is not like other memories. They say, as Randy does, that it's as present and real today as it was then, no matter how many years ago it happened.

Randy's the real deal. He deeply loves Jesus and follows him wholeheartedly. You can't easily fake the kind of heartfelt emotion I've witnessed every time he speaks of being with Jesus, and what reason would Randy have to fake it? He didn't need money or fame, nor did he desire to be thought of as semi-crazy by some of his colleagues in the medical field or professional world. But Randy met Jesus, and he can't deny it. That encounter changed him forever.

In *Dying to Meet Jesus*, Randy tells of the struggles and challenges he's faced in life as well as his encounter with Jesus when his body shut down in the hospital that day. In his new book, *Revelations from Heaven*, Randy recounts more of the conversations and the lessons learned from being with Jesus, and he helps us apply these valuable lessons in practical ways today.

These are not new revelations, as in adding to what's already been revealed in the Bible, but more like elucidations or insights of what it means to live the teachings of Jesus. For instance, God tells us in scripture we have been created for a purpose. We all want to know our purpose. What is it? How can we know if we are fulfilling it?

Well, Randy asked this to Jesus directly. The answer Jesus gave Randy perfectly aligns with what the Bible records, and yet the way he explained it to Randy gives me so much peace, realizing I can know I'm fulfilling God's purpose for me. I was so glad I brought my son to lunch that day, just so he would hear Randy explain what Jesus said about finding purpose. I think you'll agree, that insight alone is worth the whole book, but there are many more insights to help you fall deeply in love with Jesus and walk intimately with Him for a lifetime.

There's been some criticism that Christian NDEs are adding to what God has revealed in scripture. That is not at all what Randy does in this book, but rather, these revelations (or insights) help us live what Jesus taught in order to grow closer to the God of the Bible.

Of course, some NDE interpretations of their experiences will not align with what God revealed in scripture, and in that case, I advise people to trust what God said in scripture. After studying over 1000 NDE testimonies, I've concluded that what they reveal (the commonalities of their experiences) perfectly align with the Bible. But NDEs are truly an out-of-this-world experience, so each person is left "interpreting" that experience in their own under-standing and worldview.

That's why I do not advise a person to form their understand-ing, or theology, of the afterlife from NDE accounts. First, these people did not die fully; they came back. And a commonality I found was NDErs saying they came to a border or boundary they intuitively knew they could not cross and still come back to earth. So NDEs cannot tell us what's beyond the border (into eternity), but God has revealed that through the scriptures. So scripture should interpret NDEs, not the other way around.

But where scripture gives us a black-and-white picture of the life to come, these NDE stories add color to the picture God has already drawn. They help us imagine Heaven, so we will live for it, and we are commanded to imagine it and live for it: "Set your minds on things above, not on earthly things" (Colossians 3:2). *Revelations from Heaven* will help you do just that.

JOHN BURKE

Pastor and author of the *New York Times* bestseller,
Imagine Heaven: Near-Death Experiences, God's Promises, and the Exhilarating Future that Awaits You

INTRODUCTION

I WROTE A BOOK about brokenness titled *Dying to Meet Jesus*, in which I briefly mentioned my afterlife experience. To my surprise, the number-one-rated audience for this book was people dealing with suicide. I received some heartfelt communications from people who either lost a loved one, suffered from hardship, or who had become hopeless.

A few people noted their disappointment that I had not shared the entirety of my time in Heaven after clinically dying in the hospital. They wanted to know the full measure of my experience, and the epiphanies that changed my life forever.

After seeking the Holy Spirit's wisdom, it became clear to me that the revelations I once considered personal needed to be shared with others. When I began writing, what seemed too ethereal to accurately express to others flowed out with a clarity of thought I once thought impossible. That is when I realized my inspiration was not just mine, it came from the One who served as my constant Companion in Heaven.

For several years following my death, I kept private my afterlife experience. It was too personal. I kept it tucked inside my heart and locked within a personal treasure chest. In the back of my mind I feared that some might dismiss the experience that transformed my life. Besides, it was mine.

I did share it with less than a handful of loved ones by using superlatives like "amazing," "incredible," and most commonly, "Jesus is like nothing I imagined." Others could not possibly comprehend what happened. It would be like trying to explain the thrill of a mountaintop experience to someone who had never seen a mountain. Attempting to explain Heaven in a language for which there are no words to describe it, would be more difficult than nailing pudding to a wall. And how do you explain the quintessence of love? Or the spiritual truths that transformed me while in Heaven by authoring them in a physical world limited by time, space, and comprehension?

While I wrote about brokenness that briefly mentioned my near-death experience, I felt that my dearest Friend and Abba Father wanted others to better understand the fullness of God's adoration for them. We gifted several of my books to people struggling with disabilities, broken souls tormented with thoughts of suicide, and soldiers with post-traumatic stress disorder (PTSD). Apparently, the overwhelming love of Jesus Christ broke through my inability to fully express that love, just enough to draw some people closer to God so that they could discover the answer to their suffering. But again, several readers wanted to know what it was like to be face-to-face with Jesus within a tangible body.

That is when it hit me. God's Spirit was drawing me to open my heart and unpack all of the treasures I had carefully locked away. I laid them out in my mind. I dusted off the journals that I completed following my resuscitation after my heart and brain died. The memories were as fresh as the day Jesus gave them to me.

God's revelations had transformed my approach to life, fueled new meaning, and now it is time to share them with others—with you.

MY GREATEST FEAR CAME TO LIFE

Most of my life I have battled some form of disease. I spent a few of my first days as an infant in the hospital suffering from asthma and a collapsed lung. My teenage brother and sister hardly wanted to pound my back at night to release the congestion from my lungs, so mother assumed that nightly task. She would pound me on the back each morning and night while I sweated on the bed or floor, gasping in a panic. Many days and nights throughout my life I struggled to breathe, even to this day, and several times my weakened lungs have contracted life-threatening pneumonia.

When the illnesses that finally "killed" me started taking hold, I thought it peculiar that God would allow me to literally suffocate to death since as a child I have continually struggled to breathe causing me to fear suffocation more than anything else. That fear grew so strong that I even resisted going into the pool because during swimming I could not breathe freely. Just before my near-death experience (NDE),I considered how my life started with deprived oxygen and it would end the same way.

Even as I author this book, my breathing is labored. I have damaged lungs, damaged valves in my venous system, and a susceptibility to infections. I say this not to elicit any sympathy, rather to testify that God is strong in my weakness, and often uses the very impediment we experience in life as a vehicle to heal or assuage others of similar handicaps.

In like manner, as a former agnostic and NDE skeptic I have found myself speaking to people with the same predispositions I held before knowing Jesus Christ as my Lord and Savior, and previous to my own NDE. This strikes me with the same irony with which God allowed a person with damaged lungs and a fear of suffocation to succumb to a similar malady that initially caused that fear.

Now I believe that Heaven reflects a similar type of twist. Heaven is indescribable, and yet I felt compelled to try to put that experience into words despite my propensity toward denying what defies understanding. I am a very practical person, and I am clinically minded having taught surgeons and other clinicians about cardiovascular surgery and neurology within the hospital setting for major corporations. Heaven defied my ability to fully describe its majesty despite my evaluative mind that never previously settled for inexactness—that is, before my mind became bedazzled in Heaven. My rational mind was forced to give way to my spiritual mind in Heaven. To this day, I still struggle with the right words to describe Heaven because most of the words required to adequately describe Heaven do not exist in any of the world's lexicons.

MY FIRST LESSON WAS UNDERSTANDING HEAVEN'S BUILDER

If you want to know what Heaven looks like, you must first seek to understand its Builder. Everything in Heaven reflects God's glorified craftsmanship. God is Love and Heaven reflects that Love. God cherishes His children and desires to give them good gifts, and in Heaven I was lavished with gifts both spiritually and visually breathtaking—and instead of new clothes, I received a new body. God's brilliance and the Holy Spirit's comfort is reflected in the vastness of the universe; and likewise, Heaven reflects that same wondrous expanse within a cozy and uplifting embrace.

God created every living color, sound, being, and fragrance, and in Heaven those same aspects are magnified a thousandfold greater than any on this earth. In comparison, this world now oftentimes seems mundane to me whereas Heaven was infinitely more interesting and engaging with an overabundance of activities steeped in purposefulness, unlike the sometimes trivial pursuits in this world.

But of course, no creation exceeds the wonder of its creator. My greatest gift in Heaven was time spent with Jesus, and our conversations that elucidated all that mattered most. Before desiring that same experience, remember that for just about everyone, that requires dying first. Let's start there.

During that fateful time, I was dying, and I did not even know it. Everything appeared normal, and then it was not. It started during an average day. But more about that later…

I CAN ONLY OFFER A GLIMPSE OF HEAVEN

Some of the stories contained in this book are used to help elucidate incomprehensible impressions or visions. Heaven is akin to this world in some respects and diametrically different in other ways. Superior to the spiritual reality of Heaven is the transformative presence of Jesus Christ that permeates all of Heaven and those who inhabit it. My revelations happened through understanding the truths that transformed my life. Years later I would understand that these revelations were not just for me, they are for you as well.

Before my NDE, I discounted near-death experiences, just as before becoming born again I discounted Jesus Christ as my Lord and Savior. I do not come from a natural inclination to believe in the spiritual realm. My world used to be exclusively practical and world-based. Though I still struggle with the temptations of this world, I am no longer a skeptic. I would be a fool to think other-wise. All of my degrees and accomplishments used to focus me on the things of this world. It took death to focus me on the things of God. In Heaven, unlike in this world, God consumed my entire focus so that I could focus only on those things that matter most to God.

At first I felt obligated to delve into a proof of NDEs in order to validate my own experience, and then I simply accepted my vis-itation as sufficiently merited based on its profound impact on my life. To date I have lost more material wealth in sharing my after-life experience than I have gained. Professionals and clinicians with whom I routinely worked tend to view me differently. Previously, my clinical and professional peers perceived me as a rational and scientifically based individual. Much has changed since being asked about my NDE during an interview with a former pastor of mine who at the time hosted a television program on GodTV. He was but a handful of persons who knew about my time in Heaven. While discussing on television with him my decades-long research project on the principles needed to thrive in life and sharing my NDE, I instantly became the example of the person I once criti-cized. I had never shared my story with friends and acquaintances, let alone a television audience of millions.

I am by vocation and training a human development researcher, medical advisor, businessperson, and director of clinical sup-port. I started a human development firm, and before that I was a corporate executive in the healthcare field and CEO of a bio-tech company. My first "real" jobs were as a journalist, advertiser, and sales/marketing professional. I lived within the materialistic and physical realities of my environments. I became a Christian after being an agnostic. I studied the sciences and assisted with cardiovascular and neurological procedures while leading clinical teams for major corporations. My mindset was primarily fact based. Having experienced Heaven, I can now accept the realities of this spiritual place as fact—not just faith.

This book is about my observations and my interpretations of them. I believe in the accuracy of the Bible, as I will explain later, and in the Bible as God's inspired Word. I have taught in churches, completed a Christian ordination, and have participated in several Christian charities. I say this not to boast, rather to state that I am a genuine believer in Jesus Christ as my Lord and Savior. I am flawed but redeemed through Christ. I consider myself as the least worthy to express the magnificence of God's Kingdom in Heaven. Some theologians are more comfortable with my expressing my NDE as a vision, rather than a genuine encounter in Heaven. I can best explain my encounter as being more real than any involvement in this world, as I will later describe.

Much has been made of NDEs, some based on an encounter with God, and some being related to consciousness or a metaphysical experience. Some describe God as "an orb of light," or as qualities apart from any physical characteristics. A number of theologians point to the fact that in the Bible, those who experienced an afterlife did not explain their post-life experience in detail, as I have in this book, or as with several other modern era accounts. While interpretations of near-death experiences vary, a multitude of studies both scientifically and biblically based conclude that NDEs are medically inexplicable, absent normal brain functions, and not explicitly refuted by Scriptures.

My account focuses on the same Jesus Christ as recorded in the Bible. Why did I walk and talk with Jesus unlike some other strictly metaphysical accounts? I can only state my opinion, which is that my encounter was to focus on the love of Jesus Christ in a kindred way that, for me, served to dispel some of the unrelatable aspects of God and "the universe," which place the afterlife in an unfamiliar context apart from the kindred friendship I enjoyed in Heaven. My takeaway from Heaven is that God loves us more than we could possibly comprehend.

One can deny the reality of my account in Heaven, but the fact remains that I clinically died. I was a denier of NDEs before my own NDE, and I did not share my NDE publicly because it was just too personal. I felt that sharing my story would jeopardize my standing in the business and medical communities, and possibly even within some of my Christian circles. It took fourteen years before an interview on GodTV about another subject—thriving in life—exposed my NDE. After that, I felt God wanted me to make my account public, and even then I only briefly mentioned it in my book about suffering titled, *Dying to Meet Jesus*. It took almost two more years before I finally felt compelled to open my journals and share the full account of my time in Heaven in this book.

Not only did I feel released by my Lord and Savior to share my full story, but I also felt obliged to tell what I learned during my time in Heaven, and how those learnings would translate beyond just me to anyone who would care enough to read this book. At times while reading *Revelations From Heaven* you will discover my experiences in Heaven with Jesus, and at times I will share the revelations that ensued after my encounters.

What you are about to read is both practical and ethereal. Applications in this book will hopefully inspire a greater closeness to God and a deeper insight into the love that Jesus has for you. I will show you glimpses of Heaven threaded through this book as best as I can describe them. I will share with you what Jesus said to me. I will share my revelations about our purposes, our Kingdom impacts, and our most important qualities.

UNDERSTANDING THE TYPICAL NDE PERSPECTIVES

I realize that many of those who claim to have experienced an NDE recount a variable potpourri of explanations as to the essence of Heaven. Some maintain what I call a "generalist" description of Heaven with no reference to a divine presence while using positive emotions to explain a personal impression of Heaven or paradise. Some ascribe their experience with an enlightening presence in a "universalist" context, where there is either no deity or that deity maintains a state of shared consciousness. Others describe a kind of Shangri-la from a "utopianist" perspective, where Heaven in itself constitutes an idyllic place of perfection.

Many theologians tend toward a more scholarly description of Heaven from either a belief in premillennialism or postmillennialism, which essentially describes God as creating a new earth that is often described as a paradise, apart from the throne room of God. Classical Christian "theologists" believe in a "status intermedius" state where our disembodied spirits or souls await the final consummation when our glorified bodies are resurrected, however immediately after death our spirits go into the presence of Jesus Christ.

Generalists, universalists, utopianists, and theologists explain Heaven as a place. For me, Heaven is identified by a person, Jesus Christ. As we journey together, I pray that my Christian brothers and sisters will be assuaged with my firm belief in Jesus Christ as my Lord and Savior, as you will realize in this book. For my generalist friends who struggle with the legalism of Christianity, I encourage you to bear with me as I explain Heaven as more than just a place, while introducing you to the most freeing experience of my life.

For my universalist friends, it would be my honor to bring you closer to knowing God as a Friend who issues forth the peace for which we all yearn. For my utopianist friends, I too experienced paradise, and yet I also experienced the Author of that paradise whose grace I can only hope to express in some small measure through this book. For my theologists friends, I sojourned in Heaven for a brief time to confirm what you so eloquently explain from your studied position. I write to you not as a seer, but as a witness of Jesus Christ in Heaven.

MY TREASURE IS NOW YOURS

Writing has been one of my passions since taking courses at Northwestern University's renowned Medill School of Journalism. Thousands of published articles and several business books supported my love of putting ideas to print. When I wrote my first "Christian book" about suffering and brokenness, I ended that book by including a section from my journal about my experience in Heaven. At the last minute, I spoke with my literary agent asking him if I should delete this part since I did not want my near-death experience to be the focal point of my book. "No," he said, "I think it's important to the story."

I followed his advice. After many people read *Dying to Meet Jesus,* a common thread of comments appeared that indicated readers wanted to hear my full story about Heaven, but I believe God wanted more than just another account of Heaven. I believe God also wanted Heaven to serve as the way we should live upon this earth.

As before, when writing this book I struggled to share my account. At times I even wished I could place my NDE story back in my private memory bank as though no one but a handful of close loved ones would again know my secret. After all, my business had suffered since publishing the book that introduced my NDE. I faced criticisms from some people. My comfortable life changed. But then the Holy Spirit spoke to me again through a profound session of prayer between my wife and me. "Tell it all," I heard my Lord's Spirit say. "Share the truths you learned, and I will honor you." It was then that I realized my selfishness in not telling everything about what I experienced and learned.

At that moment I understood that my learnings from Heaven were not just for me. They are for you as well. Now the full account of my time in Heaven is yours for reading this book. I give you not only my story, but I also mentally sacrifice my fears in sharing my greatest treasure with those who might think of them as less than the "pearls" they represent to me. I give you Heaven and what Heaven taught me. I give you the truth. I give you my heart. I give you my profound discovery of God's Love. I pray that you, like me, will find Heaven as a light to show you the way in your life in this world.

With Love,

Randy Kay

1

DYING

O NE FATEFUL EVENING I stared at the light gray ceiling that flashed a violet color from the moonlight shining through the bedroom window. A shadow from the ceiling fan cast a figure whose arms reached along the wall to the plaster above—an ominous sign reflecting my darkened soul.

"I'm angry with You, God," I shouted while alone in bed. "I thought I knew You, and now I don't."

If rage were a color, it would be the muddied, weather-beaten burnt sienna sludge of my thoughts during those moments. *I want to say that I hate You, but that would mean that I believed in You enough to hate You.* That sentiment was birthed from the mind of a man who had served as a church deacon, taught church classes, and gave an Easter message in front of more than 1,000 congregants. I was a hypocrite, I suppose. Or at least, I felt that way now.

Just months ago I was in Washington, DC, to help launch a new "cure" for Alzheimer's after my pharmaceutical company's new drug was featured on the front cover of *Time* magazine. The FDA forced a recall of the drug after some patients in the last clinical stage developed swelling in their brains. So I was laid off. My wife and I then invested in a biotech company, which drained our resources, and then a newspaper, which exhausted the rest of our financial reserves. We were left with two young children to support and a big mortgage. All this after working on average at least 80 hours a week. This was not just a crisis of faith—it was a Chernobyl-like meltdown on a personal level.

"You need to show up this time," I declared to an unseen God, as if He might show up like the ultimate superhero. I actually waited in silence, halfway expecting the ceiling to part while a huge figure dressed in a white flowing gown replete with a white beard darted forth on a white horse. I was that desperate. But alas, no one showed up, and I actually felt like God was mocking me at this point.

"Okay, God, if You personally and audibly spoke with Moses, Noah, Abraham, Jacob, Paul, and even through a donkey, for goodness' sake, then why can't You just show up for me? I want to at least hear Your resounding voice in this room right now."

I waited for several minutes, futilely in hindsight, because He never showed up, not even a tiny whisper. *That's how much God cares for me*, I thought.

So I gave God an ultimatum. "Either You show up, God, or I…" I dared not finish the sentiment. If He were listening, surely He knew the bottomless pit from which I cried. One last chance… to believe that God was not just a figment of my imagination.

Little did I know that two weeks later God would indeed answer my request. But it would only happen after I died.

I WAS DYING

Now we're headed in the right direction, I thought while flying west from Newark Airport about two weeks after that crisis of faith tirade I had directed toward God in my bedroom. After a long day of interviews, I could finally relax. The three-hour time change forced me to get up at 3:00 a.m. my time to meet the hiring vice president at Johnson & Johnson in Summerville, New Jersey.

I had been trained in business, pharmacology, and surgery over the course of two decades, and had been licensed or certified in both business and clinical skills with a degree from Northwestern University in biology and having completed graduate business courses. After serving as the CEO of a biotech company and operations director for a major pharmaceutical company, I felt competent to lead a team of clinicians, sales, and marketing people in this minimally invasive cardiovascular division.

Two coffees in the morning and later a couple of Cokes got me through the day. After take-off I angled my body against the corner of the window seat and laid my head back. My mind replayed each interview. *Seemed to go well overall.* After a few minutes of this I faded to sleep.

I awoke from the change in altitude. My ears felt plugged as I looked over the buildings of San Diego underneath, and the Bay packed with boats. My wife picked me up at curbside with all of the questions one might expect.

"How'd it go?"

"Fine, I think I did well."

"Did they say when they would let you know?"

"In a couple of days, I think."

My mind kept drifting toward the silhouette of the ocean to our left against the evening sky. Fatigue never left me since take-off. When we pulled up the driveway, I grabbed my bag, crossed the threshold, and greeted our 10-year-old son, Ryan, and 8-year-old daughter, Annie. Then up the stairs to bed for an early slumber.

The next day an early morning stream of light beamed through the window—another beautiful day in Carlsbad, California. Everyone else slept, so I went downstairs to grab my bicycle. My calf ached. *Maybe a cramp*, I thought. Nothing would deter me from reaching the ocean. I took a sip from my water bottle. When I got there, the waves crashed like soothing music to my ears. I cycled along the two-lane road on Highway 101, entranced by the sun's reflection against the glassy ocean surface.

Normally the ocean would clear my lungs from the allergies and asthma that plagued me all of my life. The flat road posed no struggle, and yet each turn of the peddles felt like I was ascending a steep hill. I reached down to my right calf. The skin was taut, the calf swollen. Still, I could not help but be mesmerized by the ocean sounds and the sunshine spreading its warmth on this cool morning adventure. It would be a shorter trip than normal, though.

Fatigue from the long trip probably lingered, I reasoned because of jet lag. *I didn't drink enough water, so my calf is just cramping and swollen from the exercise.* I continued reasoning. By the time I returned home my chest felt tight. I started making breakfast, bacon and eggs, but needed to empty the garbage first. A short trip from the kitchen counter to the side yard seemed more like a hundred-yard sprint by the time I reached the garbage bins.

I wheezed heavily at this time, so I took a few shots of my albuterol inhaler to get relief. Strangely, the inhaler did nothing to help. I ascended the stairs to take a shower. It felt like climbing Mount Everest. I stopped to grab the railing for a rest, taking a deep breath that did nothing to relieve the increasing pressure on my chest.

"What's wrong," Renee asked as I entered the bedroom.

"I'm just…a little more…winded today," I answered.

In the shower, I noticed that my calf had swelled to about one and a half times its normal size. After getting dressed, I walked backed down to the kitchen feeling like someone had tied a ten-pound weight to my lower right leg.

Renee finished making breakfast that Friday morning as I pressed my arms against the counter heaving, trying to hide the anxiety that surged within me.

"Maybe I should…go to the orthopedic doctor," I said. "I should…get a prescription…for an anti…inflammatory."

"You're having trouble breathing. This isn't normal," Renee replied.

"I know, and my calf hurts. I think it's…from the exercise."

I wanted to believe that this was a simple muscle strain coupled with asthma. We were planning a trip to Joshua State National Park. In fact, the rented RV would be pulling up anytime. We had been planning this trip for months.

The phone rang.

"Randy, I wanted to call you before the weekend." It was the hiring vice president from Johnson & Johnson. My heart raced even faster than it did previously because of my forced breathing.

"Great to hear from you, Mary." It was all I could do to speak without pausing to breathe.

"We would like to offer you the job to manage the West, and we will bridge your service to account for the years you worked with J&J in the past."

That alone would give me almost fifteen years of service. *Thank You, God. Hallelujah!*

Mary filled in the details while it seemed like my hard-pounding heart might pop out of my chest cage. I could barely even stand on my right leg at this point.

The short drive alone to the orthopedic doctor to get some medication for the pain and swelling felt like a hundred-mile trek. My right leg shot pains each time I pressed the gas pedal or brake. Breathing offered no relief from feeling as though someone had placed a bag over my head. I hopped to the doctor's office and waited endlessly for my name to be called. Finally when the doctor walked in and saw my leg, his smile disappeared. He pressed his hand against my swollen calf.

"Lean the ball of your foot into the floor," he said. "Do you feel pain?"

"No," I answered.

"You're having trouble breathing?" *Duh,* I thought, *what led you to that conclusion…the fact that I'm gulping like a fish out of water?*

"Now press your heel against the floor," he said.

When I did that the pain forced me into a chair.

"Hurts?"

I nodded.

"You're going to the emergency room. This may be a deep vein thrombosis, a blood clot in your leg. It's not a muscle strain."

After arriving in the emergency room I was carted to radiology for an ultrasound. The technician squirted gel up my right leg and moved her probe slowly from my ankle to my groin. I heard the gurgling sound of the blood flow as she pressed into my flesh, and then she stopped to type in the results. Then she pressed again, no gurgling sound. Dead silence.

At this point I just kept thinking about the rented RV, and that sinking feeling after realizing that our trip to the mountains was not going to happen. As soon as I was returned to the ER, an intravenous line was placed to inject a Heparin solution (an anticoagulant) into my bloodstream. The first doctor entered the room.

"I'm sending you to get a CAT scan in radiology," he abruptly said. So I was once again carted to X-ray as my body was inserted through a tube.

"Hold your breath," the technician broadcast from the adjoining room.

That was a joke. I could no more hold my breath than a person being suffocated by a pillow could intentionally stop breathing.

After being situated back in the ER, a state of panic caused me to shiver from the elephant sitting on my chest, the size of my right calf appearing like a tree trunk, my heart racing faster than a NASCAR race car driver, and most fearfully, sucking in air felt as though I were sipping oxygen from a hallowed out toothpick.

"You were a walking dead man," the doctor said while holding the results of my tests. "You have six blood clots that have traveled up your leg and into your pulmonary artery, your lung's only airway. Frankly, I'm surprised that you made it this far. We lost a young surfer earlier with the same condition."

At this point my physical struggles took a back seat to the shocking reality that I was dying just hours after cycling up the coast, but that panic could not dissuade the doctor from rambling forth words that sounded like a death sentence to me.

"I would transfer you to UCSD" (University of San Diego Hospital) "for a thrombectomy to open your chest," he said, "but by the time you got there it would be too late." (I would be dead.) "So we're going to intubate you. It's going to feel strange, but that's the only way you will be able to breathe because your airway is blocked. All we can do is wait at this point."

Wait. Sucking in air, my heart flopping around like a fish out of water and burning inside—and I needed to wait? To me that seemed no different from waiting in the funeral home lobby while they prepared my coffin. The nurses and doctors came in and out with the same dour looks.

Hours passed while I stared at the ceiling in my room, the guy next to me chatting away while I replayed my life. I prayed, but not like other prayers. These prayers came from a point of desperation. *Please take care of my family. If my foggy brain slides into a coma, don't let me live like a vegetable.*

Another doctor entered my room, and at the same time a lab technician was trying to draw some blood.

"Strange," he said. "We can't draw any blood." His furrowed eyebrows accentuated his words. We both looked at my reddened skin around the intravenous needle.

"Your temperature is 101." That explained the feeling of being under a heat lamp for hours on end, and the clammy feeling my wife commented about when she touched my forehead. Eventually the technician was able to draw some blood into his vial, but he was only able to fill it halfway.

Meanwhile the patient next to me was suddenly carted out of the room. Later I would learn that he had been placed in isolation, probably contagious I presumed, though no one told me so. *Great,* I thought. *I've been exposed to whatever that guy had all of this time.*

The doctor entered my room. "You have an infection. It's meth-icillin-resistant Staphylococcus aureus, MRSA." MRSA is a type of staph bacteria that is resistant to almost all of the antibiotics typically used to treat infections.

Two of the most common killers attacked my body. Pulmonary embolism represents the third-leading cause of death, and the death rate from MRSA at the time was about 20 percent. MRSA had caused my blood to clot throughout my body, not just in my leg and lung, but throughout my entire venous system causing a traffic jam of clumping red blood cells throughout my bloodstream while damaging organs.

The next morning I felt as though my heart might push out of my chest and then it rolled and settled over and over again. Every object swirled in my mind like a jumbled image of random thoughts. My body started convulsing, flopping on top of the bed like a fish out of water, which is exactly how my heart felt.

And then everything went dark.

At first my spirit pulled out of my body, like you would pull a cottony undershirt by first picking it up from the chest area. I tried to breathe but my breath would not follow, and I felt plucked bodily out of myself and taken from that ethereal place in me by an inverse wind pulling me upward. It followed a gurgling sound like my tongue was struggling to say something—then an airy feeling like what it must be to soar in a glider, and a silence that started dark and faded into lighter shades from being drawn into the light above. I left my body in a nanosecond, every essential part of me, and I was fully aware that I was no longer in this world and that it was no longer necessary to think that I was dying.

It was the most freeing experience of my life.

2

MY FIRST REVELATION

URING THAT PERIOD, the charge nurse had stepped away from the main desk. She failed to notice that my monitor registered a flatline—no heart rhythm. Sometimes, patients will turn in their bed thereby dislodging the monitoring electrodes, or they pull the electrodes off of their skin to go to the bathroom. Some clinicians falsely assume that a flatline means that the electrodes were just accidently pulled off of the patient. Neither of these happened in my case. My heart had actually stopped.

A couple visiting me discovered my lifeless body. They alerted a nurse to the fact that my heart monitor showed a flatline and they could not awaken me, and my flesh appeared as an ashen color. According to the monitor, my heart had stopped for almost thirty minutes before I was resuscitated by the attending clinicians.

What I am about to share with you now are not just the experiences of my afterlife. I am going to share some epiphanies I experienced in paradise, what I instantly knew to be Heaven. I call these revelations. The insights I gained during my time before being revived have illuminated my life since then, and I trust that my lessons learned will help to inspire your life as well.

EXPERIENCES IN THE AFTERLIFE CAN VARY

Many accounts of near-death experiences focus on descriptions of an ethereal paradise in exclusion of any religious ascriptions. They speak of a "light," a "tunnel," of "lush scenery," or some other descriptive quality. I feel compelled to clarify that my experience was consumed with being in the presence of Jesus. I know this may offend those who do not believe in God, or who consider Jesus Christ to be only a historical figure. It may even offend some believers in Jesus Christ who cite certain Scriptures, such as John 3:13 that states: *"No one has ever gone into heaven except the one who came from heaven—the Son of Man,"* which is commonly used to refute NDE stories of Heaven as either fabricated or imagined. Paul wrote of someone—presumably himself—who went to Heaven in Second Corinthians 12:3-4.

Are these Scriptures in conflict with each other? In speaking with Nicodemus—a Pharisee and member of the Jewish ruling council—as documented in chapter 3 of the book of John, Jesus explains that a person who won't believe earthly claims won't believe heavenly ones, either. Jesus was stating that if Nicodemus, or anyone else, rejects what Jesus states about Heaven, there is no other source to which they can reference. In John 3:13, Jesus makes claim to His "exclusivity." Essentially, Jesus means that He is the one and only way to God—there are no other options. So, no, those two claims made by Jesus and Paul do not conflict with each other. John 3:13 speaks of Jesus as the only way to Heaven, and Paul is speaking of visiting Heaven.

As to NDE claims from people who did not meet Jesus, or who did not believe in Jesus Christ as their Lord and Savior, please allow me to propose what some refer to as an "invariant hypothesis." Christians can explain how they came to know Jesus Christ as their Savior in different ways, as in saying something like, "I've always known Jesus as my Savior"; whereas, others might know the very moment their life was changed through a transformational experience with the Holy Spirit.

Experiences vary, just as near-death accounts vary even though God remains constant regardless of those individual experiences. Indeed, interpretations of experiences inevitably vary from person to person. You and I could visit Venice, or the Grand Canyon, or meet a group of people at a party, and our descriptions of our experiences would not be exactly the same because of the variant filters of our minds.

Those NDE persons who do not identify themselves as Christians describe their afterlife in various ways as well. My account, while being in a space or place before settling in the presence of Jesus, was far different from the place I experienced while in the presence of Jesus. My initial experience in the light after my physical death was ethereal and sometimes extraterrestrial as though traveling through a spiral galaxy within a dimension entirely foreign to my perception of time, space, and even my common awareness of all things familiar. The light permeated the darkness in a realm of light and shadow that eventually drew me to the source of that light, Jesus. Thereafter, my experience being with Jesus was entirely consumed with the love of Jesus Christ in paradise—nothing else mattered but being in Jesus' presence.

From my perspective, I was in two different places—one just after I died, and one being in the presence with Jesus in Heaven. More than one hundred Bible verses speak of the heavens as plural, but in the space of communing with Jesus was God's dwelling place, a realm that existed where everything operates according to God's will. That place I strolled with Jesus was set apart from any other domain, a singular empyrean named Heaven that I will later describe.

So my hypothesis is that the spiritual realm can be experienced in different ways; however, an experience with Jesus Christ can only be enjoyed by those who accept Jesus as He claimed to be in His own words to a woman during the time Jesus traversed this earth as He said, *"I am the resurrection and the life. The one who believes in me will live, even though they die"* (John 11:25).

Please allow me to address all of these doubts with one important realization—God can do anything, and His existence is not predicated on any individual's beliefs. Though God never contradicts His promises or stated truths, God's modus operandi is to reveal Himself, even if He must use seemingly absurd vehicles such as a burning bush, a donkey, the wind, or countless flawed people, like me. According to ancient writings, eight people went to Heaven without dying, including Enoch, Noah's great grandfather (Genesis 5:22-24) and Elijah (2 Kings 2:11).

In the New Testament of the Bible, Stephen, Paul, and John all experienced visions of Heaven. As a former agnostic, I understand others' skepticism about any rigid adherence to Jesus Christ as the "only way," but as someone who met Him face-to-face, I can state emphatically and without reservation that Jesus is indeed the way, the truth, and the life—and that no one can meet God except through the One with whom I journeyed in Heaven. I sincerely hope that you will someday be equally awed by Jesus' overwhelming presence in paradise. If I could simply transfer my experience of Heaven into your soul and spirit, you would likely cave to the floor in a flood of tears ushering forth indescribable awe and joy, as I did.

If the debate is whether near-death experiences are real, I could remain silent as I did for fourteen years after my own NDE. If the debate is whether Jesus Christ is real, I will not remain silent. I will shout that indisputable fact to anyone who will listen. And I hope that includes you. And, for anyone who calls me a lunatic, liar, or idealist for declaring the personal reality of Jesus Christ, I simply say this—you are loved more than you know.

As mentioned at the beginning of this chapter, I experienced a crisis of faith only two weeks before dying. God answered my desperate plea to show Himself to me, but it required that He stop my physical heart to release my spiritual heart in Heaven so that I could see Him face-to-face.

EXPERIENCING MY FIRST ENCOUNTER

My first recollection after my body ceased functioning was that of my spirit rising above my body, which I faintly saw from below. A brilliant light pulled me upward, like the sun, only this light did not burn. It soothed. My senses were piqued, clear, and my visions were lifelike, unlike the indistinct accounts of dreams or hallucinations.

I saw gargantuan figures battling in the far distance upon fields of grass and rolling hills. Not sure of what was happening, all I could do was cry out the name of Jesus, all the while feeling peaceful without a care in the world.

Next, my feet settled on a cushiony ground. A soft figure snuggled against me as He placed His arm around me and pressed His soothing face against my cheek. His bristles were soft and His skin smooth. It was Jesus. Being with Him felt as though we had been pals for eons. I knew it. My awareness was piqued. My senses more pronounced than ever before. I smelled, saw, felt, and understood things more than at any time in my life. For the first time in my life I could breathe deeply, inhaling fragrances never before realized. The light emanating from Jesus illuminated everything around me.

"I am with you, my beloved," Jesus said. "Always."

I caved to the ground in awe of my Lord and Savior. His hand rested on my left shoulder as He grasped my right hand to pull me up. I was sobbing with breathless adoration being in the presence of the Almighty, my best Friend, consummate Love.

"Trust Me," He said.

I stood as Jesus' left arm pulled me into His side. I felt at home. No worries, no fears, no regrets...absolute comfort.

Some wish to know how Jesus appeared. His face impressed me most since a robe covered His body, but even that did not influence me overall. His face was symmetrical with thick eyebrows, almond shaped eyes, straight nose, olive skin, full cheeks and lips, strong jawline, brownish-green eyes, pointed chin, and a full head of dark hair. His serene physical appearance seemed surreal at first, and then I understood that the quintessence of Jesus' appearance was a divine embodiment of love and kindness and gentleness that made His outward characteristics seem irrelevant to how Jesus appeared to me. I presumed that the light flowing from Jesus was the burgeoning emittance of love, like we might visualize from the moon's reflection of the sun. If anyone could paint both a radiant and comforting picture of love, that would be Jesus.

The first takeaway from my intimacy with Jesus was that His exclusive focus was on me, just me. I knew that the cares of the world rested on His shoulders, but when we were together, cheek to cheek, I felt like I was the most important person to Jesus.

Never in my life had I felt that kind of absolute devotion. I don't know how Jesus did that, but I have talked with other NDEers who also clinically died—their hearts stopped—and each one experienced a similar if not same phenomena. He sees you as though you are the only person in Heaven and on earth, was my takeaway.

Revelation #1: You are like the only person in the world to God.

You may have heard the saying, "When you were born, the mold was broken," meaning that no one else is just like you. More so, God sees you as though you are the most special person in all of creation. When Jesus looked at me, His eyes glistened with love. I truly believed that He saw *only* me. I don't understand how He did that. Jesus assumed the cares of the world, and yet I possessed God's exclusive attention. That same absolute attentiveness applies to each of us.

This overwhelming revelation translated into not only my personhood, it also unveiled my inimitable purpose in life. In Heaven, God exposed to me my special imprint. After being initially awestruck and caving to my knees, realizing that I stood in the presence of the King of kings and Lord of lords, Jesus and I strolled together as best friends. I journeyed along with my Companion both awestruck by Jesus and comfortable with Him at the same time. Because our hearts were kindred in Heaven, my sense of knowing God's truth seemed almost instinctive.

I knew that my time in Heaven served a purpose, and I believe that purpose includes my sharing some deep insights with you. Jesus revealed my uniqueness in Heaven, exposing my truest self. I know that He also wants to expose your singularity and specialness as well. Before you were born, God fashioned you and me for a reason. That reason is for a Kingdom impact. But before you can make that impact, I want to tell you how special you are to God.

YOU ARE MORE SPECIAL THAN THE ANGELS

Please allow me to explain why you are so important to God, if I may be so bold. Perhaps the most common question others have asked me about my time in Heaven is whether I saw angels. The answer is "yes." Their tall, towering figures were translucently clear and formed like chiseled Olympian bodies cut from stone and draped in white linens through which their long brass-colored arms protruded. Their eyes appeared more like fire than pupils. And the voice of one angel reverberated an echo more powerful than the volume of several humans. I know these descriptions may sound bizarre, and not very humanlike. Indeed, these angels were more awesome than any other creature I saw around me.

Now, here is what struck me about the angels' presence. Their awesome sight appeared to command reverence, although only God was worthy of being worshipped. Conversely, Jesus appeared to me in a plain robe, curly brown hair over His ears, hands and feet like mine; in fact, He appeared as a very ordinary man compared to the angels—more like me. If not for the overwhelming depth of love I felt from Jesus, I might have been tempted to speak with one of those colossal angels because their mere brilliancy commanded attention. It was then that I understood how legions of angels could have abandoned God in favor of the masquerading *"angel of light,"* satan (2 Corinthians 11:14). They were that compelling.

As for me, Jesus elicited congeniality. He felt as a relatable friend whose love commanded reverence more so than His appearance. I felt entirely at home with Jesus; and frankly, I was a little scared of the angels even though they followed Christ's commands with a simple motioning of Jesus' head, hands, or eyes. As for me, my Lord's hands simply hugged me with reassurance.

"What you see are My angels, and yet you do not know them," Jesus said to me.

"They are foreign to me, Jesus, but not You. You are...I can't even explain it."

"You know more than words, My child," He said, "your heart tells you who I am to you."

"I want to say my forever Friend, Lord," I said. "Before meeting You in this place, I thought You were a little bit scary, but not now. It is like You have traveled with me for my whole lifetime, and I was the best with You, and the worst apart from You. You were my best Friend all along, and I didn't even know it."

"So be it. What you say is true. There is none closer than Me. You see around you all that we created, and they are good, but you are of My Spirit, beloved. You see with your eyes that which you desire. Now see with your heart that which I desire."

With those words I felt within my heart a bursting desire to serve my Lord and Savior, Jesus Christ. He was greater than all of creation and still the humblest of all. I wanted to worship Him with more than I could possibly express.

Now allow me to turn the attention on you. Our spirits were conceived by God's Love. That makes us special. In Heaven I felt more special than even those majestic angels, though now, amusingly, I can better appreciate those amazing "bodyguards" that Jesus may send us from time to time. My point is that the glory of God, the Spirit of Jesus Christ, rests within the kindred—us. He is perhaps less striking than the angels, and yet Christ is more spectacular than any other in Heaven, and certainly more relatable. The fact that amid all of the splendor in Heaven and on earth, Jesus doting over you and me above all else, should cause each of us to feel wonderstruck.

My motivation for serving Christ became magnified in Heaven. All of us should try to grasp God's absolute devotion to each of His children. Once we grab onto the quintessence of God's overriding attention on us, the translation to us must be to please God above all else. To please God is the ultimate challenge for the human race.

How Do I Know if I Am Pleasing God?

We can tell whether we are making a Kingdom impact by assessing whether an action does one of two things: it either draws us closer to God or it draws others closer to God. Of course, a Kingdom impact can do both and yet sometimes, as with prayer, it only draws us closer to God.

Maybe you know that the Lord's Prayer includes the sentence: *"Your will be done, on earth as it is in heaven"* (Matthew 6:10). This speaks to making a Kingdom impact. You probably have heard that a thousand times. But maybe you never really thought through what that means to you, personally. God imprinted His will within your spiritual DNA even before you were born. He called out your name in Heaven, and He placed within you the will to do *His will.* We can never be satisfied in this life unless we remain true to that spiritually genetic "will" that separates you and me from every other person on earth and distinguishes you from each person in all of history. Jesus made this abundantly clear to me.

I am not referencing simply your characteristics. The personality or behavioral style that psychologists and trainers teach, like whether you are an INFP or Type 3, only compares your general style to the millions of others around the world. God did not create you from a group-think perspective. He created you as an "N of 1," a term the scientist uses when a single patient is the entire trial. Meeting the Creator of humankind taught me this much.

You are the "apple of God's eye," as stated three times in the Bible—Deuteronomy 32:10; Psalm 17:8; Zechariah 2:8—meaning that God remains absolutely focused on you as uniquely special to Him. You are the favored child, the most loved, and that is true of all of God's children. God's attention on you is absolute, just as I felt it in Heaven. Mind you, each one of God's children draws God's same singular attention and imprint. Only God can do that. No one else in my entire lifetime has come close to that level of devotion.

To say that you are special would be a gross understatement. You are the last of your kind. A failure to fulfill your singular purpose on this earth will leave a void in this world forever. No one else can be you, just as no one else can complete the work that God ordained for you from the beginning of your existence. Jesus made that revelation from Heaven clear to me as we journeyed together.

Most of us will be forgotten within three generations in this world, but not within the spiritual realm of God's creation. Jesus taught me that He longs for us to establish our influence on earth that creates a feeling of His being home on earth as it is with Jesus in Heaven. Our prayers and passionate service to God establishes a home for Jesus in this world that remains everlasting on this earth. Our devotion to God creates an abiding influence of His divine revelation.

I discovered during my walk with Jesus that there exists a vacuum in this world that extends throughout history because of unfulfilled purposes. It lingers like a spiritual black hole such that the light of Jesus Christ cannot penetrate the darkness, all because of lost opportunities for God's children to be the light of Christ in this world. I learned that bringing the light of Jesus Christ happens by enjoining our acts of love for others with God's love for us.

While ascending to Heaven I viewed a darkness that I later learned resulted from lost dreams, drawing me to pray, just as I witnessed Jesus interceding on our behalf. As believers in Jesus Christ, the will of God is poured from Heaven to earth whenever we heed the calling of God to make a Kingdom impact in this world. That impact fills the darkness, the emptiness, the void created by lost opportunities with the light of Jesus Christ that creates life to the full. I could see these dynamics with my spiritual eyes that perceived not just material realities, but intentions as well. What can be seen in Heaven and what can be felt, blended into an awareness of what was beyond just appearance to the manifestation of intentions.

People who do good for others fashion an everlasting imprint in the spiritual realm that blesses countless people. That makes you and me special in God's plan. Without you, God's intentions for this world remain uncompleted. This world would become an unfinished piece of art without your presence and contributions. The chain of your influence extends to countless people such that if God opened your spiritual eyes to reveal how many people were touched by you, as Jesus did with me in Heaven, you would be astounded. Not hundreds, not thousands, I saw millions of people touched by one lone soul.

Know this: you are not just a speck in this world, you mean the world to God. When Jesus cupped my cheeks with His hands, His emerald-brown eyes revealed more than a gaze. His hands felt more profound than a casual touch. I felt sanctified. What does sanctification mean? In Heaven it meant that Jesus imbued me with His holiness. It felt like being filled with water after being parched, only that water was Christ's Spirit quenching my heart, filling me with God's love so that my heart supernaturally spilled out God's abiding love from the wellspring of my spirit. In the world I strove to be more Christlike. In Heaven, Jesus imparted that grand desire to the full.

Jesus conveyed upon my soul an intimacy beyond any previously felt connection. Jesus was wholly devoted to me as I longed to be faithful unto Him in return. Our longing in this world should be to honor that devotion by also devoting our lives to Jesus Christ, thus making our Kingdom impact complete. Just as Jesus was fully devoted to me, He expected my full devotion to Him as my one and only God.

Will We Experience Family the Same Way in Heaven?

Some have asked me whether our devotion to God means sacrificing the family unit that many of us enjoy in this life. The plain answer is no. All relationships in Heaven are enhanced, with one qualification: relationship to the fullest in Heaven stems from God.

I was fully cognizant of my loved ones left behind, yet even more aware of the undivided attention that God lavished on them. This realization assuaged my concern that Renee might not be able to financially provide for our family as we had planned, or that I would not see my son and daughter grow up, or that I could not care for my aging parents. Understanding that God had assumed my paternal and spousal position in Heaven allowed me to implicitly trust in God's providence. In Heaven, God fully assumes the role as Father and as Husband (Hosea 2:16; Jeremiah 31:32).

This explains why in Heaven we will be aware of our marriage partners and our positions as a son or daughter and as parents; however, God will satisfy all of those desires for which we yearn in this world so that all relationships will be rooted in the abiding love of Jesus Christ. We will remain "spiritually affectionate" toward those family members from this life, as I was with my grandmother in Heaven, without the need for familial affinity except that of being a child of God. Being *"heirs of God and co-heirs with Christ"* (Romans 8:17) translated into absolute devotion to God in Heaven, and an absolute feeling of kinship with my brothers and sisters in Christ.

JESUS SHOWED ME THE PAST

In Heaven, Jesus showed me a life review similar to vignettes you might see through a flashback. They appeared as fast-paced movie scenes with me as the imbedded main character. Each scene elicited God's grace and comfort, even for those situations in which I failed. While witnessing them I was actually reliving the smells, sensations, and the sentience of others as well as my own feelings.

Jesus showed me a scene while praying with my grandmother so that she could receive Christ; and the same when I prayed with my father as he confessed Jesus Christ as his Lord and Savior; and then he showed a frail boy lying within a hospital bed. I had previously met this boy when I was a teenage agnostic while working in the hospital as a volunteer. I served him a meal.

"I'm dying of cancer," the boy had said to me decades earlier.

Not knowing quite what to say, I simply responded, "Oh."

"Don't worry," he said. "I'm going to Heaven, and you'll be there someday too."

"Oh, I don't believe in Heaven, but I'm sure if there is one, you'll be there," I answered.

"I'll pray for you," he said.

A few days later I stopped by the boy's room again. His bed was empty. I checked with the nurses' station, and a nurse said, "He's not with us anymore."

"He went home?" I asked.

"No," she said. "He died a couple days ago."

That was my playback in Heaven. Little did I know that one day his statement, "You'll be there someday too," was today, now, as I viewed those moments with the boy in retrospect. I had forgotten this part of my life until God played it back to me in Heaven. Now I understand that this boy's prayers helped bring me to know Jesus Christ as my Lord and Savior.

I believe God showed me this story, and the other stories of salvation, to reveal to me the Kingdom impact of our prayers. When we pray, "God's will be done on earth as it is in Heaven," we are literally praying God's will into existence on earth. We are making a Kingdom impact. And that impact is yours and mine to make—no one else in this world can make it for us.

WHY LOVED ONES CANNOT RETURN TO VISIT THE LIVING

Because purpose defines our reason for being here, the loss of a loved one in death leaves us with an indelible hurt. That loved one can no longer support us on this road of life. We often feel left with a hole in our ability to thrive because their loss deprives us of the full measure of joy we so earnestly seek.

Would it not be easier if God allowed our loved ones to visit us once in a while? Maybe a nice chat by the fireplace? A familiar embrace? A chance to say what was left unsaid?

As I looked across the vastness of Heaven untouched by darkness in the glowing light of Jesus Christ, a massive summit separated the light of Christ from a grey murkiness on the other side. I had the distinct feeling that was the place where I ascended through the darkness after dying as Christ's brilliancy pulled me into Heaven. A tunnel appeared in the distance similar to the whirling funnel of a tornado. It contrasted so strikingly to the lush scenery in Heaven bathed with daylight, hills dotted with what appeared to be vineyards, and frolicking figures both ethereal and distinct.

"Jesus, what's that?" I asked while pointing to the funnel over the hill.

"The place between here and the world from which you came," Jesus said.

I knew instantly that a spiritual chasm existed between Heaven and earth. Once on the other side of Heaven, the same burdensome feelings and disappointments with which we struggle in this world would oppress anyone who crossed that great divide to return to this life. Indeed, soon after awaking from Heaven in the hospital, the peace and comfort I had realized in Heaven was gone. I was no longer free of my failings. That stark reality initially haunted me in the hospital bed in striking contrast to being in the full presence of Jesus.

My point in sharing this experience with you is that if God allowed your loved ones to cross that great divide, your loved ones would lose the perfect comfort and faultlessness they now enjoy in Heaven. You would not want to sully their joy, would you?

I believe that is why God has returned many of us to testify of Heaven, so that our loved ones in Heaven can continue to flourish while we who recovered in our mortal bodies can declare the reality of the afterlife. Those who have passed from this world have fulfilled their purpose in this life. You and I have not.

When tough times burden your soul, please dwell on the best that you can imagine, and then multiply that by a "million times" to approximate the splendor of your future with God in a place where the harmonization of all things good is not only a dream, it is your future.

MY ODE TO HEAVEN

My purpose in life before my NDE was to honor God, and that remains much the same, with one important change. Now, I speak of things that cannot be seen as having seen them. Some of my travels exposed me to some of the most breathtaking places around the world. I marveled at the pounding waterfalls sliding over the mountaintops of Yosemite National Park, pondered the panel of the Sistine Chapel painted by Michelangelo entitled, "The Creation of Adam," which famously shows God reaching His finger to touch Adam's outstretched hand. I have gazed at centuries-old olive trees on the Mount of Olives, imagining one reaching over Jesus while He agonized there just before His arrest, and I cruised on the Mediterranean Sea during a similar storm experienced by the apostle Paul as he traveled to evangelize the known world. I do not think any of these wonders compare to the magnificence of Heaven.

So after returning from Heaven and as I began recovering from my injuries, a period of melancholy consumed me. I missed Heaven. During these moments I started penning a poem about

Heaven as a cathartic process of assimilating to the afterlife of my afterlife. Though I do not consider myself a poet by any stretch, the following is what I wrote:

> Jesus gleamed at the peak with power found,
> And the life, breath and love of every sound,
> Seen brightly through the mountains' domes of green,
> God's watching throughout, favor all around;
> Artistry blossoms into waters clean,
> And the sky sparkled with a daytime star,
> On this side of eternity afar.
> Trees reached their arms to Thee in praise, oh my;
> And flowers along rivers flowing by;
> The sound of every living thing is God's.
> His wind blew waves to shine His light on high,
> God's light cleansed away all that made men sigh.
> His light did spread through clouds that never teared.
> God's glory bathed the righteous from all feared,
> Washed with scents of sweet flowers in the air.
> Now a lifetime from first love, I despair;
> And pondering that walk, if I could see,
> A glimpse of His face making sorrow cease,
> My longing soul would dwell in perfect peace.
> I desperately long to journey back,
> Walk that path, open my soul to unpack,
> When my heart rests in the arms of Christ...oh,
> To rest anew through Heaven's afterglow.

3

ADOPTING A CHRIST MINDSET

N ow I am going to get "woosoo" with you—a word I will use for the ineffable things of God for which there are no words. I also use that indescribable term to try to explain those truths that sometimes appear contradictory to our common understanding. Here it goes: God does not value us for our achievements.

> Revelation #2: God does not value His children by their actions. Rather, He values their hearts.

You and I are off the hook in terms of earning God's acceptance. I did not observe any hierarchy in Heaven, such as Abraham residing in the Beverly Hills version of Heaven while "doubting" Thomas lived in the Bronx. As much as I could tell, Heaven is egalitarian with one benevolent Ruler, Jesus Christ. Residents of Heaven traversed through "homes" in every place they dwelled. They lived harmoniously as extended families within exquisitely designed communities comprised of a contiguous blending of various structures surrounding the throne of God.

No one was more prestigious than another. While our status in Heaven is not dependent on any worldly or heavenly merits, that does not excuse us from doing good works. Indeed, seventeen Bible verses make it clear that we were created to do *"good works."* However, pleasing God by doing good works should not be confused with the value God places on you and me. Human value, from God's perspective, is fixed the moment we become born again (John 3:3). Understanding our value in Christ underpins our ability to overcome obstacles, because feeling valued is the antigen to fending off the foreign spiritual pathogen we call fear.

FEAR STEMS FROM THE UNKNOWN

When the Coronavirus 2019 (COVID-19) pandemic spread around the globe, fear paralyzed much of the world. Many businesses closed. Many people isolated themselves. Social distancing became the norm. Many wore face masks, and some remained isolated in their homes for months. Prudently, people at risk of dying from this disease took precautionary measures to safeguard themselves against the potentially deadly virus.

After 100 million cases worldwide had been identified with 2 million deaths and 72 million recoveries having been reported as of January 26, 2021, the mortality rate of 2 percent proved to be less than the death rate of the hospital-acquired strain of the MRSA infection that contributed to my death. I remember thinking during these times: *If they only knew.* If everyone who fears death only knew how baseless their fears are in comparison to the absolute peace I felt after my own death.

While my body started shaking and my heart fluttered before dying, all of my thoughts centered on wanting it to stop. At some point the hospital room seemed full of a "reassuring presence" and that is when I knew that I was about to die. Suddenly my body settled with no awareness of my body's existence, except that for a brief period my thoughts transitioned to a sense of peace. My assumption is that there was a period after my heart stopped when my brain remained active within my lifeless body in a vacuum of stilled awareness while my senses had become dormant. After my brain ceased, I was in an ethereal funnel pulled by a light from above.

After being resuscitated, the first words I heard from one of the clinical attendants was, "Mr. Kay, can you hear me?" That is the first time I felt present within my body again. Death to me is essentially nonexistent today. I certainly empathize with the angst sufferers felt from diseases like COVID-19, since I experienced similar affects from MRSA; however, I no longer consider death the end of life. That was certainly not my attitude before dying.

In this world, before Heaven, I was more of a hoper than a believer. I would hazard to guess that many Christians sometimes question their faith, especially during tragedies. Post-Heaven, I am a true believer. I walked with Jesus. I became aware of Christ's absolute dominion over everything. Whenever Jesus motioned to a field of flowers, they started blooming. Wherever He moved, life sprouted forth. Even the golden-brown translucent path upon which we walked appeared teeming with life. Everything in Heaven quivered in response to the King of king's commands.

Now I look back and think: *Was the paralyzing fear of COVID-19 merited?* Here is a general answer I surmised: only one fear is acceptable to God, and that is fear of Him. Fear of God for the believer is more accurately defined as awe. Scripture tells us that the fear of God is the beginning of wisdom, and the beginning of wisdom is to depart from evil. How do we depart from evil? By doing the opposite, which is to pursue God—to wholeheartedly desire His presence. When in the presence of God, reverence replaces fear with the ensuing confidence that God has authority over all things.

In Heaven, fear was irrelevant. Did I fear—perceive as a threat—God in Heaven? No, I was struck with an awe never experienced before or after living in this world. Being in the presence of God, the name given to Jesus multiple times in the Bible, elicits reverence. Reverence in relationship to God leads to wisdom, and wisdom results from obedience to the all-knowing authority of Jesus Christ. Fear in relationship to this world equates to a distrust in God. The only antidote to fear is trust in the One who loves us most, and that happens through growing in love with God. In the presence of Jesus, I desired only to please Him because He loved me infinitely more.

The COVID-19 pandemic unmasked a vulnerability in the human condition. Isolation from each other mirrored an isolation many felt from God. Complete trust in God, as I experienced in Heaven, dispels all manners of fear. During the pandemic, governments imposed shutdowns of businesses. Many lost their livelihoods. Panic raged through much of the world. No one knew much about the COVID-19 virus, and many feared the worst. This pandemic exposed not only humankind's susceptibility to contagions, it also exposed a spiritual distancing from God within our world.

Fear disables our ability to relate to God. Believing in the providence of God dispels fear. Allow me to state this emphatically based on what I heard from Jesus while walking with Him: "Only at My *appointed* time will you return to Me in Heaven." Only when God says it is time to die will you and I die and never return to this world. A virus cannot tell us when to die. A car smashing into a vehicle cannot tell us when to die. Even a criminal holding a gun to our head cannot tell us when to die. Only God can do that.

So if you and I are to trust God, we should also no longer fear dying. At no time after my heart stopped beating did I feel as though I was dead. My consciousness remained although my body ceased to function. No believer should ever be conscious of death because Jesus Christ has overcome the consequence of death.

WHY DOES GOD ALLOW BAD THINGS TO HAPPEN?

Sometimes we wonder why God allows bad things to happen, or seemingly turns a "blind eye" to others' cruelties. At one point during my journey in Heaven, Jesus turned His head to open a window to the world from which I came.

"What do you see?" He asked me.

"I see spirits hovering over people, Lord."

"You see the unseen, My beloved. You see those beholden to Me, who speak My truth, and you see those who are not of Me, who deceive," Jesus said.

"Your angels?"

"And those who have departed from Me who were once Mine." I knew these to be the fallen angels, or demons.

"My beloved, those who hear My truth, and obey, they are like the wise man who turned away from dark clouds to avoid a storm. And those who listen to the deceivers are like the foolish man who chose to defy My truth. They obey the whispers of the defiler and so they defile others."

Jesus sacrificed Himself so that no one should perish (2 Peter 3:9), and now He appeared as a grieving father seeing wickedness defile His loved ones. The only time I witnessed Jesus' sadness was during that time when He saw the corruption of His loved ones. His overwhelming love reached to those who heeded God's truth—those who listened to His words and obeyed them.

His heart aches for those who deny Him. I know from my time with Jesus that God does not cause His children to suffer, but that He will always redeem for good what this fallen world and the powers of darkness inflict upon us. That is God's promise. In some cases God may allow the powers of darkness to inflict people, as with the biblical Job, but always for the purpose of returning evil for a greater good.

If we blame God for not saving us from trials, then we must also blame Jesus for not saving Himself from the cross. For God's children, suffering inevitably leads to redemption, just as it did for each of us because of Christ's suffering on our behalf. My friend, please think of your suffering as a living sacrifice. In my experiences, many of those who have suffered the most have sought after God most. They became closer to God in the process. Those devotees to Christ will gain immeasurably greater Kingdom rewards because of their sacrifices.

When bad happens, God always redeems what was lost for something of greater gain. God does not ignore those who suffer, He weeps with them. God grieves for the lost. He beckons everyone to His truth and will deny no one of their free will to deny Jesus Christ or to accept Him.

ANGELS AND DEMONS WERE BATTLING FOR SOULS

In the end, COVID-19 proved to be less devastating than some originally feared. Meanwhile, other related travesties happened as people suffered from depression caused by losing either their income or from fearing their own death. What we learned from this pandemic is that fear can paralyze people more than any other factor. Indeed, the devil and his minions—fallen angels who dared to think of themselves as equal to God—use fear to separate us from the love of Jesus Christ perhaps more than any other factor.

Those seven-or-so-feet-tall figures I saw in the distance while ascending to Heaven were the angels and demons battling in the netherworld. They battled with each other; however, their battle was not for their own lives, but for the lives of others, people like you and me. The angels appeared untarnished; however, the demons appeared ancient and decrepit like warmed-over corpses. That is how I imagine spiritual battles within our own lives in the netherworld. In my case, I believe those spirit beings were battling for my soul, and whenever I called out the name of Jesus Christ or declared His authority in my life, demons fell.

Angels and demons battle for the rights to whisper lies or truths to peoples' souls in this world. These whispers from demons elicit oppression, despair, avarice, and a host of other disparaging impressions that isolate individuals from God. Ultimately, their aim is to compel a person to take his or her life in order to destroy God's appointed purpose for that person.

Angels whisper God's truths, whereas demons whisper deceitful ideas to confuse people; and, if demons win the battle, they can convince even believers that good is evil, or that lies are truth. They can oppress their victims through deceit, convincing them that they are worthless. Angels whisper the edifying words of God that uplift the downtrodden soul and give hope. I could sense these spiritual dynamics lucidly in my spirit, though in Heaven I maintained an overriding confidence that God's providence would always prevail.

Angels can only speak what God tells them to say, which is always the truth. In Heaven, I witnessed these spiritual dynamics in a way that cannot be fully explained even though I understood precisely what was happening in the spiritual environs of this world. Both angels and demons can morph their appearance, but only demons can possess disbelieving humans with their spirit beings. Angels in Heaven could only influence God's believers with God's truths, but under God's authority they never possess anyone.

You may ask if demons inflicted me with the disease that ravaged my body. I am not sure. More likely God allowed my suffering that was caused by the flawed nature of this world for a reason, and maybe that reason is you. I am sure that the spirits of darkness (demons) spoke lies to me that all hope was lost. Indeed, I felt this way at times before dying. I suffered from a disease potentially more life threatening than COVID-19. But as with any suffering—whether allowed by God for a reason, imposed upon someone through the complicit actions of people who refuse God, or influenced through the spiritual forces and authorities of the unseen dark world who impose their powers in the fallen spiritual realm inhabited by evil spirits—God always rescues those who place their trust in Him. Always.

GOD TURNED MY FEAR TO GOOD

At the time of my dying, the MRSA infection coursed through my body from an infected intravenous line. This type of pathogen destroys organs as it essentially eats away human tissue. It can settle in the lungs, as with COVID-19, and my lungs had already been damaged by asthma and Chronic Obstructive Pulmonary Disease (COPD). I slowly suffocated to death from pulmonary emboli (blood clots) exacerbated by the MRSA. Yes, I became fearful of losing my life and my family's security at the time. Fears ratcheted my soul as I dwelled on the imminent possibility of death. But like all cases of fear, the cure exists on the other side of what caused it.

Whether fear of death, public speaking, or an unknown virus like COVID-19, it only takes getting through the event to overcome that fear. Think of a trial that caused you to fear. You got through it. Not knowing the future creates a fearful expectation of what might happen. Death represents the ultimate unknown. What the physical mind cannot comprehend in the mysterious, the undiscovered, and the untested, the spirit can fathom beyond the mind's capacity to understand.

My greatest fear, death, turned into my greatest joy in meeting Jesus. Fear stems from the absence of faith. Worry results from unfounded anticipation. Confidence arises from crossing the bridge between our fears and worries to the calming influence of what God invariably turns for good. Take it from someone, me, who feared death and the inability to breathe more than anything else. Each morning I awoke to a counter filled with vitamins, supplements, and pharmaceuticals to fend off the possible effects of illness, the greatest of which would be my inability to breathe. My affliction in the hospital stopped my ability to breathe. It killed me.

I would not trade that experience in retrospect, because on the other side of my fear stood the One who gave me infinitely more than my wildest dreams could have envisioned. Meeting Jesus face-to-face resuscitated my soul so that I could inhale the very breath of God. Being given a private tour with the Creator of the lush paradise in which my soul found itself in Heaven birthed a new purpose to serve God full time in building a future filled with creativity in helping others.

Here lies the truth of our reality apart from our own understanding: only that which God first created in Heaven is everlasting. God is Truth. John 14:6 tells us that Jesus said, *"I am the way and the truth and the life. No one comes to the Father except through me."* Colossians 1:5 further explains that our faith and hope is stored up for us in Heaven. God is Spirit, so we know that truth can only be revealed in a spiritual language between God and His children. The full manifestation of our faith and hope only exists in Heaven, as I experienced it in my spirit. In Heaven was the only time I felt perfected.

THE KEY TO AN ENLIGHTENED LIFE IS A SPIRITUAL LIFE

Our life in this world will eventually end; however, what exists in Heaven will never end. I learned that the key to an "enlightened life" is to live more fully in the spiritual realm of life with Christ instead of the physical reality of what appears possible in this world. To express more goodness by becoming more heavenly minded. To transcend from a mindset of physical boundaries to a Christ-centered mindset that focuses on Heaven's reality requires absolute trust in God.

Not only me, but countless others have tried to explain the reality of Heaven, and of God. When I attended a gathering of Christian NDEers in Texas, it felt like a "Heaven reunion" to me. My brothers and sisters in Christ shared their experiences in Heaven that sounded identical to mine. In Heaven, the senses are intensified. Many of us spoke of numerous shades of colors never before seen, newfound fragrances more striking than any on earth, and about how everything in Heaven sprouted life. Heaven appeared as another dimension, as John Burke explains it in his book, *Imagine Heaven,* unlike the three-dimensional space in which we live on earth.

Unlike this world, in Heaven nothing dies, and everything thrives. Even relatives and friends appeared vibrantly youthful. Beyond the beauty of Heaven, most of the NDEers I have met treasured their meeting with Jesus foremost. We felt alltogether comfortable with Jesus and abundantly loved. Although we remained aware of our life on earth, nothing in this life felt condemning. We were forgiven as though all of our faults never even existed. Only peace and comfort remained—and that incredible impression of Love as a person, Jesus Christ, and not just as an emotion.

Would you like to experience Heaven on earth? Sure, who would not want to experience that life of abundance in this world. All of the Christian NDEers in John Burke's multi-decade study, including me, left Heaven having been indelibly changed. There is an ole adage: "Once you've been to the city, it's hard to go back to the farm." Well, this world is the farm, and Heaven is the shining *"city on a hill"* (Matthew 5:14 Living Bible).

Indeed, the "city" I viewed in Heaven sparkled like a cut diamond with abodes of various heights and magnificently adorned designs unlike any architectural elements I have witnessed on earth. In the center I saw angels standing around a court surrounded by a floor made of deep blue stones that gave forth what appeared to be a blue flame through which the angels walked; and before the angels rested a glorious figure whom I knew was God the Father, whose white hair and robe flowed elegantly through the wind. I still recall the ethereal wonder of Heaven and the consuming love of Christ as if it is still happening. The memory of it remains fresh to this day, almost fifteen years later.

OUR FAITH CHALLENGE IS REAL

The challenge in this physical life is that believing remains primarily an exercise in faith minus the reality of absolute conviction. We hope that the foundation of our faith is justified; but until we see Heaven, at that appointed moment when God calls us home, we simply hold on to that hope like an anchor that keeps us from drifting into a sea of doubt. Is Heaven real? Is God real? These are not just the questions of unbelievers. Most Christians, if they are completely honest, at least maintain a thread of doubt in their minds, especially when trials hit.

To experience Heaven on earth, we need to adopt a spiritual mindset—and specifically, a Christ mindset. What are realities in heaven can only be seen through the spirit. And it is our faith that presses us to walk out, here on earth, what is shown to us in God's Spirit. Faith is the starting point—it beckons us to move in obedience. And obedience always requires action on our part.

"Faith by itself, if it does not have works, is dead" (James 2:17 NKJV) begins with the word "faith." Faith establishes relationship with God. Being conformed to the image of Jesus Christ compels us to do good works. Trying to do good works before establishing the desire to do them is a little like the proverbial way of "putting the cart before the horse." The horse, or driver, is the Spirit of Jesus Christ. The cart is filled with all the good works that we are called to carry out.

Being heavenly minded, that is focused on the spiritual truths of God's Kingdom, will transform us by the renewal of our minds (Romans 12:2). A renewed mind focuses on what God established in Heaven. Heaven contains everything that is good, and right. Heaven is an impartation of God's truth come to life. Heaven is not just a reward, it is a place of absolute truth, love, and life.

4

SEEING WITH THE EYES OF OUR HEART

MY POINT OF greatest suffering in dying was followed by my greatest joy in Heaven. In Heaven, I not only saw joyful figures frolicking about, I sensed joy in everything around me—the luscious green hills, the cascading waterfalls, the flowers of all colors sprouting forth life—even the blue sky seemed to smile down at me. I reaped the rewards of my suffering in Heaven, but the odd thing is that the closest people to God whom I remembered on earth had also suffered the most.

Probably the most astounding discovery I made while studying cases of people who suffered in this world when I researched the topic after recovering from the hospital, is that persons who suffered the most, causing them to desperately seek after God, appeared to have the closest relationship with Jesus Christ. This is because brokenness can often lead to breakthrough. A broken heart helps us better see others through the eyes of our spiritual heart.

When trials strike, we can go in one of two directions. We can either blame God and wallow in our miseries, or we can seek after God by immersing ourselves in His presence and truths. Running away from God produces just more despair and suffering. Running toward God eventually produces peace and comfort.

MY BROKENNESS TURNED TO JOY

Life after my time in Heaven was not just a "bed of roses." My after-life recovery required constant bedrest to guard against a stroke, and then walks of increasing length to strengthen my muscles that forced me to sit every few feet before caving from exhaustion. It felt like I might never walk normally again, and my calf was permanently swollen from damaged valves. Since MRSA had gotten into my bloodstream, it caused infections in organs such as my heart, which is called endocarditis, requiring me to rebuild my cardiovascular strength. Because strong anticoagulants were required to guard against my state of hypercoagulability, severe migraines resulted from what doctors feared was hemorrhaging in my brain.

The first time I took a walk at home I needed to stop next to a lamppost, breathless and close to tears, realizing that I would need to test my endurance like never before because I had accepted that job with Johnson & Johnson requiring over 50 percent travel. My first visit to the church that prayed for me during my hospitalization proved embarrassing. I was called to the stage and collapsed in front of the congregants after the pastor announced my "amazing recovery."

I was thirty pounds lighter and I think most of it came from lost muscle. I will never forget my first business trip to Seattle from San Diego. Renee drove me to the airport, about two months post-discharge, sooner than the house rest prescribed by the doctors. I looked out the passenger window toward the sky thinking *I cannot do this impossible thing. Lord,* I prayed, *I can only do this if you give me supernatural strength because I can barely walk.* Upon arrival I was met by the representative who drove me to a hospital which required me to stand six hours in the hospital operating room while we observed a cardiovascular procedure using our company's devices. It was excruciating and often I needed to lean into the back wall for support.

These painful experiences lasted for weeks, and at any time I expected a reoccurrence of the blood clots and infections that caused my demise. But, my attitude toward life had changed. I no longer became stressed about the little things in life. God had instilled a new mission in my life—to serve others with the love of Jesus Christ. *What's the worst this life can throw at me other than death?* I thought. I worked as "unto the Lord," undaunted by the corporate responsibilities that used to keep me awake at night. But, then crises hit again.

My daughter experienced mini-strokes as my wife and I awoke to nightly terror screams. I needed to manage damaged organs with respiratory treatments and cardio exercises while traversing across the country. Several skin infections resulted from latent bacterial strains from my hospital-acquired infection requiring frequent antibiotic treatments. Then as my damaged organs appeared to be healing, I faced two bouts with cancer and one of these required surgery. Just as I began healing from those attacks, several of my loved ones died. Finally after paying off most of my $300,000 hospital bills, my corporate division was sold, and this resulted in my being laid off. To ease the brokenness, my wife used to joke that I must be a descendant of Job, the man mentioned in the Bible whose well-ordered life had been ripped to shreds.

Despite all these, I will never again doubt God's love and His desire to redeem what I lost for a greater Kingdom impact. It was only through the darkness of my brokenness and suffering that

I could appreciate the brilliancy of God's love—but never will it shine so brightly as it did in Heaven.

Though Heaven remains a vivid memory now, the presence of God I felt while in Heaven still lingers after times of trouble like a long overdue nap. His Spirit soothes me with the music of an angelic choir. The Holy Spirit now bathes me in the confidence of God's assurances. "Trust me," He first spoke to me in Heaven.

Recently, my body was prostate on a gurney in the emergency room as I struggled with my third case of pneumonia.

"This time it's in both lungs and we think you have both bacterial and viral infections, and you could be clotting again," the physician said.

This is it, Lord, I thought while looking at the squares of white panels on the ceiling. The light from the emergency room desk that was separated from my dimmed room by a partially opened curtain eked forth a lambent glow onto my bed as I thought back on the time when I faced death in the ER over a decade ago. I closed my eyes.

I was there again, remembering Heaven, imagining the eyes of Jesus, trusting in His promises. I was not afraid. I was ready. I would be young again in Heaven, with thick hair, and unwrinkled skin that glowed translucently. I would work as unto the Lord, always, never to be hospitalized again. Never to be sick again. Never to return.

No, God spoke to my Spirit. Not yet.

Subsequently, while recovering, I shared the great news about Jesus Christ with hospital staff members and some patients over several days during my hospital stay. A patient in the other bed of my hospital room prayed with me to receive Jesus Christ as his Lord and Savior.

I told him that in Heaven there would be no sun or moon, and the vistas in Heaven would give off an iridescent glow, people would speak in a different language that was understood by all, everything would be alive, several choruses would be sung in harmony, and generations of his family would be welcoming him in a place unconfined by time or space, with the love of Jesus permeating everyone and in everything that never dies, and all of creation will be thriving in a constant state of growth. "That will be your experience in Heaven," I said to the older man.

"You sound like someone whose been there," he said. I could only smile without telling him that indeed I had tasted of it all.

My latest suffering was well worth it. I could endure the trials that would have caused me to question God as I did before meeting Jesus in Heaven because I could reason from my spirit mind in the language of Heaven—the language of God's love.

I VIEWED JESUS CHRIST INTERCEDING FOR US

My greatest challenge in describing experiences in Heaven arose when Jesus formed impressions into visions that I perceived in my spirit as the materialization of His truth. One such example occurred when Jesus revealed to me an outspreading of His presence in the form of different color grades pierced by a brilliance with no hue, like a pure drop of water. Defining the ethereality of Heaven in these terms defies common understanding, just as the concept of an omnipresent God defied the understanding of people during the ancient times of Moses and when Jesus Christ walked this earth. If you were to claim that God could communicate anywhere at any time to those generations, they would likely accuse you of being a lunatic. "No way could anyone communicate from here to some distant land," they might say.

But now we understand the concept of universal communication because of digital, analog, and electrical transmission through electromagnetic waves. We know that invisible wave frequencies are decoded by receivers tuned to the same wavelengths to produce images and sounds transmitted from faraway places. A similar dynamic occurs in Heaven, whereby God's Spirit transmits His presence to countless people. I am not suggesting that God communicates with us through this exact method of synchronization using wavelengths. Rather, God "synchronizes" with His children in a way science has yet to discover, and in a way we will most likely never fully understand.

The color grades I observed in Heaven to me represent an entirely new meaning now. I perceive God's rainbow that He sent as a *"covenant between me and you and everything living around you and everyone living after you"* (Genesis 9:12 The Message) after the flood in the time of Noah as having a direct relationship to the colors surrounding the throne of God that I viewed in Heaven. This I do know—God is all places, all the time. And just as with modern technologies where people can turn off their TV or hang up on a phone call, we as humans can turn off God, refusing to answer His call. Furthermore, those colors representing God's presence revealed to me a profound dynamic about how God relates to us.

This woosoo moment impressed upon me the intercession of Jesus' Spirit, the Holy Spirit, to those in need. I knew it. My spirit comprehended this phenomena in a similar way that we feel that "aha moment" when the truth imparts a revelation to us; only this time, I actually saw God's intercessions with my spiritual eyes, and I felt His presence as a comforting warmth within my chest.

During this time Jesus and I did not speak with words, but impressions. Jesus impressed upon my spirit that He constantly intercedes for people experiencing trials, for those facing seminal decisions, and for those experiencing other pivotal moments in their lives. It also brought to mind the story of Shadrach, Meshach, and Abednego from the biblical book of Daniel, in which the Babylonian King Nebuchadnezzar II ordered these three Hebrew men be thrown into a fiery furnace for refusing to bow down to the king's image. Once in the furnace, the king observed not three figures, but four. The fourth being *"like the Son of God,"* Jesus (see Daniel 3:25 NKJV). Miraculously the three condemned Jews survived the furnace and the king subsequently ordered that no one must speak against the Hebrew God.

Friend, Jesus told me that in Heaven He intercedes on our behalf in much the same way. When we go through our "fiery furnace," whether an illness, the loss of a job, or any other point of suffering, Jesus is right there with us, saving us from destruction. I saw it with my spiritual eyes. That pure light that cut through the colors of the rainbow showered over people in this world—and only in Heaven did I notice the millions of people being saved by Jesus Christ's presence "taking the heat" for us, each and every second of every day. That seems unbelievable to my human mind, but to my spirit mind in Heaven it consumed me with love for God's infinite grace and mercy desiring to save us from all harm, refining us through the furnace, forging a newness of purpose and impact through the most challenging trials—and in the vast majority of cases, leaving us unscathed by our enemies' attempts to destroy us.

In Heaven I saw accidents that never happened, diseases that never materialized, and intended attacks that turned against the attacker, both in my life in this world and in your life. God works His greatest miracles in our afflictions that were defeated before we knew they even existed. Oftentimes we praise God for saving us, when in fact God more often saves us without our even being aware of it. It has been said that the memory is kind, but in Heaven memories serve to assuage our thoughts by showing the grace of God in all things.

LIVING LIFE AS A FIRST-TIME EXPERIENCE

> Revelation #3: We can only see God
> through the eyes of our heart.

Shortly after leaving the hospital, I began a journal recording of my experience in Heaven. After several pages, I stored my completed journal in boxes before we moved from our house after the kids moved out so that we could enjoy a home requiring less upkeep. During quiet times I would recollect about my time with Jesus as though it were fresh. It was like glancing out the window at the scenes of my childhood hometown while feeling exactly like the boy who viewed those scenes as a child. I was not perceiving Heaven with my physical eyes. I was reliving Heaven with the eyes of my heart as though yesteryear was now.

When I unpacked my journal, I noticed that my recollections were identical to what I had recorded years earlier. I tried reasoning why my recollection of Heaven evoked a clarity of mind that no other memory in my lifetime even closely resembled. I could only faintly imagine my past in this world, but getting still with God ushered my spirit mind's return to Heaven with all of the emotions and awe I previously felt in that paradise.

When reason failed, I asked God to inspire me with the answer as to why the vividness of my memory from Heaven transcended any other experience in this world. Soon thereafter, I received my answer. In Heaven, everything is viewed through a "first-time mindset," like the childlike thrill of a first-time experience. Do you remember some of your first-times? Perhaps the first time you received Christ as your Lord and Savior? The first time your awestruck eyes beheld something majestic? Your graduation? Your marriage? The birth of your child? These firsts form an indelible impression within our minds. Our brain has chunked together some of these first-time experiences apart from the millions of experiences in our lifetimes. They are uniquely special and set apart to be remembered forever.

Now, here is how the mind of the heart thinks in Heaven—everything is seen as the first time, even though it may be seen over and over. My wonderment in walking alongside Jesus never departed. Second or third views of the natural beauties, villages, and joyful people astounded me as though I had never seen them previously. The mind of my heart (my spirit mind) perceived everything afresh. In Heaven, I viewed each moment like a child tasting his first candy, only better—because I was there again.

So after I left Heaven, my spirit mind remembered Heaven as though it was now, and as if my recollection was as real as being in the now. The "aftertaste" or "afterview" of Heaven lingered for a lifetime. I think now that it would behoove each of us to think more from the vantage of a first-time experience, like a child, as if everything experienced had become new again. This perspective might also enable us to better communicate with God, and with one another.

The flip side also proves true, meaning that if we view each person as though it is the last time we will see that person, we will consider that individual more deeply. Considering the finality of our experiences immerses us in the moment. When Jesus stretched His arms out to me before I left Heaven, I noticed the scars in the palms of His hands. Why would Jesus keep the scars in His resurrected body, you may ask? Because, I believe, Jesus wanted to remember His final goodbye to His beloved followers. Jesus wears the scars of His crucifixion as emblems of His continuous willingness to sacrifice Himself for us.

My brain could not reason why Jesus would remain in a perpetual readiness to offer Himself to us, but to my spirit mind, it made perfect sense. Jesus Christ will forever remain the unblemished Lamb of God, even in Heaven. In Heaven, all things are made pure through the pervasive indwelling of Christ's Spirit. He is also the Lion of Judah, ever ready to defend His children and to reclaim them from the evil that grips this world. To genuinely know these two sides of Jesus, we must relinquish our brain to our spirit mind.

SPEAKING THE LANGUAGE OF HEAVEN

Thinking with the spirit mind compels us to speak the language of Heaven, which speaks of the love we gain from being the offshoot of Love Himself. The next time we see a loved one, we could think of meeting that person as though it were the last time we will see that person. We might forgive more by reimagining the abuses that scarred that person with a fresh perspective. We might love God more fully by viewing Him through the eyes of a child. The language of Heaven always speaks with perpetual Love, and it is only heard through the guileless filters of our spirit.

Consider the language of Heaven as akin to the mindful state of intuition. The dictionary explains intuition as the ability to understand something immediately, without the need for conscious reasoning. Unlike intuition, a heavenly impartation does not require understanding. When I was in Heaven, I did not reason what I perceived in my spirit. I just absorbed it.

I was like the spiritual servant whose eyes God opened so that he could see into the spiritual realm, seeing *"hills full of horses and chariots of fire all around Elisha"* (2 Kings 6:17). Indeed, as I was rising toward the light from above immediately after my physical death, I looked over the hillsides and saw warriors battling before my eyes. I saw these things because my spiritual eyes had been opened. My entire being was spirit at that point.

You can see the same things that I perceived in your spirit, but only if the eyes of your heart, your spiritual eyes, are opened. The apostle Paul, a fellow NDEer (see 2 Corinthians 12:2-4), wrote the following while under the inspiration of God's Spirit as documented in Ephesians 1:16-18:

> *I have not stopped giving thanks for you, remembering you in my prayers. I keep asking that the God of our Lord Jesus Christ, the glorious Father, may give you the Spirit of* **wisdom and revelation**, *so that you may know him better. I pray that the* **eyes of your heart** *may be enlightened in order that you may know the hope to which he has called you, the riches of his glorious inheritance in his holy people.*

The *"eyes of the heart,"* as Paul explains, imparts the Holy Spirit's *"wisdom and revelation,"* drawing us to a closer intimacy with God. William Shakespeare said, "The eyes are the window to your soul."

More can be revealed by looking into a person's eyes than just about any other physical observation.

When God looks through the eyes of our heart, He sees everything about us. When Jesus looked into my eyes in Heaven, His eyes tunneled into every dark place within me and infused His light in place of that darkness. What did this do? It created peace and comfort and a profound understanding of God's grace and forgiveness. Heightened senses allowed me to see beyond the trivial into the ethereal realm of another dimension that thrives in the presence of God's supreme love. I was never more alive than I was in Heaven. My new body felt strong, youthful, and devoid of any maladies or woeful concerns.

In that moment when Jesus first looked into my eyes, I understood the absolute forgiveness of God. I felt washed by His righteousness such that He did not even recall my failures. The Bible in Psalm 103:12 explains that when we genuinely seek God's forgiveness, He removes our transgressions as far as the east is from the west. In other words, He forgets them. He loves us that much. After being forgiven, God sees us anew as though it were the first time.

In Heaven, like me, you will not be condemned by your failures. Rather, you will understand the redeeming value of God's forgiveness. Nothing in the eyes of Jesus spoke condemnation. Quite the contrary, I knew the depth of God's redeeming love such that I was made pure through Christ. That is because my spiritual eyes could blend feelings and appearances to produce a synergistic understanding of God's will. No longer was my mind in Heaven focused on my cares, they focused on the cares of God.

SEEING THE IMPOSSIBLE

"So we fix our eyes not on what is seen, but on what is unseen, since what is seen is temporary, but what is unseen is eternal" (2 Corinthians 4:18). Have you ever wondered what lies within the "unseen"? Maybe at times you have stopped for a moment and been dazzled for no reason. You felt profoundly aware of something beyond your ability to describe it. That momentary unveiling of the sublime is a constant state of awareness in Heaven.

As a spirit being with a defined body much like my youthful body on earth, but with heightened awareness, I knew things beyond the pale of words in Heaven. No longer burdened with my earthly maladies, like asthma, and certainly not with the diseases that killed me, I was freed to see different grades of colors, variations of wonderful fragrances, and an accentuation of inspiring sounds that combined into an abiding realization of it all being good.

Good—that word apart from God ceases to exist. What I mean by this is that nothing entirely good comes from this world, it comes from God. In Heaven, everything is good because God reigns supreme. Goodness flows out of Him as supernaturally as streams from the ocean. What I am about to tell you may blow your mind, but it ties into the abiding presence of goodness in all things of Christ.

I saw a river flowing from Jesus that stretched throughout Heaven, and it started at the feet of Jesus. Wherever Jesus walked, life sprouted forth, and the *"river of the water of life"* described in Revelation 22:1, gave life to everything. Amazingly, everything in Heaven thrived in abundance because of that flowing river. I saw it with my spiritual eyes because I was a spirit, and I was with Jesus in Heaven.

You may have questions at this point. "Were there people in this lush place?" Yes. Their countenances exuded joy and their numbers exceeded my wildest expectations. "Were there animals?" Yes. They roamed freely and included all types and kinds, including (for those pet lovers), dogs and cats. (I must admit that as a dog lover and not a cat lover, I jokingly had wondered if cats were in Heaven.) "Did you taste of any foods?" No, I only hungered for more of Jesus Christ, though I did thirst for the water from Christ's river of life. "Are there genders in Heaven?" I noticed no physical separation of male or female given that our heavenly bodies had been spiritually transformed into the nature of God with consummate love devoid of carnal desires. All of my desires were fulfilled, unhindered by the distorted nature of physical yearnings that lead to fatuous love, empty love, jealousy, possessiveness, or infatuation.

Everything in Heaven was racially, ethnically, and characteristically accepted with no need to judge one creation from another. No bias could be felt in Heaven. We viewed one another apart from race or ethnicity as one would fondly view the different eye colors or distinguishing characteristics of a close loved one. Every one of God's creations appeared without any need to assess whether it was good or bad, right or wrong—it was all good, and each human being resonated the righteousness of Jesus Christ.

Colors, shapes, and sizes simply blended into a mosaic of God's wonderfully creative artistry. And there was no awareness of ethnic variations or any prejudices that we experience in this world, because differences in Heaven were mere expressions of God's creativity, not identifiers to distinguish one from another. Rather, differences were reflections of God's artistry and abundance. Each impression was heartfelt, and acceptance was unconditional.

Now, here is the point of how this all ties to our seeing through the eyes of our heart in this world. When we catch glimpses of Heaven on earth—such as that epiphany that defies description yet elicits comfort, peace, joy, and love—we are seeing through the eyes of our heart. I viewed everything in Heaven through the eyes of my heart. The key to bringing a little bit of Heaven into our life in this world, is to steep ourselves in the presence of God so that the Holy Spirit can turn what seems mystical or mysterious into what is self-evidently real.

In Heaven, you and I, like every living thing—and by the way, everything in Heaven is living—will be in the presence of God all of the time. Everything in Heaven imbues Christ's presence. He ushers forth the river of life (Revelation 22:1). He breathes life into everything. There is no way of escaping God in Heaven because His presence is imparted to everything.

GOD LOVES LIVING WITH YOU

The only way to realize the abundance of life in this world is to seek the face of God. That is, spend every waking minute of each day dwelling on Jesus Christ, and being still to hear God's voice in return. Impossible, you might say? Not if you consider that God's Spirit resides with you always. I remember Jesus' words that struck me as an epiphany like none other: "I am with you always." I had previously heard the Scripture to that effect, but when Jesus said it I became overwhelmed with the awareness that God literally never leaves the presence of His children because Jesus absolutely loves being with you and me. He never wants to leave our side, even when we rebel.

The revelation that God wants to have an ongoing conversation with us, struck the innermost part of my understanding. In

71

this world we have become conditioned to believe that we need to find a special place such as a prayer closet or find a special time perhaps in church on Sunday or laboriously devote ourselves in dedicated prayer, worship, and study during allocated periods, like first thing in the morning. Sometimes completing these tasks lulls us into a complacency that, if we do these things routinely, we can better justify ourselves before God. Jesus taught me that although disciplined attention to God is good, we need to make continuous fellowship with the Spirit of Jesus Christ a "normal way of living." That means talking with God's Spirit as though He is a constant Companion, which He is.

Now, I often involve God in the smallest things. For example, just today I was trying to decide which pasta sauce to choose. Being undecided, I asked the Holy Spirit to tell me which one to choose. Immediately, I knew exactly which one to select. Sound silly? Consider that Jesus' first miracle on this earth arose from a seemingly trivial comment by His mother at a wedding party after the wine ran out. Jesus turned water into the best wine of the evening, because He cares about what is important to us, no matter how trivial.

The old adage says that "The devil is in the details." To the contrary, the devil can only be in one place at any point in time. God, on the other hand, is in the details because only God knows everything, and only God is ever-present.

Considering that Jesus walks each step, breathes each breath, and thinks each thought that we make because He desires to be with us whether during the good times or the bad times speaks to the affectionate nature of God. Thus, dwelling on God need not be laborious. We can say anything, do anything, and think anything without fear of offending God, because He loves us warts and all. So when watching some form of entertainment, ask the Spirit of God to reveal to you what He sees.

When meeting with someone, ask the Spirit of God to reveal what He wants you to learn and share in that relationship. When you have doubts or questions, ask God to provide you with His answers. When alone, ask God to give you wisdom. When you fail, ask God for another chance. When you feel broken, ask God to comfort you and then expect Him to do it, if not now, soon. Jesus made it abundantly clear to me that we must expect that for which we ask, because the evidence of faith is not hope, it is expectancy. You do not need to imagine the Spirit of God being with you, because in fact that is exactly what is going on—always. Nothing you can do can stop God from loving you—nothing.

Know that God wants what is best for you even if your vision of what is better is different from God's absolute best. Trust Him. Jesus made it convincingly clear to me in Heaven that He does not want a part-time relationship. In Heaven, being in fellowship with God was continual, without effort. In this world, God knows our full attention requires constant discipline, and I felt Christ's mercy since He understood how hard that is for each of us. His readiness to grant forgiveness for my inescapable failures impressed me since Christ desired to forgive me infinitely more than I desired to forgive myself. "When you fall, My beloved," Jesus said to me in Heaven, "look to Me and I will lift you up."

Relationship with God need not be occasional. It should be constant because His Spirit abides within each believer in Jesus Christ. In Heaven as on earth, Jesus is my Friend, my Pal, my ever-present Companion. Whether you know it or not, the same applies to you.

Knowing Jesus Christ as a constant and familiar Friend is that simple—and that profound.

This Life Appears as a Workstation

Consider this life as a workstation, and when we retire we go to Heaven. God placed us in this world to do good works, but He views our heart foremost. Quit thinking of success in terms of achievement. Success is who you are in Christ, not what you are in this world. When the heart is centered on Christ, the will to do God's bidding just spills out of us regardless of our position or circumstance.

Colossians 3:23-24 states it like this: *"Whatever you do, work at it with all your heart, as working for the Lord, not for human masters, since you know that you will receive an inheritance from the Lord as a reward. It is the Lord Christ you are serving."* Working for God requires full attention on Him. The doing part spills out of the being part so that anything we do, whether sweeping the floor or leading a business, must be done with a Christ mindset.

In Heaven, everyone works for Jesus who functions as the Foreman, if you will, and our mindset will be focused on executing God's will. Our works will glorify God in all things such that now I believe that this book was originally authored in Heaven, as strange as that may seem. I believe that I was capable of writing poetry in Heaven that might make my favorite poet, Robert Browning, proud. I was capable of teaching others as an oracle of God because my Christ mindset in Heaven had been fully established. Every intentional activity in Heaven is more significant than any duty we might perform in this world.

How we will live in Heaven represents the model for how we should live on earth. All of God's children function both in the present and future. We plan for the future; and if our plan aligns with God's plan for us, the outcome of our plan makes a Kingdom impact. What we accomplish according to God's plan in this life does not end when we die, it continues into Heaven. There exists an eternity on earth that extends into Heaven and includes everything that we do according to God's Kingdom purpose—which extends beyond our mental grasp.

For example, in Heaven every Kingdom work I accomplished in this life extended into Heaven. In this world, I sometimes functioned as a teacher, and in Heaven my ability to expound on God's truths continued unfettered by the confusion that sometimes hinders my ability to understand the truth in this world. I can teach you now about "heavenly truths" only because of what was established for me in Heaven. My ability to author this book you are reading now began in Heaven almost fifteen years earlier because God spoke it into being long before my afterlife experience happened.

God is pouring out His purpose for you and me now based on what He conferred to us in Heaven. Using a crude analogy, Heaven operates as the "manufacturing plant" for every Kingdom purpose we accomplish in this lifetime; and when we get to Heaven, that Kingdom purpose will continue in much the same way.

God speaks what is commanded in Heaven into being so that it can be manifested in this world, irrespective of time and events. *"Before the mountains were brought forth,"* as it says in Psalm 90:2 (NKJV), the God of "I AM" was called forth to birth Himself in this world as the Messiah, Jesus Christ. The "I AM" God establishes our life in Heaven, directs our steps now, and perfects our purpose in Heaven. In Heaven, everyone, including me, seemed to function in similar ways that they functioned in this world; however, their activities were exclusively dedicated to God's purpose, and their ability to carry forth those activities were made perfect. In Heaven, artists produced astounding works of art, gardeners produced breathtaking outcomes, organizers rallied people to worshipful events—people in Heaven were not just busy, they were executing the will of God.

If your head doesn't hurt too much at this point with woosoo thinking, please allow me to distill this down to you here, now. When you consecrate what you are doing to Jesus, you are ful-filling what God created you to do in Heaven; thereby you are manifesting God's will for you in this present life. You are doing what God called you to do. And, when you reach Heaven, you will be executing that work to perfection.

Consider now your greatest accomplishment in this world. Maybe you were a terrific parent. Maybe you started a thriv-ing business. Maybe you produced an amazing creative piece. Whatever you are most proud about today, having honored God with your mastery, you will see your proudest Kingdom achieve-ment perfected in Heaven, and you will continue to produce several other perfect masterpieces in Heaven. You will not just be busy in Heaven—your works will be flawless. This is because your Christ mindset will be all-consuming.

WHAT IS A CHRIST MINDSET?

A Christ mindset comes from Isaiah 40:13 (New English Translation), *"Who comprehends the mind of the LORD, or gives him instruction as his counselor?"* The verse is also quoted in the New Testament in First Corinthians 2:16: *"'Who has known the mind of the Lord so as to instruct him?' But we have the mind of Christ."*

Having a Christ mindset means we adopt Christ's point of view, comprehending His values and desires as a compelling mindset, not just a disciplined practice. It means to absorb God's thoughts irrespective of our limited perspective.

In First Corinthians 2:5-6, Paul contrasts the unbeliever, the self-focused person, with the believer, the God-focused person. When we exhibit a Christ mindset, it contrasts with our common mindset of fulfilling our wants. It requires the wisdom of God to direct our steps, which cannot be understood without God's Spirit (verse 14). When we have a Christ mindset, we live primarily within the spiritual realm of Christ (verse 15).

Living with a Christ mindset represents a huge paradigm shift for most people. Most function as busybodies, attending to what life throws our way. The floor gets dirty, so we mop. Product sits in the warehouse, so we sell. The kids need a ride to school, so we hop in the car. A job needs to be done, so we do it. If honest, most of us would confess that we live as functionaries most of the time.

The key is that whatever we do, our heart must compel us to do it for God—even the mundane. Jesus delighted in every little moment in Heaven while we sojourned. He saw each effort of mine as an expression of my character. Being aware of God's concern for our minutiae is how we should live, knowing that God is in the details. In Heaven, God orchestrated even the details of life while empowering each of His children with God's Spirit to unleash their creativity so that each person could enhance everything of value. Heaven was not just a place of busyness; it was a place of intentionality.

LIVING THROUGH GRACE

> Revelation #4: The flip side of a worldly point of view is that our hearts will determine the merit of our contributions in Heaven.

God will not look at you on the day you die and say, "Hey, you did not achieve your best." No, He will look upon you as you truly are in Christ, period. An elderly friend of mine read my book, *Dying to Meet Jesus*, and said, "All this time I thought that when we get to Heaven, God would judge me for what I did and did not do." That is a common misperception about Heaven.

Each one of my fellow Christian NDEers with whom I have interacted say essentially the same, "I didn't feel judged, I felt accepted." Some, like me, experienced what is called a "life review," but even the failures were not condemning, they merely reflected the grace of God by revealing the damage those failures caused, and the redeeming purpose that God forged through them.

When I met Jesus, I was not a saint. My opinion before Heaven told me that God was angry at me. I tried living a good life, but I failed (sinned) more than I care to mention. In this world those failures circled in my mind like vultures preying on a wounded soul. But in Heaven, my conscience was clear. Not because I did nothing wrong—I did a lot wrong—but the grace of Jesus Christ was sufficient to cleanse me of all unrighteousness. I felt redeemed, forgiven, thankful, and welcomed.

Now, my desire to do good is not from a fear of being judged; rather, I want to please my Lord and Savior because He loves me so very, very much. I can now tell every single human being on the face of the planet, "God is not angry with you." The God I met loves even those some consider unlovable. Jesus told me that no one is unredeemable. Not only does God love you, He likes you.

That represents a gargantuan difference in how to live through grace. When you come face-to-face with Jesus Christ, you will understand the full measure of God's grace in your life. Being on the other side of this world will impress upon you that spending time with God was the most important expenditure of your entire existence on earth. Nothing illustrates this better than the story of when Jesus visited the home of Mary and Martha in Luke 10:38-42:

> *As Jesus and his disciples were on their way, he came to a village where a woman named Martha opened her home to him. She had a sister called Mary, who sat at the Lord's feet listening to what he said. But Martha was distracted by all the preparations that had to be made. She came to him and asked, "Lord, don't you care that my sister has left me to do the work by myself? Tell her to help me!"*
>
> *"Martha, Martha," the Lord answered, "you are worried and upset about many things, but few things are needed— or indeed only one. Mary has chosen what is better, and it will not be taken away from her."*

Spending time with God is paramount to a thriving life. Conflict arises from spending too little time with God. Our thoughts drift toward the demands of life when Jesus is simply saying that we need to remain focused on Him as our abiding Friend and Counsel. My only regret in Heaven was that I had not spent enough time with God.

Time with God is time abundantly and everlastingly spent.

WHAT THE HOMELESS MAN TAUGHT ME

Some have asked me if I saw any of the "spiritual giants" noted in the Scriptures such as Abraham, the common patriarch of Judeo-Christianity, or Mary, the mother of Jesus on earth. No, I did not. Even if I had met one of them, they would have appeared as no more significant than anyone else in Heaven.

Previous to Heaven, my dream was to someday meet Abraham Lincoln, but knowing what I know now, this is no longer a desire. Everyone in Heaven is cherished by God regardless of their accomplishments. All of the saints in Heaven considered themselves as of paramount importance to God, yet they remained humble, desiring to serve others. I considered others to be more valuable than myself while at the same time I considered myself more valued by God than any other, as strange as that may seem. Indeed, God shows no favoritism (Acts 10:34), although we will feel infinitely valued by God in Heaven. There will be no desire to get God's attention, because His attention will always be on us.

In this world, status is highly regarded. Whether consciously or unconsciously, we tend to think of wealthy or acclaimed people as more significant than ourselves. My friend, Steve, who was homeless for years, said that no one in this world looks at homeless people eye to eye. Little can homeless people comprehend that God not only sees them eye to eye, He cherishes their souls. I know this because when in Heaven, Jesus revealed to me a person who was formerly homeless in the world. He was clothed in a purple garment richly adorned with pearls and gold. If I had not known better, I would have thought of this man as royalty, when in fact he, like all the saints, was of "royal blood" having been adopted by the King of kings.

At no other time did I realize the former status of a person's life before they reached Heaven, except for an awareness of this once-homeless man. Jesus nodded His head after I said to Him, "So this man used to be in rags and now he's in riches." It then dawned on me why Jesus would reveal the man's prior status to me. In Heaven there is no such thing as status, and yet in this world our purpose is often defined by our position in life.

One of the most common questions asked of children is, "What do you want to be when you grow up?" Perhaps answers include, "A teacher," "A sports player," "A doctor," "An astronaut," etc. Rarely will a child answer, "I would like to serve others." From early on we were taught to define our purpose in life as the attainment of a position or status, and those programmed expectations defined our purpose as a vocation or stature.

But that was not how I perceived God's measure of someone's purpose in Heaven, or His intention for us in this world. That former homeless man taught me that a person's stature is solely defined by their relationship to the King of kings, and that no person merits a higher status than another in God's Kingdom. Purpose, subsequently, amounts to accomplishing God's objective for us moment by moment, person by person, and situation by situation.

The former homeless man appeared to be feeding a group of saints formed in a circle around him. One by one, he placed a morsel in their outreached hands, which ironically juxtaposed with a vision I had of this man being served food in a soup kitchen on earth.

"Those you see around this man served those like him in the world," Jesus said. "Those who serve My beloved in the world will be served abundantly more in Heaven."

This told me everything I needed to know about our noblest purpose—to serve one another. Whether that be a plate of food given to the poor, discipleship, or assuming the burden of another, Jesus blesses the helping hands of persons who care for those in need. This runs contrary to how much of the world operates. The modus operandi in this world is to serve oneself before serving another.

HOW GOD SEES US

I can reasonably deduce now that pretty much every value in this world contrasts with God's values in Heaven. When Jesus shared the so-called Beatitudes during His Sermon on the Mount (Matthew 5:3-16), He highlighted the diametrical differences between the Kingdom of Heaven and the kingdom of this world. The following are the comparisons:

THE KINGDOM OF HEAVEN	THE KINGDOM OF THIS WORLD
Blessed are the poor in spirit.	Blessed are the rich in things.
Blessed are those who mourn.	Blessed are those who make merry.
Blessed are the meek.	Blessed are the assertive.
Blessed are they who hunger and thirst for righteousness.	Blessed are they who hunger and thirst after self-righteousness.
Blessed are the merciful.	Blessed are the avengers.
Blessed are the pure in heart.	Blessed are the worldly.
Blessed are the peacemakers.	Blessed are the instigators.
Blessed are those who are persecuted for the sake of righteousness.	Blessed are those who are victorious for the sake of getting their own way.

When I realized the values God esteems in His Kingdom, everything else in this world lost much of its value to me. It was difficult for me to accept this world's values since those in Heaven elucidated the differences between the spirit, which is governed steadfastly by the Spirit of Christ, and the flesh, which is governed by the shifting ways of this world. The world's values and God's values are antithetical.

The same inverse valuation applies to a person's worth in this world in contrast to how God sees that person in Heaven. Consider the people God chose to bring forth His Word to the world:

- David—the least of his brothers, an adulterer, and murderer
- Paul—a Pharisee who persecuted Christians
- Mary Magdalene—a prostitute
- Jacob—a cheater
- Moses—a stutterer
- Naomi—a poor widow
- Jonah—a coward
- Elijah—a suicidal man (at one point)
- Martha—a constant worrier
- Peter—a doubter
- Noah—a drunk

I could go on, but you get the point. God uses flawed people. Moreover, He never uses perfect people in this world to convey His perfection because, frankly, there are no perfect people in this world. Why does God more often use hugely flawed people to communicate His truth? Perhaps it is similar to the reason why God used even a donkey and burning bush to share His truth. God continually reminds us that only God can impart perfection to an imperfect vessel.

The moment we think that we have all the answers is the most dangerous point in our lives. I know this as a former agnostic. I thought that God did not exist. Ironically, God used someone—me—who did not believe in God to reveal His absolute reality in Heaven.

Humility is the most prevalent characteristic of everyone in Heaven, and the least evidenced quality of those in this world. That is why God oftentimes uses opposites to convey His perfection. Weak people cannot boast of their own strength; they, like me, can only boast of God's strength. A perception of our weakness is the beginning of wisdom. Those farthest from God, coincidentally, are the most arrogant, the proverbial know-it-alls. Speaking personally, the more I know, the more I realize that I do not understand most things. Please do not think that because I caught a glimpse of Heaven that I am more enlightened. No—because of my experience, I am just more grateful to God.

We will all have an eternity in Heaven to learn the infinite wonders of God's creation, just as I witnessed people in Heaven teaching and learning from each other in much the same way that we learn information today, only God's impartation was instilled in Heaven through progressive revelations (see Ephesians 2:6-7). I gleaned more ideas during my brief period in Heaven than in some of my post-graduate studies.

We can all imagine how our learnings will exponentially increase to eternity. The difference in my heavenly learnings from my earthly learnings was that in Heaven my intuitive grasp of reality produced more gratitude toward the author of all knowledge Himself, God.

Gratitude is a constant state of mind in Heaven, as I believe it should be in this world. I suppose that if I met Abraham Lincoln in Heaven, I would simply say, "Isn't God wonderful?" All of the great leaders throughout history were foremost servants to the people they led. Servants acknowledge their masters. In this world, a "master" may be a boss, a parent, or a politician. For the Christian, the master should always become the servant. Though I worshipped Jesus in Heaven, wishing to serve Him, I always felt that Jesus was serving me. That in itself was mind-blowing.

Servanthood flows supernaturally from God. Success in Heaven is not a measure of one's attainment, it is a given. However, from my perspective in the spirit, my personal success was measured by the degree of love I felt for my Lord. My mission in life is simply to love God more and more.

> Revelation #5: The extent of our love for God determines our Kingdom success.

PUTTING GOD FIRST

One man shared with me that he had only recently discovered his purpose in life.

"Really? You're turning 80 and you're just finding that out?" I said to him.

Imagine that, an 80-year-old man finally discovered his purpose in life. Surely this accomplished man had discovered his purpose long ago. I considered how this man had been the most accomplished attorney in all of San Diego, the seventh-largest city in the nation. He never lost a case as a prosecutor. That is right, *never*. The records confirm this man's stellar achievement. And now this man, who lives in one of the most affluent areas in the world, was telling me that he only recently had discovered his purpose. His purpose? Living day by day, moment by moment, waiting on the Lord for directions about what to do next.

Guess what the man does vocationally now, at the age of 80? He raises white doves and releases them at memorial services and weddings. Often he shares the love of Jesus Christ with people mourning their lost loved ones, like the father whose teenage son pulled the trigger of a gun the boy placed in his mouth. Word spread that Joe could understand the heart of parents who grieve the loss of their children, because Joe's teenage son committed suicide, and his young daughter died in an accident.

Now, here is the shocker. Joe's ministry is not the reason for his godly success and fulfillment. As deeply impactful as his ministry can be to people at their lowest point, the doing part of Joe's second career only represents the surface of God's pleasure in Joe. God rejoices that Joe's heart desires Him, causing Joe to seek after God. The end result is that Joe feels compelled to do good.

I know Joe. I know him as a kind, loving, generous, and faithful follower of Christ. The love of God just spills out of him supernaturally. I also know that Joe knows the value of what is most important. Shortly after losing his only biological children (he has one adopted son), and after his wife left him, Joe took stock of his life, the $30,000 show horses, the luscious acreage around his multimillion dollar home, the priceless artwork, and the three cars parked outside, and inwardly said, *These things are nothing.* He sold most of them. He now gives liberally to those in need. His success is defined not in dollars but in devotion to God.

STORING TREASURES IN HEAVEN

In essence, the greatest treasure in Heaven is closeness to God. Those who lived in closeness to God in this world will experience an even deeper relationship with Him in Heaven. Those who gave only a perfunctory acknowledgment of God in this world, though saved by Jesus Christ's grace, will experience a lesser treasure in Heaven, meaning that their closeness to God will not be as intimate as those who were closer to Him in this world. The best analogy I can think of is when a distant relative arrives to live with someone, that distant relative needs to grow their familiarity with the person at whose home that relative will live. Whereas a close relative will feel instantly at home in the presence of the homeowner because of their familiarity with that homeowner.

Regardless of whether someone made a last-minute confession on his or her deathbed, or daily sought after God in this world, everyone in Heaven appeared immeasurably closer to God than at any time in this world, including me. The key takeaway: do not wait to earnestly seek after Jesus Christ in this world. Believe me, you want to be as close to God as possible in Heaven for all of eternity, because the degree of closeness to God in this world is magnified infinitely more in Heaven. A life of abundance in this world translates into closeness to God.

Living with abundance has nothing to do with things and everything to do with relationship, foremost our relationship with God. Not that God does not want His children to have good gifts. Indeed, God enjoys lavishing His children with gifts (Matthew 7:11). However, the treasures in Heaven that God speaks about in Matthew 6:19-21 cannot be found in achievement. These verses mean that if one places one's treasures in Heaven, that is where one's heart's desire will be established. Verse 21 expresses the key:

"For where your treasure is, there your heart will be also." Many interpret that verse as saying if your heart is focused on God, then your calling will be significant in this world. Those persons substitute the need for a genuine relationship with God with works and traditions that lull them into complacency.

I used to think that way. If I read my Bible each day, prayed, attended church, worshipped, fellowshipped with other believers on occasion, and participated in a ministry like leading a small group, then I could maintain a disciplined walk with Christ. My life would be significant because I lived as a good and decent man. Indeed, some people thought I had it "together." But inwardly I was a mess. I got angry when people offended me. I even cussed in traffic on occasion! If my beloved church family only knew…

But God knew. He knows everything. He knows our thoughts and our motives. Nothing escapes God's eyes—not even that occasional risqué television series or those passing desires to…well, you get the point. The fact is, we can never be good enough to "please" God all of the time. My "please rate" would barely earn enough godly points to buy a cup of coffee in Heaven. The rich young ruler discovered this truth after approaching Jesus one day. The story is told in Luke 18:18-23:

> *A certain ruler asked him, "Good teacher, what must I do to inherit eternal life?" "Why do you call me good?" Jesus answered. "No one is good—except God alone. You know the commandments: 'You shall not commit adultery, you shall not murder, you shall not steal, you shall not give false testimony, honor your father and mother.'" "All these I have kept since I was a boy," he said. When Jesus heard this, he said to him, "You still lack one thing. Sell everything you have and give to the poor, and you will have treasure in*

heaven. Then come, follow me." When he heard this, he became very sad, because he was very wealthy.

In response to Jesus calling out the young ruler, you may wonder, *Really? We have to sell everything to follow Jesus?* No, but each of us must be *willing* to sell everything if required by God. Moreover, we must treasure our time with Jesus more than anything else.

> Revelation #6: The *doing* part of pleasing God cannot be achieved before the *being* part of wanting to please God is achieved.

Finding purpose is the equivalent of seeking after God in all things. It means a full-time relationship with God, not a part-time one. It means being, more than doing. The important key is to put God first, which means we need to transform the "have to" of life to the "want to" of life. We know that we *have to* obey God in order to live a purposeful life. But when *having* (needing) to do good becomes irrelevant because we *want* to do good, the Spirit of Jesus Christ has taken control. When our need to obey God becomes a driving force compelling our mindset, then we have arrived. Our will is established in this world just as God willed us in Heaven.

No doubt you have heard the saying, "You can't take it with you." My experience confirms this completely. Standing before the Author of Love, I knew that my being infused with His Love was paramount. Apart from God I could do nothing. I owned nothing in Heaven and yet I possessed everything of value in Christ. Consumed in His presence I felt empowered. The doing part came later.

LIVING THE IMPOSSIBLE

Jesus says in the Bible, *"With God all things are possible"* (Matthew 19:26). Anything? Yes, as long as that "thing" aligns with God's will. The key to living out our purpose is to meld our will to God's will, so that the two are synonymous. If that sounds like an impossible task, then stop thinking of it as a task and think of it as surrendering our will to God each and every moment.

It is time to reach into the "impossible" now, so that we can grasp the possible. When Jesus walked on water, He was defying what is possible. When God parted the waters for Moses, He was defying what is possible. When Jesus rose from the tomb, He was defying what is possible. When Jesus returned me from the dead, He was defying what is possible. God lives in our "impossible."

Now it is time that I woosoo with you again. Remember that word means entering the realm of our impossible to reach God's possible. Remember that time when my body struggled to survive. I clinically died. My heart stopped. I entered into that space scientists cannot explain—the heavenly realm of what is after life. My impossible became God's possible as my body failed and my spirit soared. This is the part where some may think I am more wacko than woosoo.

Breaking through the impossible to God's possible is spiritual, not physical, and living fully in the spirit is foreign to most. In the afterlife my spirit body was being pulled by a bright light through a vacuum of space. No longer was I cognizant of my body. I was entirely at the effect of someone or something sucking me upward, and I experienced no fear during this time, just tranquility. At that moment, a myriad of colors fused into oblique forms melding into mountains, streams, and trees through which the wind blew life into everything. The glory of God was birthing a new world before my eyes.

Afar from the paradise where I stood with Jesus, I perceived an expanse of space that appeared unfinished, or obscure. It appeared as a galaxy blended with an amorphous mix of waters and land. I could not make sense of that space except to think of it as a melting pot, analogous to the mixing of colors on a surface; but instead of colors, what I saw appeared like a melding of terrains, waters, and atmospheres that remained distinct yet fluid. My impression was that another reality existed beyond Heaven, still under God's authority, but apart from the paradise in which I existed, and perhaps even apart from the finished works of God who indwelled every person in Heaven and breathed inspiration into everything.

Now I realize that Heaven—or the paradise mentioned by Jesus Christ to the penitent thief who hung next to Jesus when He lived on this earth—is set apart from this world by a chasm that may appear just as I explained in the preceding paragraph. And I also sensed that from the beginning of time God created this earth and our galaxies from the "soup" that I perceived in the distance. If that does not sound too woosoo to you, then allow me to take this a step further. In that space between what is well defined as the earth, the galaxies, and Heaven may exist a realm of creativity from which God can turn His word into form. A crude analogy would be when a painter uses a palette to mix paints to form a piece of artwork. God's "palette," in this case, might be what I described; however, God's "brushstroke" is actually His Word.

Consider John 1:1-5:

> *In the beginning was the Word, and the Word was with God, and the Word was God. He was with God in the beginning. Through him all things were made; without*

*him nothing was made that has been made. In him was
life, and that life was the light of all mankind. The light
shines in the darkness, and the darkness has not overcome it.*

In Heaven I could visualize how God spoke life into all that
lived, and now I can easily envision how God could speak into
the great chasm I observed, to create this world and everything
within it. The Word of God in Heaven was literally the spoken
word of God that commanded everything into being and spoke
truth into others.

In this world, our words can be powerful. They create an effect.
Our speaking encouragement to another in this world uplifts that
person and even creates a thriving mindset within that person that
favorably impacts their overall well-being. However, when God
speaks, He actually creates all that is good. In Heaven I heard
Jesus speak to a tree, and it produced fruit. When Jesus spoke to
me, a new level of understanding arose within me. Whenever Jesus
spoke, it was as though His personhood of truth gave life to everything around Him. That is the power of God's Word to create and
to breathe life.

Nothing in this world compares to the power of God's Word.
That Word, beloved of the Lord, is Jesus Christ. There was even
a time in Heaven when I could not see Jesus, but I could hear His
Word, and it seemed to me as if His spoken word was the same as
if He were physically embracing me. Wowsa!

OUR FUTURE IS IN GOD'S PAST

God's Word represents the quintessence of His character just as
Jesus represented on earth the incarnation of what God spoke into
being. The Word of God speaks Truth, and only God personifies
Truth. While in Heaven I witnessed God's Truth born out in real

time, such that when Jesus spoke His Truth, a shift occurred in Heaven that ushered forth new creations, including what I sensed were inspirations for all of God's children in Heaven who chanted resounding praises in response.

Jesus spoke into being trees that took root, homes comprised of what looked like multi-colored stones, and a birth of creativity in His children that appeared to magnify their works. When Jesus said to me, "You will bring my Light into the darkness" as we strolled together, He motioned to a place I instantly thought to be my future home in Heaven. It appeared as a vision to me, unlike the vivid realities of Heaven I viewed previously, and it appeared as a type of ranch with animals rustling around. A white porch surrounded the green farmhouse estate. As a child I dreamed of living on a farm and this vision excited my senses.

I asked Jesus about this vision, and He informed me that my future is in God's past, and I deduced that Jesus was showing me a glimpse of my future. Perhaps this helps explain why our mindful context of Heaven differs from our spiritual context of Heaven. Heaven may be in a different plane from us, rather than a different place. Expressing Heaven defies our linear way of thinking because it is multi-dimensional and not bound by any human context.

Thus, I understand now that my memories of Heaven do not fit the paradigm of most stories in this world, because what happens in this world is chronological and well-defined within the context of time and space. In Heaven, most of what I experienced was represented as a fusion of adventures not bound by time or even spatial dimensions. God explains in Isaiah 55:9 that "the heavens are higher than the earth," and so are His ways higher than our ways.

During my recovery I journaled many of my experiences but there was not a step by step walk through Heaven that I could tell you. Typically, stories are told as going from "point A" to "point B," but my experience was more like viewing familiar scenes and people, and then my observations were transformed to nothing I had ever seen before, and I perceived their aspects in varied ways as though peering through a "spiritual kaleidoscope."

Mine was a transfiguration to places both familiar and foreign, and the events may not have been sequential, they may have been juxtaposed or assimilated from thought to perception to reality. If that sounds confusing, please believe me when I state that my experience was not at all confusing. I can tell you that my experience in Heaven was more real because what I witnessed did not have to be defined by mere events or causal factors. What happened I could only explain in the context of how I understood its meaning, and Jesus imparted to me an awareness I had never fully realized in this world.

I think this represents the challenge posed by some writers about their NDE experiences. Even Jesus said that He did not talk about heavenly things very much because we could barely understand earthly things. Telling about Heaven does not fit with the instructions I learned in writing classes at Northwestern University. It also does not fit neatly within my scientific learnings having spent countless hours covering cases in surgery, and teaching students about physiological, behavioral and scientific knowledge for over 25 years.

If I attempted to just explain what I saw in Heaven, and when I saw it, or even how I felt when seeing it, the reason why I saw these things might be lost within the scintillating effect of being in Heaven with Jesus while missing the point of why God allowed me to experience Heaven in the afterlife. My thinking was transformed in Heaven, and my point in writing this book is my attempt to elucidate those newfound insights.

Today, my memories of Heaven are now relegated to my recovered notes and the complex interaction between my brain chemicals and neuronal receptors within the temporal lobe of my brain, but, my spirit is constantly reminded of my time in Heaven.

Part of what I learned is that Heaven should not be considered as being of the utmost importance. Matthew 24:35 records Jesus as telling us "that Heaven and earth will pass away, but my words will never pass away." I treasured my Lord's words more than anything, because He spoke life into everything.

As I now try to synthesize all that I learned while walking with Jesus, I remember one very important moment. A soft wind soothed me in Heaven as I heard these words either directly from Jesus or imbedded within the wind itself: "You are at home wherever I am with you." That profound understanding is for you just as it was for me. Jesus is our home.

I am now at home with Jesus typing these words so that you can know that even though today is Heaven's yesterday, God is before you and with you now, and every moment of your life matters in the scheme of eternity because God has "plans to give you hope and a future" (Jeremiah 29:11). Your actions are memorialized in Heaven.

What you do according to God's plans expresses a Christlike fragrance rising up to God (2 Corinthians 2:15), and I bear witness to the fact that your sweet fragrances are pleasing to God.

A FINAL RELEASE OF THE DOVES

I watched my friend, Joe, release his white doves on Ponto Beach during an Easter sunrise service. My daughter released these doves from their white boxes as they emerged in direct ascendance toward the blue sky. One could not avoid thinking about God's Holy Spirit, represented by the doves rising to the heavens after being held captive in their container.

In Heaven, I faintly saw birds in the air that appeared to leave an afterglow, and to me that represented the lingering presence of God. After Jesus was baptized by John, *"the Holy Spirit descended on him in bodily form like a dove"* (Luke 3:22). This is why Christians use the dove as a symbol of God's Holy Spirit. I think God revealed His everlasting presence to me in the form of those birds in Heaven as a way of assuaging my angst after Jesus informed me that I would return to this world.

Those doves Joe released on the beach now represent a special meaning to me. This world contains us. It boxes us in. We yearn to spread our wings in flight toward Heaven. We await someone to open the lid of our prison, to free us to fly. Someday, we hope, we dream…that we will be freed of this fallen world. But the only way God can completely free us is to release our spirits from our bodies on the day that each of us will die.

Those doves that were freed on Ponto Beach flew up toward Heaven into the sky until they reached a certain altitude, and then once they got their bearing, the doves started flying home. My friend, Joe, had trained them to return to his ranch. The sky was not their home. They needed a place to rest. Something inside them called them home. Indeed, those birds I saw in Heaven represented God's Holy Spirit who would call us home after our spirits are released from our bodies. They also served as messengers of God's promise to me that one day I would return to live with Him forever.

When Jesus told me that I would be returning to this world, I felt saddened for the first time in Heaven.

"Lord, no." I felt like a child waking on Christmas morning to open his presents, only to be told by his parent that he would have to return to bed.

"Your purpose has not been fulfilled, My beloved," He said.

"So tell me what's my purpose." I felt as though I deserved an answer since I would be leaving paradise. Doves are homing pigeons whose mission is to fly and return to their cages. This world in comparison to Heaven seemed like one of those cages.

That is when I met the butterfly. Butterflies live for a brief time, maybe a year. They are meant to be free. The multicolored design on their wings softens the atmosphere. Should one of these beautifully painted butterflies rest on you, you need to be still, or else it will fly away. And that, my friend, makes all the difference.

5

THE BUTTERFLY

THE POWER OF PRAYER

That acrid smell of hospital disinfectant invaded my nostrils after awakening from my thirty-minute decease. A couple stood at my bedside singing the same song I heard in Heaven. At first, I thought the angelic voices after my cardiac arrest were actually the couple's voices resonating within my mind. But then I remembered the angelic voices in Heaven singing a worship song so ineffable that nothing in this world can compare, not even an assembly of the world's greatest symphonies.

That same, identical, worship song I had heard in Heaven was being sung by the couple alongside my bed after I awoke from my once-dead body. Somehow, God had enjoined the worship of these two people by my bedside with the worship of His angels in Heaven as one glorious paean. I remembered what Jesus had said to me in Heaven, "I am sending you back, beloved. Many are praying for you now." I learned in that moment about the power of prayer.

The analogy that comes to mind is a tipping point. Please excuse the crude word picture, but it is like a cup rests in Heaven, and each time someone prays for something, it is like they are pouring milk into that cup. At some point when the cup is filled, God pours out the milk as answered prayers onto earth, inaugurating God's will on earth.

> Revelation #7: What we pray on earth is enjoined in Heaven such that God can pour forth His will on earth.

The cup represents God's established purpose for each person. The prayers of His saints are the milk. Milk as we know it is the beginning food for life. A newborn born into this world survives on his or her mother's milk. Spiritual milk—prayer in this case— also provides nourishment for birthing God's will on earth. When a sufficient amount of prayer fills the cup, God pours out His will from Heaven and establishes it on earth.

God births His purpose for us through *"prayer and supplication"* (Philippians 4:6-7 NKJV). We know that God understands our needs even before we ask them, but there is some heavenly shift that happens when God's people pray. I know that I was returned for a purpose because of the prayers of others. I know that those who prayed first listened to God's will. They said something like, "God, I sense, or know, that You are not finished with Randy in this world yet." They knew it because they listened to God's Spirit; and once they heard God's will with their spiritual ears, they enjoined God's will in Heaven with their prayers on earth.

"I'm going to return you, My beloved," Jesus said to me in Heaven.

"Why," I asked. "At least give me an answer if You are going to take me from this paradise."

"I am returning you for a purpose, beloved."

"Please tell me." I implored God to just tell me. *At least I deserved that much.*

What happened next changed my life forever. And I hope it will change yours. You see, in Heaven, change is always for the *best*. On earth, change is sometimes for the better. But in Heaven, change is always for God's best because change in Heaven expands God's influence.

WHAT I LEARNED FROM THE BUTTERFLY

A butterfly rested on my right shoulder. A mosaic of soft colors flowed over its wings. The colors appeared like a felt painting, in shades of blues, reds, greens, and yellows more brilliant than any colors in this world, with variations of hues unlike any I had ever seen. It nestled softly, lightly, lovingly on my shoulder.

"This butterfly is the wisdom that will guide you, My beloved," Jesus said.

I dared not move, knowing that butterflies are sensitive to movement and not wanting it to fly away because it imparted so much tenderness in my heart.

"Just as you must remain still, My beloved, so it is with My wisdom."

Be still, and know that I am God. I remembered the verse from Psalm 46:10. I knew that if I moved too abruptly, not waiting on God, not resting in His presence and not listening to His will, I would lose God's guiding wisdom.

"Lord, I know what You are saying. I need to wait on You."

"My Spirit has told you this," He said.

"So it's about just being with You, spending time, listening."

Jesus smiled softly; His eyes beamed with joy. My pleasure in pleasing my Lord exceeded any amount of satisfaction I had experienced with anyone in the world—more than the approval of my parents, teachers, or bosses—more than anyone's accolades. I felt my Lord's comforting approval not just in words, but through understanding God's truth, inspired with the determination to abide by that truth.

I had been a Type A person for most of my adult life in a Type A world. Within school, the corporate world, even in my own home when raising my children, I expected more from others and myself. I am sure that my parenting suffered by transferring some of those expectations onto my children, and even my wife.

As a young child, my father strived to improve our lives after leaving the poor side of town in Keokuk, Iowa, faithfully serving in World War II, and then raising me in an apartment in the modest part of Skokie, Illinois, near Chicago. I never felt as though we lived in a lower-class lifestyle while growing up, until visiting the jaw-dropping houses of friends. The first time I saw a home with a balcony, I thought as a grade school kid, *I want what they have.*

My worldly striving began after tasting the finer things in life. I studied hard to earn A's. I played football to please my dad, a former All-State middle linebacker. When Princeton and Northwestern approved my applications, I chose Northwestern because my dad had always dreamed of going to that school. I joined a fraternity at Northwestern, became president, then joined eight other organizations and ran for president in each one.

My grades suffered because of my over-involvement with activities, but that was okay, because I thought that others perceived me as an "important guy." I worked out at the gym to impress the ladies and my fellow students. I eventually became a corporate executive, entrepreneurial CEO, etc.—so what? These activities and positions never satisfied in the long term. I strove for success from a worldly viewpoint, and by golly, I achieved it for a fleeting period in my own mind, but not in God's mind.

The problem with worldly achievement, of striving for the elusive goal of being the best, is that someone or something always appears to confirm that we are not the best. We need to try harder to get to the proverbial next rung in life. However, the next rung invariably leads to just another rung.

> Revelation #8: On the day we die, what matters most is how we lived our life for God.

Truly, the revelation that only service to God matters in Heaven deflated every other achievement. Before you think that the results of our works—our jobs, our toils—are fruitless, please know that they are in fact beneficial, but only if done with the intention of serving God and others. A job well done for God merits approval. Volunteerism done for those in need merits approval. Sacrificing for our children merits approval. Even washing the car as a caretaker of what God has given to us merits approval. The key is to do everything as a living sacrifice to God (Romans 12), as unto the Lord (Colossians 3:23).

"Everything you have done for Me is good," Jesus said to me.

My thoughts after Jesus said this: *Whatever I did to merit the approval of this world was wasted; and whatever I did to honor God with my works, including the responsibilities He gave me even in the smallest things, earned treasures in Heaven.*

What are treasures in Heaven? As noted previously, the greatest treasure in Heaven is closeness to God. The closer we get to

God, the more goodness can usher forth from us. Consider the fruits of the Spirit cited in Galatians 5:22-23: *"But the fruit of the Spirit is love, joy, peace, forbearance, kindness, goodness, faithfulness, gentleness and self-control. Against such things there is no law."*

These qualities have characteristics not inherent in themselves, they are discoverable only by God. Our imperfect expression of these qualities on this earth cannot be ascribed to a perfect God without missing the quintessence of them. However, in Heaven we are perfected through Christ, untainted by the effects of this world, such that these qualities are inculcated upon our soul in Heaven through what we established in this world, and united with Christ's Spirit to fulfill our soul.

The good works we accomplish in this life serve as impressions upon our soul that carry over into Heaven. Every good work that I did in this world translated as a treasure within my soul. I finally became in Heaven the person I had always wanted to be in this world. All of the good I had accomplished in this life served as reminders of the goodness of God. My treasures in Heaven were translated into a deeper love for God. If you want to be "rich" in Heaven, love God more in this life. The more love we have for God, the greater will be the abundant flow of His goodness to others.

EXPRESSING TREASURES IN HEAVEN

Our treasures in Heaven are spiritual, not material. They exist as expressions of the fruits as explained in Galatians. I saw in Heaven many wondrous sights, but one in particular struck me as evidence of heavenly treasures. Afar off I saw pillars of what looked like billowy linens, flowing down into fields of rippling waves. Figures frolicked on these cushiony fields, not unlike children jumping around an inflatable jumpy house, though much more elegant. Some appeared as gargantuan angels dressed in robes, and others as children.

My thought was that these children had died in their childhood, infancy, or even before they were born. Their most striking quality revealed itself to me as joy because their faces reflected peace during their merriment. They did not simply dance in abandonment, there was a purpose to their enjoyment. They exuded a perpetual reverence to God as evidenced by their worship, and a kindness of heart that deeply imbued the same within my soul. Conversely, those whose despondency caused them to abandon their purpose by taking their own lives in suicide grieved my Lord even though His grace redeemed those who sought Christ's forgiveness.

Later I would realize that God showed me this appearance for a profound reason. Their impressions conveyed to me those same fruits as explained in Galatians. Somehow, the joyfulness of these spirit bodies was an impartation of their personas that resonated the glory of God in my heart. This happens because everyone in Heaven reflects God's expressions.

Please catch the immense subtlety of what I am trying to express: Our purpose is reflected in who we are when steeped in the presence of God. Those frolicking figures were not only expressing their joy, they also imparted the glory of God to me. Think about that—even in play, others will be affected by your countenance, your presence; and, when your presence is a reflection of God's Spirit within you, it changes others. Our God-given purpose mirrors God's intention for others.

Your and my overarching purpose is to glorify God in everything we do. But we cannot glorify God without the glory of God shining through us, and (from 1 Thessalonians 5:16-18) that takes:

- Worshipping/praising God both individually and corporately, with others
- Knowing God's written Word, the Bible, which builds faith, and listening to the Holy Spirit's silent whisper to our soul, or conscience, which builds relationship with God
- Encouraging people and remaining open with other believers
- Being equally thankful to God for the good as well as the bad
- Rejoicing because God loves us beyond measure
- Maintaining an ongoing conversation with the Spirit of Jesus Christ as though He is standing or sitting next to you, which is true spiritually

In so doing, we are building spiritual treasures in Heaven. My apologies if you thought that treasures in Heaven would grant you a bigger house than your neighbor's. Those villages I saw in Heaven contained designs more spectacular than any mansion on earth; however, there were none more outstanding than another. Abodes were shared and comprised of what I can best describe as lingering sentiments of warmth for each inhabitant within structures combining naturescapes with cozy villas reflecting stones like opals. Though I was not a resident of any of these places, I could observe them from afar. While beautiful, they did not represent God's treasures to me. Treasures in Heaven were reflected as an abundance of God's presence to those who lived as unto God.

My dream to this day would be to drive up in a 1965 red Corvette to greet my loved ones in Heaven one day; and, I still think that God might allow me to do that just for fun. But the desire will not be for my glory, but to reveal God's generosity in satisfying the desires of my heart. My greatest treasure in Heaven was more of God.

I know that many think that people like Billy Graham, Mother Teresa, and Abraham Lincoln earned a bigger mansion in Heaven, but that simply is not what I perceived. Yes, they made a hugely positive impact in this world, and yes, they earned treasures in Heaven. Again, those treasures come in the form of expressions of God's Love, not in status. From my experience, we will not desire more "things" in Heaven, we will desire more closeness with God.

When Jesus said, *"My Father's house has many rooms,"* or mansions in John 14:2, I do not believe that He was referencing Buckingham Palace. If you were hoping to trade in your one bedroom apartment for the Palace of Versailles overlooking the ocean, sorry to disappoint you. In Heaven, you will not even desire that. I did not observe any French Normandy, Tudor, Colonial, etc. style of houses.

The Greek translation in the Old Testament for what we think of as a mansion actually means dwelling. I do not know if anyone even needs to sleep in Heaven—I did not observe anyone snoozing. There was, however, a communal sense of God's Kingdom, in that everyone lived in harmony with one another. There existed no conflict, like needing to move in with the in-laws (P.S. I love my in-laws), or to put up with that nasty neighbor.

Everyone got along swimmingly in perfect harmony. That is because our spirit bodies did not carry over any of the bad elements of our nature. I did not desire anything of the flesh, nada. (Although, I suppose if someone had offered me a chocolate... sorry, just being silly.) I actually craved nothing but God's presence.

What I did observe were purposeful people filled with the fruits of God's Spirit. Geez, in Heaven I did not care where I lived as long as I lived with Jesus, and that was guaranteed.

MAKING THE MOST IMPORTANT DECISION OF YOUR LIFE

If you think that your purpose is complete in Heaven, I suppose the answer is both yes and no. I did not hear those words from Matthew 25:21 that I longed to hear once I got to Heaven: *"Well done, good and faithful servant!"* That is because my purpose had yet to be fulfilled. I challenged Jesus as to why He could not just call it a "job well done" and let me stay. Here is how that conversation went:

"Lord, if You are sending me back, then please tell me what I am supposed to do."

"My beloved, if I were to reveal to you your purpose in full, you would not remain dependent on Me," He answered. At that point I felt Him pull me even more tightly, and all the while the butterfly remained on my shoulder.

"What am I supposed to do?" I insisted.

"Remain focused on Me, beloved," He said. "And then moment by moment your purpose will be revealed to you."

At that, the butterfly flew away; and as it did, I remember seeing its beautiful trails as a sparkly mist covering me in warmth.

That was it—a moment-by-moment revelation from God as to what to do next. Remember that I was a Type A? Well, a Type A tries to think and live big. Sometimes the goal of a Type A looks like a celebrity status on the world's stage, sometimes it looks like a person respected by everyone, and sometimes it seeks after a promotion. Heck, I hazard to guess most people seek some form of adoration. Again, in Heaven, the only desire one seeks is to please God.

> Revelation #9: The only adoration that gains God's approval is our adoration toward Him.

6

HEAVEN AS HOME

I REMAIN A BIG believer in goals, and I think God does as well. The goal of Jesus Christ on earth was completed only after He allowed Himself to be tortured, hung on the cross, and raised from the tomb. Indeed, He said on the cross, *"It is finished."* The Greek word *tetelstai*, means paid in full.

Now, please pay attention because this point is very important. Jesus paid for the debt carried by everyone who has sinned, failed morally. This hearkens back to whether we are judged in Heaven for our actions. For the believer, the answer is no—we have already been judged and found "not guilty" because Jesus became a proxy for us. He assumed responsibility for our wrongdoings.

JUDGING WITH FORGIVENESS

Many struggle with the judgment of God. My time with Jesus surfaced a surprising revelation about God's judgment. It happened during my conversation as Jesus pointed to masses of people devoting themselves to God's inspirations in Heaven.

"Which of these is the least of them?" Jesus asked me.

"No one," I answered.

"There is one, beloved. Ask yourself this question," Jesus said.

When talking with Jesus, His attention always focused on me. I felt at the center of everything He said, and so the answer seemed obvious to me.

"I am the least of these," I said.

Jesus looked at me with those piercing yet gentle eyes that saw every thought and every feeling within me.

"No," He responded. "I am the least of these. Beloved, because I became the least for all, those who inherited My Spirit could become worthy of My Kingdom."

I remember now in hindsight what Paul said in First Corinthians 15:9: *"For I am the least of the apostles and do not even deserve to be called an apostle, because I persecuted the church of God."* Paul felt unworthy because of his sins. Before knowing Christ as his Savior, he had murdered Christians. My revelation was that Jesus needed to become the least of humankind so that He could cover the guilt, the shame, and the stains of all who confessed their unworthiness to the lordship of Jesus Christ. Jesus Christ had reached the lowest point of anyone in this world so that He could reestablish relationship with those who assumed His mantle of forgiveness.

I teared up in understanding the full measure of Christ's sacrifice. "Oh my Lord," I said. "How could I have ever doubted Your love? I feared Your judgment when all I needed was Your love."

Jesus hugged me tightly and kissed my forehead. "My child fear not. Never did I seek to judge you. Always I wanted to forgive you, My beloved. But in those times when you judged yourself, I reminded you that I found you worthy of Myself."

Jesus wiped my tears from my cheeks and reached His hand soaked with my tears and dipped them into the river of life. "Judge not yourself. When you stop judging yourself, you will stop judging others."

Those words penetrated my soul. During my life on earth, I had judged others all too often. My daughter often felt judged because of her drug use. My son felt judged. My wife felt judged. The only one who did not feel my judgment was my dog, and even that proved untrue when he wet the floor. All this time I felt guilty for judging others, when all I needed to do was stop judging myself. I could do that in Heaven, being in the full presence of Jesus Christ; but on earth, that would be a constant struggle. I felt guilty for judging others, ashamed, but most of all I felt guilty for my own failures.

Jesus stopped pointing to others and then He rested His hand over my heart. A warmth penetrated me with soothing comfort. I felt entirely at peace. No longer would I need to struggle with the judgment of God. I simply needed to rest in Christ. When my eyes looked at others in Heaven, I loved them, because the love of Jesus Christ had penetrated my soul.

To this day I feel a more profound sense of being forgiven. The depth and greatness of Christ's love no longer convicts my soul, it frees me to love others. Because Jesus Christ became the least of us, He freed us to love those considered the least of humankind—even the "unlovable."

Friend, if you struggle with God's judgment, please know that our struggle is not with God, but with ourselves. People tend to filter their perception of God through their own prejudices. They view a wrathful God ready to pounce on their misdeeds. That is not the God I know, the one I met in Heaven. The God of Jesus Christ can no more forgive those who stubbornly refuse the lordship of Jesus Christ than we can forgive others without the power of God's Spirit empowering us to forgive. Our fallen nature deprives us of our capacity to forgive.

Forgiveness is the desire of Jesus Christ. Our damaged self wants to hold on to our misguided perceptions of right and wrong. Only when we relinquish our need to be right can we assume the righteousness of Jesus Christ.

The judgment of God is not the execution of God's will, it is the absence of genuine Love. We cannot inherit a perfect world if we bring into that world our imperfections. Assuming the mantle of Jesus Christ is the only way to true forgiveness, and submitting to Christ's authority is the only way to love those who persecute us. Without Christ, we will continually fall victim to our own failures. With Christ, we no longer need to strive, because Christ has assumed full responsibility for our failures. Our sole responsibility is to place our burdens at His feet and confess our sins so that Jesus Christ can cleanse us of our self-righteousness.

"Beloved," Jesus said during our journey of forgiveness, "I am your all, and all of you is what I seek."

Friend, God does not want you to die or to suffer. Plan B is in effect. Plan A was total obedience to God in the Garden of Eden, and we blew it. So the only way an independent-from-God person could become re-dependent on God was through the controlling influence of Jesus Christ's Spirit. There is no other way, and Jesus Himself said so in John 14:6. The good news is that you breathe today. All you have to do is say something such as:

> *"I have done things that are bad. I have sinned. I know that I don't deserve Heaven, but I can't imagine a world without God. I know that You are Love, God. I know that You are God, Jesus Christ. You suffered on the cross to save me. And I ask for Your forgiveness. I don't want to be in control of my life anymore. I want You to control me*

with Your Spirit. Take my life, my Lord and Savior Jesus Christ. I give You my all."

Oh my, I am in tears writing those words because I know how much they mean to God. I was with Him. I know the joy of the Lord over the salvation of one lost soul. You mean the world to God. He loves you with all of His heart. Even if you do not think of yourself as worthy of God, He found you worthy of Himself.

If you said those words or similar words for the first time, there is a celebration in Heaven going on for you right now. Wowsa! Party in Heaven! The celebration I saw in Heaven was like fireworks or shooting stars birthing new creations and an amalgamation of everything that was beautiful and pure. Tell people about what you just did. Be joyous about it. That was the most important decision of your life.

I would never want to disappoint Jesus, but I know that I fail time and time again. I know what it means to be face-to-face with Jesus. Believe me, on the day that you die, you will want to know Jesus as your Friend, as I did.

CHOOSING HEAVEN OR HELL

I once met a young man in Texas who died from a drug overdose and went to hell. I sat across from him in absolute shock as he described the sense of hopelessness and despair that greeted him in hell after he died. I am delighted to say that this young man professes his faith in Christ today. In fact, he is a youth pastor.

His story and numerous others reveal a diametrical difference between Heaven and hell. Simply put, Heaven is a place where God lives, loves, and rules—hell is a place without God, devoid of love, and ruled by the fallen angels who rebelled against God from the beginning of time. This is not just some fairy-tale theory. It is a verifiable phenomenon.

Jesus told the story of a rich man being in Hades, or hell, after his death, and of a beggar named Lazarus whom the *"angels carried to Abraham's side"* after dying. The King James version of the Bible uses the phrase "Abraham's bosom," which was an expression referring to the "paradise" Jesus anticipated following His crucifixion (see Luke 23:43). We learn from this account in Luke 16:19-31 that the soul is alive and conscious after death and *before* a bodily resurrection. The rich man was in torment in hell. He looked up to see Abraham with the former beggar.

The formerly rich man cried out to Abraham and a discussion ensued:

> *"Father Abraham, have pity on me and send Lazarus to dip the tip of his finger in water and cool my tongue, because I am in agony in this fire."*
>
> *But Abraham replied, "Son, remember that in your lifetime you received your good things, while Lazarus received bad things, but now he is comforted here and you are in agony. And besides all this, between us and you a great chasm has been set in place, so that those who want to go from here to you cannot, nor can anyone cross over from there to us"* (Luke 16:24-26).

That account as told by Jesus Himself should send chills to those of us who know the love of Jesus Christ. Some believe that all religions lead to Heaven, but if that were true, then frankly, Jesus would have sacrificed Himself for nothing. Certainly, Jesus sacrificed Himself for us, like no other religious founder throughout history, in order to save us from the effects of hell.

WE TRIED TO DISPROVE GOD AT NORTHWESTERN UNIVERSITY

I did not experience hell, but at one time I was on the road to hell. As a devout agnostic, I used to criticize Christians whenever the opportunity arose. I hated the hypocrisy of Christians. To me, they boasted of their own righteousness while condemning my lack thereof. I agreed with Mahatma Gandhi when he said, "I like your Christ, I do not like your Christians. Your Christians are so unlike your Christ." So I spoke through my apartment window to an unknown God saying, "If You are there, I need to know You as personally as I know my loved ones."

First, I needed to disprove all religions since I believed that each religion only represented the flawed people who created it. At Northwestern University I teamed with some researchers to disprove all religions using a building-size computer system called Vogelbach. We programmed datapoints from each of the major religions comparing ancient documents with each religion's earliest recordings. We could disprove all religions as simply a fusion of beliefs, or as a set of opinions created by a self-professing oracle—with one exception.

The God of the Bible was confirmed through thousands of ancient documents more substantiated than even the oldest known literary works such as the Kesh Temple Hymn dated to around 2500 BC. The Bible has more manuscripts, more dated manuscripts, and more accurately copied manuscripts than any other ancient book in recorded history. It contains the earliest recordings of any ancient writings. There proved to be more than a 98 percent agreement between the 25,000 known manuscripts of the Bible with no major contradictions, versus less than 50 percent for most of the other ancient religions of the world.

Other major religions are based on the writings of one man, mostly textually unsubstantiated documents, meaning that the earliest dated documents are too varied to form a consistent confirmation of their accuracies. Christianity is a monotheistic belief versus an amalgamation of beliefs as with most other religions. Far Eastern religious writings do not make a claim to be God's word, as does the Bible. Neither does the Koran claim to be direct words from Allah, unlike the Bible's claim. Only the Christian Bible claims to be God's words.

Having invalidated all of the other religions except Christianity, our team needed to invalidate the Bible's claims in order to disprove the religion of Jesus Christ, which we could not. Especially given that each of the sixty-six books of the Bible produced an astounding prophetic accuracy of 1,000 percent. No other religion came close to even 10 percent.

People and places in the Bible were validated through other corroborating documents, even those from other religions. Jesus was a common historical figure accepted by some of the other religions, like Islam. And, although Christians do not always reflect the nature of Christ, countless lives throughout history were radically and positively changed by their belief in the God of the Bible.

Our team of agnostics even evaluated the character of each religious figure or founder. We discovered that Buddha struggled with conflicting thoughts and never espoused himself as a prophet. Muhammad sometimes exhibited rage while owning slaves. Some gods explained in Hinduism stole, abandoned mates, and imbibed hallucinogens. We could find no moral lapses in the life of Jesus.

As to those who believe in a non-descript universal presence, our team determined that no one can relate to a cosmic force or to an impression or even to a feeling. Research in human development confirms that only humans are capable of establishing deep con- nections, and that belief in a universal presence deprives believers of a relatable person. A belief that god became the universe, or that god existed primordially as the universe deprives individuals of any form of familial relationship. These type of believers relate to god in the same distant way that someone may feel while looking up at the stars. The concept of God in the flesh—Jesus—and in the image of humans allowed for an intimacy that the universe could not provide.

Our researchers also disputed the theory of reincarnation. Unlike animals, only humans can reason the divine and regulate social relationships, because humans maintain an exclusive abil- ity to:

- understand others' complex thoughts
- reason abstractness to determine others' mental states
- reflect and imagine the undiscovered to allow creativity

It made reasonable sense to us that God would place His Spirit in human receptacles, and not in animals who, though capable of affection and thought, cannot fully relate to a higher being.

All of our objective researchers agreed that they would hate to be reincarnated as a naked mole rat or as a condor. That alone made reincarnation seem like a silly theory. I personally deter- mined that if the God of the Bible truly existed, He would need to create humans in His image for the sole reason that He could relate to humans most intimately.

But all of that research at Northwestern was not enough for me. It took a concussion from a near-fatal car crash to overcome my disbelief as my head catapulted through the windshield, confirming my hardheadedness. Before the crash, I thought of myself as invincible. After some "indefinable influence" tugged at my heart to seek after the God of Jesus Christ, I did the "impossible." Lo and behold, one day I entered a church and later said the same prayer that I presented to you earlier. I met Jesus Christ in my spirit.

HEAVEN IS OUR REAL HOME

Fast-forward several years later, and I met Jesus face-to-face. My born-again experience occurred in the realm of the ethereal. My experience in Heaven was as real, if not more real, than it would be meeting you in a grocery store. If you think that you will live in a perpetual unknown after you die, think again. In Heaven, everything is ten times the reality of this world. Because in this world we are limited by our five senses. In Heaven, there are senses beyond our ability to define them through our experiences in this life.

Not only are the five senses heightened in Heaven, there also exists the following additional senses, some of which I cannot fully explain:

- *a sense of knowing*
- *a sense of blendedness with others*
- *a sense of Jesus Christ as a kindred Person*—not ethereally, but as being a noticeable, observable, visible figure
- *a sense of multiple places*—viewing life in its entirety, not as isolated parts
- *a sense of belonging* as evidenced by joy, peace, and comfort

- *a sense of the micro with the macro*—viewing the growth of the minutia and the macro of creation; everything was living and could be seen as living harmoniously
- *a sense of immersion* and an exclusive focus on what matters most
- *a sense of perpetual awe* while being in the constant presence of God
- *a sense of wholeness*, an immutable completion of perfection
- *a sense of acceptance*, no need to judge or qualify anything

One might say that these are feelings. In Heaven they are not just feelings. They are a state of being—constant and ever-present. They are as real as smell, touch, hearing, sight, and taste. Feelings represent a temporary emotional reaction or belief; whereas in Heaven, a lucid consciousness placed me in a piqued state of readiness without any anxieties that can accompany heightened senses in this world.

Think of it this way. Do you remember the butterfly that Jesus showed me to illustrate wisdom? If that butterfly were born on earth, it would start as a caterpillar. Now, imagine that the IQ of the butterfly is 150. It could think reasonably and intelligently. From its perspective as a caterpillar in the cocoon, the yet-to-emerge butterfly would consider its memory as a caterpillar foraging on plants using its tiny legs and squeezing its muscles in an undulating wave motion. The caterpillar's perspective on the earth came from a limited exposure to the ground, vegetation, and anything within the plane of earth.

Instinctively the caterpillar would prepare for its metamorphosis into a butterfly. Soon after it emerges from its cocoon as a butterfly, it flies into the sky. Instead of an earthly perspective, it visualizes the sky and earth from a different viewpoint. Because of its intellect, the butterfly can try to assess its experiences from this new vantage, but there exists very little context within the added dimensions of this newfound atmosphere. No words can describe the butterfly's experience because the vocabulary it learned previously did not include anything beyond its previous point of reference.

A new dimension for the butterfly in the sky can be compared to Heaven's new dimension when we, as humans, leave our "cocoon"—our earthly body—and assume a new spiritual body in Heaven. Our heavenly body is more beautiful, like the butterfly. It is vibrant and fitted within an environment that includes both our previous domain, that are our familiar natural surroundings on this earth, and our new ethereal domain, including supernatural surroundings in Heaven. Like the caterpillar turned into a butterfly, our experience in Heaven will be both familiar and otherworldly. And like the butterfly, this otherworldly dimension in Heaven will feel like home.

> Revelation #10: The longing we have
> for something greater is the hope
> of Heaven, our everlasting home, for
> which God ultimately designed us.

Heaven as our true home may seem foreign in concept, but in reality, that longing feeling that poets and other artists have tried to explain in the ethereal represents God's design for us. We, like the butterfly, long for something more than the earth and our cocoon can provide. We long for Heaven.

God also designed us for a purpose in this world. Like the caterpillar that grows and builds in a constant state of activity, we must fulfill our purpose in this world before we can turn into a "butterfly" and fly away to Heaven.

God designed you for a purpose in this world. It is the reason you and I live here, now.

LIVING ON PURPOSE

I remember the first time I got fired. It happened shortly after I graduated from Northwestern University having learned to write (Journalism), conduct business (Finance and Business graduate courses), and understand the sciences (Biology co-major). One of the most successful companies in the world issued me a qualifying test to determine my intelligence quotient (IQ). "You're the only one who completed all of the questions correctly with a score of 100 percent," the Human Resources person told me. *Great*, I thought, this placed me in the "genius" category. I was an agnostic at the time with no idea as to my impending lesson about humility.

I thought I was hot stuff. Procter & Gamble (P&G) flew me to its headquarter city in Cincinnati to launch a new product in their healthcare division. It was an incontinent undergarment, which on the surface seemed like an unattractive assignment at first. Still, this first healthcare product represented a major deal to P&G since it was entering the healthcare field with grandiose expectations of expanding into an entire line of surgical gear. "You are the top achiever in the field," my manager told me. Wow, my head swelled with illusions of gaining a corner office. I bought several white dress shirts and three suits on clearance. P&G flew out a marketing executive from New York City to work with me.

About a year later, my employment was terminated after I started several product evaluations but failed to increase prices after the trial periods ended. Customers were getting P&G's new product at a grossly discounted rate. But, *Hey*, I thought, *I had the most placements in the nation. They can't fire me. It was a simple misunderstanding. No one told me that I couldn't continue to offer the product at a money-losing discount.* This self-professing "genius" at the time made a stupid mistake. I became a failure overnight.

Shortly after, I was hired by Johnson & Johnson, the largest healthcare company in the world, but it took years of humbling to help me understand that my ways are severely limited, and that God's ways are infinite. You see, in comparison to God, our "IQ" is probably commensurate with a 5-year-old's, or worse. God is all-knowing and we are always learning about newly undiscovered realities.

Heaven from our physical perspective is like the distant galaxies, and this life in relationship to living in Heaven is more akin to a baby playing within its playpen with no idea as to the vastness of the world outside. Our stature apart from Christ is commensurate to that of homeless person, but once we become born anew through Christ, God considers us like royalty (1 Peter 2:9).

We may think that we are hot stuff when viewing ourselves in comparison to this world's standards, but God sees us much differently. He thinks we are *"fearfully and wonderfully made"* (Psalm 139:14)—because we are made in His image. The standards of this world do not apply in Heaven. When Jesus looked into my heart, which was always, He saw Himself in me. Imagine that—God sees us as a reflection of Himself. That, my friend, is more important than any degree or status this world confers. Our relationship to Jesus Christ alone makes us remarkably special.

Being made in God's image tells us a lot about our purpose. It begins with asking the following question: What is God's purpose? Have you ever tried to answer that question? Please allow me to take a bold stab at answering this question: God's purpose is to love you. If that sounds too woosoo or esoteric, consider First John 4:7-21:

> *Dear friends, let us love one another, for love comes from God. Everyone who loves has been born of God and knows God. Whoever does not love does not know God, because* **God is love**. *This is how God showed his love among us: He sent his one and only Son into the world that we might live through him. This is love: not that we loved God, but that he loved us and sent his Son as an atoning sacrifice for our sins. Dear friends, since God so loved us, we also ought to love one another. No one has ever seen God; but if we love one another, God lives in us and his love is made complete in us. This is how we know that we live in him and he in us: He has given us of his Spirit. And we have seen and testify that the Father has sent his Son to be the Savior of the world.*
>
> *If anyone acknowledges that Jesus is the Son of God, God lives in them and they in God. And so we know and rely on the love God has for us.* **God is love**. *Whoever lives in love lives in God, and God in them. This is how love is made complete among us so that we will have confidence on the day of judgment: In this world we are like Jesus. There is no fear in love. But perfect love drives out fear, because fear has to do with punishment. The one who*

fears is not made perfect in love. We love because he first loved us. Whoever claims to love God yet hates a brother or sister is a liar. For whoever does not love their brother and sister, whom they have seen, cannot love God, whom they have not seen. And he has given us this command: Anyone who loves God must also love their brother and sister.

Notice that *"God is love."* His personhood is love. He exudes love and does everything with love because that is who God is as a Person. In Heaven, that was the most striking revelation to me. I knew love as an emotion or as an action, but when I met Jesus, He exuded Love as innately as we express our character every day. Most of us need to feel love, but God is Love, so it emanates from Him as His persona since God is the Author of love, expressing Himself to anyone who would hear His voice or word. In other words, anyone who spends time with God will know His love and will exude that love to others.

Notice the words before *"God is love"* in the Scripture passage from First John: *"If anyone acknowledges that Jesus is the Son of God, God lives in them and they in God. And so we know and rely on the love God has for us."*

Reliance on God means total dependence on His leading. How can we be totally reliant on God? Remember the butterfly I experienced in Heaven. Jesus told me that wisdom would be my guide. Wisdom is God's expression of His truth through our understanding. Gaining wisdom depends on our total attention on God apart from the cares of this world. Wisdom draws us to love God with our heart, soul, mind, and strength through the renewal of our mind.

> Revelation #11: Wisdom is the voice
> of God telling us what to do.

HEAVEN WAS THE ONLY PLACE
I COULD LOVE FULLY

I learned while being with Jesus that divine love cannot be reasonably compared with the love most people in this world experience because of one important reason: God is not only the Creator of Love; He is the personification of Love. Comparing the person of Love to an emotive response would be akin to likening a songwriter to his or her song, the former is the creator of the song, and the song itself inspires listeners; but never will the song be the same as the songwriter. And if you have ever been to a concert, you probably know that the impact of being in the same arena as the songwriter singing her or his song far exceeds just listening to the songwriter's music on the radio, just as being in the presence of the Author of Love far exceeds any other experience known to humankind.

Being in the presence of God infuses us with divine love for God, and for each other. Love as an action or emotion will never surpass the Author of Love. Moreover, God emanates agape love, which equates to Christ-centered love. Agape love as described in the Bible is perfect love. How did this affect me being with this perfect Love? Jesus exuded Love to me as supernaturally as the sun gives off heat. Christ's love warmed the souls of everyone in Heaven and inspired me with a profundity of Love never felt before or after Heaven. The closer we get to the sun, the warmer we feel, just as the closer we get to Jesus, the more loving we become. I can tell you that soaking in the presence of Jesus made me love others abundantly more than at any other period in my lifetime. If you want to love more, get closer to God.

First Corinthians 13 is commonly referred to as the "Love Chapter." Verses 4 through 7 describe the action or definition of love:

> *Love is patient, love is kind. It does not envy, it does not boast, it is not proud. It does not dishonor others, it is not self-seeking, it is not easily angered, it keeps no record of wrongs. Love does not delight in evil but rejoices with the truth. It always protects, always trusts, always hopes, always perseveres.*

I used to think that these verses describe how we should act in true love, but after meeting Jesus face-to-face (see 1 Corinthians 13:12), I realized what Paul explains in verse 10 as *"completeness,"* knowing fully the essence of Love as a Person, not just as a feeling. I realized that the descriptions of love in 1 Corinthians 13 actually reference God's character. Because Love is the personification of God, the demonstration of these qualities arises from simply God being God, and the practice of these qualities can only happen for us when we are with God in Spirit. Paul explained that now we see the essence of Love dimly, but in Heaven we will see Him face-to-face, and only then will we be completely able to love being fully immersed by Love Himself.

That my friend, is the quintessence of Love, and I was consumed in Heaven by that Love, and God's Love lifted me, it inspired me, it empowered me, and it made me the loving person I had always desired to be but could not fully attain in this world. That, beloved of the Lord, is your future in Heaven. Your striving will cease, and you will be the very best of you. For now, the goal for us is to draw closer to the Son of God so that the warmth of

His Love can be felt more deeply. Once Love becomes our driving force, our purpose in this world can become effortless.

OUR PURPOSE IS A JOURNEY

Too often we view purpose as an end goal. Perhaps you have heard this sage insight, "It's not about the destination. It's about the journey." Many interpret this as a call to just enjoy life and take in situations and environments without any need to interpret them. The Zen approach is to find that "inner peace." The God approach is to find that inner voice from the Holy Spirit who speaks truth.

Absolute truth can be hard to grasp when our experiences filter through our observations. For example, if I were to try to explain to you the color blue without any visual to help me, I would explain it as a reflection of something blue I have seen in life, like a flower. Describing the color blue without a common point of reference is like trying to describe Heaven to someone who has never been there.

I know that I am getting woosoo with you now, but please bear with me. Truth is interpreted from our point of view, as referenced through our experiences. In the time of slavery, many slave owners believed that they were justified in buying and indenturing another human being. In fact, many slave owners cited Scriptures like Paul's admonition in Ephesians 6:5: *"Slaves, obey your earthly masters with respect and fear...."* From a biased frame of reference just about anything can be justified, including slavery. Mind you, God hates slavery. In Heaven there are no slaves. And yet, I consider myself as a servant of God.

My point is that our interpretation of the truth can be apart from God's truth. Perhaps the most dangerous point in our life, whether as an agnostic or as a theologian, is when we think that we have figured out God. In Heaven, I knew so much more than I understood in this world, not because of my personal enlightenment, but because of God's fullness as expressed in Heaven.

The analogy that comes to mind is if you were reading about the thoughts and feelings of people during another time in history, say the Civil War, and then instantly you are transported into the White House while sitting next to Abraham Lincoln during his historic meeting with Frederick Douglass, a former slave, on a hot day on August 1863. The two men look eye to eye, compassionately, feeling the immensity of their struggles. You hear their conversation and the emotions each feels in the midst of bloodshed all around them. At this point, you fully understand the depth and breadth of the impact of the Civil War from the perspective of these leaders who carried the weight of the world on their proverbial shoulders.

You are there. You know the truth not as it is recorded in the history books—you know the truth because you are part of that history. That was me in Heaven. I met with the One who carried the weight of the world on His shoulders. He was not just someone I read about in the Bible or imagined as a historical figure. I knew God not only by faith, but by total immersion, and this will also be your experience in Heaven. I knew then the truth. And the truth is that God so loves this world that He is willing—present tense—to sacrifice Himself for you and me. Truth, my friend, is not what we think it is from our perspective. Truth is what God thinks, period.

Followers of Jesus Christ know that servanthood represents self-sacrifice. Slave owners used others to serve themselves. First John 4:20 says, *"For whoever does not love their brother and sister, whom they have seen, cannot love God, whom they have not seen."* How can we love others? It does not come naturally. It happens supernaturally through the Spirit of Jesus Christ. Our walk with Christ aligns our truth with God's Truth.

God imprints His will upon our will so that we can express His love to others. When Jesus said, *"I am the vine; you are the branches"* (John 15:5), He meant that we must be spiritually grafted into Christ to bear out the fruit of God, which is love. When we are grafted into Love—God—we can love others.

This directly relates to wisdom. Remember, wisdom is the voice of God through us. If we are not grafted into Love—Jesus Christ—we cannot hear the voice of God speaking to us. Just as Jesus told me that I needed to be still, and wait upon Him, so it is for each one of us.

Wisdom will guide our purpose moment by moment, situation by situation, and thought by thought. Purpose is not a destination—it is the journey in Christ. To this day, I vividly recall my walk with Jesus in Heaven. Memories from Heaven are not like memories from a dream or from a situation in the past that we experience in this world. My memories from Heaven place me there, in the moment. I can hear God's voice speaking to me, I can feel His soft face, and I can see His emerald brown eyes just as if I were there right now. I believe that is because I no longer doubt the existence of God in Heaven. I know beyond a shadow of a doubt that God and Heaven are true. I would be a fool to think otherwise.

A RECENT EVENT TAUGHT ME ABOUT MY JOURNEY

I experienced an example of how to again overcome my propensity to define God's purpose for me as only the destination during a meeting with my sister in Christ, Lenna, at a bookstore while I was signing my most recent book. God wanted me to understand that His purpose is a journey. Lenna traveled a long distance to see me. It had been almost twenty years since I last saw her at the church we both attended. She shared with me a word I had given her at this church. To me it seemed like a trivial statement, but for her it was life changing. I said back then, "Lenna, you are going to enter a new ministry. You will be rejected by some of your closest acquaintances, but you need to stay true to your calling even though others might think you're crazy."

She ran up to me at the Barnes & Noble table and said, "Randy, that word you spoke to me changed my life. I had been intending to go to a new job, but I had this desire to start a ministry. People told me that I was crazy to not take the job, but I pursued my dream just like you said, and for almost two decades I have been living out my purpose in a way that has made a greater impact than I could have possibly imagined."

It struck me that my purpose was fulfilled in simply speaking some encouragement to my sister long ago. I did not plan it. I did not expect that my statement was anything other than a word of encouragement. But my seemingly trivial action dramatically changed Lenna's life, because I felt God wanted me to say that to her. I was listening to the Voice of wisdom.

Please start thinking of your purpose as both future and present. You may be planning for something in the future, but God uses your present circumstances to birth His purpose for you in return for the loving benefit of someone else. It may be a simple word of encouragement, or a silent prayer, or helping carry someone's groceries—acts of kindness in obedience to the Holy Spirit's prodding. Get still, listen to the Voice of wisdom, and boldly speak and do that which God places on your heart. God's children do not just "hang out" in life. They remain ever purposeful, while listening to God's wisdom in the stillness of their soul.

Now for another woosoo moment—viewing how God sees us from Heaven. For a brief time while journeying with Jesus in what became a nature hike in Heaven surrounded by villages that blended together in a divine and mysterious beauty against the azure sky within verdant hills teeming with life of every kind, I could see Jesus' eyes glisten as He looked over His most beloved creations—people. His eyes bowed down to view this world.

"What are You seeing?" I asked Jesus.

"I am looking to see who is wise," He said.

It struck me as odd at first, and then as always in Heaven, God's wisdom taught me exactly what Jesus meant. It harkened back to the days when I was a child, and my mother was speaking to me while my mind drifted to someplace else, like the ice cream truck parked outside. She would say, "Randy, are you listening to me?" In a similar way, Jesus was looking down to see who is listening to Him.

Imagine that. Right now, God is looking down from Heaven to see if you and I are listening to Him, or if we are distracted by the cares of this world. When we listen to God with our spirit and our mind, by getting still and dwelling on God, we hear the voice of God that translates as wisdom speaking truth to our soul. God checks in with us to see if we are listening.

"Are they listening?" I casually and half-jokingly asked Jesus.

"Those who are wise, My beloved," He answered. And then a smile spread over His face.

Our purpose is to do God's will every moment of every day during our lifetime. However, our purpose can only be fulfilled through soaking in God's presence and listening to Him in the stillness of our soul. God's Spirit is the engine required for us to drive into our divine purpose. That purpose is a journey with a multitude of God-ordained appointments along the way. One important principle tells us how to prioritize our lives: Put the God things first, and the other things second.

GOD OPENED MY GRANDMOTHER'S MIND AND SPIRIT

While on a business trip in Texas, the Holy Spirit impressed on me that I needed to call my grandmother, Gramma Kay. Mary Kay, not the famed makeup executive, lived during her younger years on the poor side of a Mississippi River town in Iowa during the Great Depression repairing shoes for less than a buck a shoe. Some of the teens on the wealthier side of town called my grandmother, my granddaddy who was disabled by a stroke, and their three sons, "white trash." Some people called them "hicks." Growing up, Gramma always took good care of me, though the smell of mold and sound of rickety floors that eerily creaked at night caused me to resent sleeping over as a kid.

I never recall Gramma mentioning Jesus or anything about God. In fact, she taught me a racial slur once that even as a boy I felt necessary to correct. "You shouldn't say stuff like that, Grammie," I said. Later I supposed that being considered as the lowest class of people in town may have caused Grammie to want some other class of people to scrape the bottom of the social bracket just so she did not have to consider themselves as "trash." That did not justify any form of prejudice, but it did explain the anger from never having quite enough despite working multiple jobs to afford a saggy bungalow in support of three spunky boys, two of whom, including my eventual dad, would go off to "the war," as she called World War II. Come to think of it, I never saw my grandmother just sit and relax. There were always chores to do.

As a woman in her eighties, she then lived in a nursing home on a special unit for patients suffering from dementia and Alzheimer's. I called the nursing home from my hotel room.

"Hi, my name is Randy Kay and my grandmother, Mary Kay, is in your nursing home. I would like to talk with her, please," I said to the receptionist.

"I'm sorry Mr. Kay, but your grandmother will not know you," she replied.

"Just put me through…please…bless you for it," I responded.

The receptionist connected me with Gramma's room. An attendant picked up the phone and told me the same thing as the receptionist, "She won't know you."

"Please, please just hold the phone to her ear," I said. So she agreed.

"Gramma, this is your grandson, Randy," I said.

"Randy?"

"Yes, Gramma, do you know me, do you remember me?"

"Yes," she answered. "How are you, Randy?" I could imagine the attendant's jaw dropping at this point.

"Gramma, tell me about a time we spent together." I wanted to further check her mind's ability to know me.

"That time when I visited you and your dog licked me in the guest bedroom," she answered. I chuckled while also remembering how my Golden Retriever named Puff had licked my sleeping grandmother years earlier. Now I am sure the attendant was sitting down after seeing that my grandmother's mind had returned to reality.

"Gramma, how are you?"

"Not good."

"Why? What's going on?"

"They put me in this place," she said. "I hate it."

"But Dad loves you, Gramma. He was only doing what he thought was best."

"I hate it. Nobody cares." Then I got still to hear God's voice of wisdom.

"Okay, Gramma, do you know that Jesus Christ loves you?"

"No," she abruptly responded.

"Gramma, do you want to ask Jesus to become the Lord of your life?"

What seemed like an infinity passed in silence. "Yes," she finally replied.

What followed was my reciting a prayer similar to the one I noted earlier in this book, and my grandmother repeated every word. After praying that prayer, she said that she felt "loved." And then her mind faded into oblivion shortly after that, no longer recognizing me as her grandson.

God had opened her mind long enough for me to respond to the Voice of wisdom telling me to call Gramma. Two months later, she died. My purpose during that window of time had been fulfilled, and later I would learn its full effect.

God Records Our Life

When I was in Heaven years after speaking with Gramma, the Lord opened my eyes to view several vignettes. As I previously mentioned when seeing the boy with cancer who prayed for me to know Christ, God revealed to me my life in review. This time, He showed me my grandmother—in Heaven. My once plump and grey-haired grandmother appeared slender, youthful, and beaming with joy, much like she appeared in an old photograph I had seen of her as a young bride. She smiled at me.

I know that some who died and experienced Heaven tell of meeting their deceased loved ones at Heaven's "pearly gates." At the time of my death, my grandmother was the only close relative who had previously died, but I did not see her at those proverbial pearly gates. My first experience in Heaven happened while being face-to-face with Jesus. Only after spending time with Jesus did I shortly thereafter notice my youthful grandmother standing several feet to my side.

"You will see her again," Jesus said to me. I knew that my grandmother saw me, just as I saw her in the distance, because we acknowledged each other with a smile. I said, "I love you," to her, and she cupped her hands over her heart showing the same Cheshire grin with which she always greeted me after opening the torn screen door on her front porch when I was a child.

Her hair was brown, not grey, her figure svelte, not paunchy, and her hands smooth, not calloused as before. I think she wanted to hug me, but our meeting in Heaven would be short as she waved mouthing something that appeared like, "I will see you soon." Then she disappeared into a place I cannot to this day adequately describe, only to say that it appeared as a faded impression similar to a Monet painting come to life, in a blurred reality that extended from the clearly visible paradise in which I stood with Jesus.

> Revelation #12: God records all of your life, but failures will not be condemning for the believer—they will only reveal God's grace in a redeeming fashion; and the positive things in this life will overlay everything with God's loving influence so that they will all appear as good and pleasant.

The revelation that God will never condemn us in Heaven applies to believers in Jesus Christ. I have spoken with those who said that they experienced hell as unbelievers. Their life review did not soothe them, it troubled them.

We call an admonition given in love, conviction. When God convicts us of our wrongdoings, it comes as a solution to cleanse our soul by praying for forgiveness. God can call us home at any moment. In the blink of an eye, each one of us will emerge from our "cocoon" to enter Heaven. Let us make sure that our life in review at that point comforts us by asking Christ to forgive our iniquities. A clear conscience in this world translates into an even deeper sense of peace in Heaven because every act on earth done for the sake of honoring God counts as a sacred offering.

My life review in Heaven left me feeling deeply appreciative to Jesus for His grace and desirous to serve Him more faithfully because of that grace. I remember thinking, *If I had one more breath to breathe, I would want it to be while thinking of how much God loves me.* Herein lies a revelation that surprised me from my experience in Heaven: Even fondly thinking about Jesus honors God as a form of worship, because spending time with Jesus in thought is an everlasting form of devotion that God records in much the same way that we would record memories in a photo album.

You might ask, "Is there a literal Book of Life in Heaven as referenced several times in the Bible?" Nothing is allegorical or metaphorical in Heaven. It is all as it seems. Jesus gently placed my hand over His heart as we were walking. "Your name is written here," He said. The answer, beloved of Jesus Christ, is that your name is written in God's heart.

GOD GRIEVES FOR THE LOST

I know that many people enjoy the thrill of watching a scary movie or episode, just like many enjoy the thrill of a rollercoaster. Be careful, though. A rollercoaster ride evokes a physical thrill. Ghoulish scenes, on the other hand, elicit something spiritual. What we see and hear can invade our soul, either positively or negatively. A worship song can usher us into a spiritual longing for God. It positively impacts our relationship with Christ.

A horror flick, a salacious novel, cuss words, blaspheming the name of Jesus Christ, or a pornographic sex scene will not only elicit a physical response, but a spiritual one as well. Whenever we entertain our carnal desires, we are essentially telling God, "God, I want to take a break from You for a moment and just indulge myself, so please turn Your head away from me for a while." As silly as that may seem, that is exactly what we are saying to God, and I have done that to God all too often. Thankfully God remembered none of those in Heaven, because I had sincerely repented of my misdeeds; and as to the sinful propensity that remained in my earthly body, that was redeemed for a heavenly body free of sin.

God records our brief deviances not to punish us, but because He remembers all of the details in our life—both the good and the bad. The good news is that if we sincerely repent of our "slippery slide" away from God, He takes His eraser and wipes it off

His record book. It no longer exists. You will not see it again in Heaven. However, if we allow that spiritual toxin to seep into our consciousness unchecked, it turns into a bad habit and becomes tattooed on our soul, in a manner of speaking. Once that happens, we no longer feel compelled to repent of our sin. Our damaged heart accepts that aberration as the norm. The King James Version calls this a *"reprobate mind"* or a *"depraved mind"* (Romans 1:28).

God forbid that anyone should go there. More importantly, it grieves the One who loves us more than anyone else. It hurts Him. Yes, God has feelings. The shortest verse in the Bible is, *"Jesus wept"* (John 11:35). I saw Jesus weep. His eyes looked down as He pondered the lost souls still living.

"I desire that no one will perish," Jesus said to me with a faint smile. My impression during that moment was that God absolutely loves to forgive, desiring to give good gifts to His children, and that He laments over the destructive toxins that defile His beloved.

Only once did I overhear the conversation of one of the unknown saints in Heaven that I witnessed. A conversation between a woman with long straight brown hair, a man with black kinky hair, and a thin young man with a goatee appeared a few feet from Jesus and me. They held each other's hands while standing under a tree. The woman spoke directly to Jesus, but her head did not turn to Jesus while He stood next to me. Instead she looked in the center of the ring formed by these three, as if Jesus was standing there just as He stood with me. She said, "Thank You, Lord. We lift up (she said a name that I did not record) that he might know your forgiveness." That was the sentence I recorded in my journal.

I learned then that even those who have passed from this world to Heaven are interceding for their loved ones in this world. I knew that the prayer was for someone in this world because no one needs forgiveness in Heaven. You see, in Heaven prayers are said with absolute conviction that God will do precisely that for which the saints pray. Here, in this world, the common prayer is more like a hope than a belief that in, fact, God will do what is asked.

When I turned to Jesus after viewing those three praying, I could see His downturned face as though He were thinking of those for whom the three prayed, the one who did not know Him in this world. Perhaps Jesus was sending one or more of His angels to do battle on His behalf. Perhaps Christ's Spirit whispered God's truth to the lost one for whom the three prayed. I do not know. What I do know is that Jesus was answering the woman's prayer in the moment that I walked with Him while I viewed those three saints. It was a holy moment. It was a time to save someone who had lost his or her way.

That brief moment with Jesus represents the only time in Heaven when I actually felt sad. In Heaven, every care felt by God affects His children as well. We feel as God feels. Sensing my Lord's sorrow for the lost is when I knew that I had to go back. No longer did I feel the need to challenge Jesus as to why He would return me to this fallen world. I knew that my purpose was to express the heart of God to a broken people.

SENDING YOU POSTCARDS FROM HEAVEN

As sometimes happens, someone asked me about an experience related to the loss of their loved one. The man's daughter died years ago after drowning when the young lady's hair became caught in a bathtub drain. His loss weighed heavily on this gentle soul's mind.

"I had the most pleasant dream the other day," he said. "My daughter and I were exchanging pleasantries in a beautiful field of flowers. I really wanted to stay there."

Immediately I began assimilating the father's dream with my experience of Heaven after feeling that this was no ordinary dream.

"What people often don't fully comprehend is that our loved ones in Heaven are in constant communication with Jesus," I said to the man. "So when a strong impression of peace and assurance happens to us, like the dream you experienced, I think we can consider these as postcards from Heaven."

The man smiled. "What do you mean?"

"I mean that your daughter may have been sitting with Jesus in a field of flowers in Heaven, and then she said to Jesus something like, 'Lord, would You send a message to my father to let him know that I am here, in this place with You, and that I am having a wonderful time.'"

The man's eyes peered into the distance for a brief moment. "I never thought about it that way."

"Everything that is good and pleasant comes from God," I said. "When we grasp just a semblance of reality apart from this world, as in that special inspiration that arises from God's love, we can begin to realize that seeming coincidences that result in what is good are not really coincidences at all. They are God's orchestration of our life from His throne in Heaven."

"I'm so glad that I mentioned my dream to you," the man said. I could see his shoulders relax, his back straighten, and his chin turn up as if God's inspiration to his soul matched his posture.

"Maybe now you can start reading more postcards from your daughter in Heaven, because even though your daughter cannot communicate directly with you, Jesus is in constant communication with you and your daughter, and Jesus delights in sending those uplifting messages to you, like the one I believe your daughter may have relayed to Jesus for you to experience in your dream."

These "postcards from Heaven" always come from the one Messenger, Jesus Christ, who seeks to uplift our soul. They will never haunt us. Postcards from Heaven bring a piece of Heaven to fill the void in our heart. They connect us to those with Jesus, and they give to us a glimpse of Heaven. Postcards we might receive in this world often are signed, "Wish you were here." Postcards from Heaven are signed by your loved ones in Heaven with, "I will see you here one glorious day!"

If I could convey one important message from those in Heaven to those in this world besides the fact that Jesus loves you more than you can imagine, it would be: "I am not dead." Please heretofore stop thinking of those in Heaven as having died. Today, now, they are thriving, more alive than ever in this world, and some of them are praying for you right now.

Your loved ones think fondly of you, regardless of the past and sometimes because of the pleasant memories of your past with them. Only good and encouraging thoughts reside in Heaven.

Death in this world is something that each of us will experience—yet none of us will encounter death as the end of our life.

7

THE CHARACTER
OF HEAVEN

JUST BEFORE WRITING this, I learned of the death of a friend's 23-year-old son who tragically lost his life after being shot and killed by someone from a gang while chasing down a hit and run driver. The Arizona news stations hailed Joey as a "Good Samaritan."

Joey impressed me because of his ready smile and the fact that, even at a young age, he was always trying to right the wrongs of others. He would be the first to defend someone being bullied, and the first to volunteer when help was needed even if it meant doing menial chores.

Seeing him in the lobby of a church not too long ago, I thought, *This young man is going places. He has a very bright future.* Now he is in Heaven having left this world in the prime of his youth. At first my heart grieved both for my friend and the fact that this youth could no longer shine his light in an often dark world.

The Greek historian Herodotus, in the year 445, originated the phrase, "Only the good die young." It means that highly regarded people who are morally upright, kind, and compassionate tend to die at a younger age than most people. Certainly, that would be the case with Joey. He appeared kinder and more empathetic than most of his peers. Why did God take Joey so young?

One of the scenes Jesus revealed to me during our stroll was a group of children joyfully playing in an open field of flowing grass. They chased butterflies and petted creatures like mellow wildcats, but with a different and "softer" appearance than those I have seen in zoos. These creatures were large like lions, and playful like dogs.

Heaven is not a wispy place inhabited by vapory figures floating in the clouds. What I viewed in Heaven elicited images and feelings beyond the exact details I viewed, yet very much distinguishable by characteristics as vivid as the physical figures we see on earth. The glory of God transformed everything similar to how a master portrait artist recreates a photo from scratch using hand-painted brush strokes. In the case of Heaven, God recreates all that we see on earth through the brushstrokes of His glory and artistry.

In Heaven, everything is made better than what we experience on earth, in a time-space continuum that defies any comparison on earth, albeit there were activities galore that reflected not simply busyness, rather each activity serves a God-given purpose. But nothing...nothing compared to being in the supreme presence of the Son of Man, Jesus, God.

Most of the time with Jesus, He interpreted my thoughts and spoke accordingly. I wondered why these children were not grown adults, like most.

"These are the ones who left too soon," He said.

Too soon? In Heaven, answers often come through impressions. I knew instantly that some of these children had died as infants. But I also knew that each one carried a fulfilled purpose despite their leaving this world "too soon." I knew it because I sensed their lingering impressions, like Joey's, that left a remnant of virtue in this world, like a baby's innocence, or a youth's vitality, or as in Joey's case, the lasting signature of doing good.

Nothing pains the heart like the death of a child, especially a son or daughter. Their survivors are left with thoughts of what the departed one could have accomplished if just given a full life. But God does not see life in the context of our expectations. He sees life from the perspective of His Love. We cannot see beyond the other side of death; however, God lives on the other side of death. Death is no more than a "stubbed toe" to God.

God views the essence of a person, not just the actions of a person. I wrote about this earlier. He sees the heart. We view the physical expressions of a person and sometimes the quintessence of a life. We know that feeling as when someone gives off a good vibe or a bad vibe. We sense something about a person and occasionally it happens with a first impression; often, it happens after getting to know the person. That lingering impression finds its way to Heaven as the vestige of a person.

> Revelation #13: A life is never wasted.
> Even the young in Heaven leave a lasting
> legacy that lingers in this world.

So now when I think of Joey, I picture him in Heaven with Jesus. No doubt he is viewing the grandeur of God's creations. Maybe Jesus will dip His hand into the river of life, and sprinkle it over Joey's head, baptizing Joey with peace, joy, and revelations as Jesus did with me. The river of life that originates from Christ's presence reveals a freshness of God's impartation.

In their childhood, Renee and I would take Ryan and Annie to the ocean on a hot day and run into the cool ocean to escape the heat. Just as a cool immersion in water refreshes us to escape the heat, so does the warm river of life refresh the soul. It serves as an awakening of God's comforting Spirit and a relief from the cares of anything else, and it is especially appreciated through a child's innocence. Truth is, we are all more like children in Heaven, restored to the innocence of how God created us to be in the most idyllic setting conceived by Him.

GOING FROM BLACK AND WHITE TO COLOR

In 1939, producers wowed America with the Wizard of Oz movie starring Judy Garland. If you like millions have watched the film, you know that it starts in black and white. Judy meets a gypsy who is later revealed in her dreams as the fake Wizard of Oz. A tornado knocks Dorothy out, and she enters the dreamland of Oz. Dorothy awakens to view Oz in vivid colors.

Usually we think of dreams in reverse—dreams are often remembered as a vague monochrome, and reality appears in lucid colors. However, the brilliant writers for the Wizard of Oz did the reverse, partly to showcase the company's new three-strip color process. I prefer to think of this life as being in black and white, as with the movie; whereas, Heaven appears in millions if not billions of colors.

When people ask me what Heaven looks like, I sometimes liken it to Dorothy moving from a black and white world that includes both kind and harsh people to a never-before-seen world of color with only nice people. This world may seem like our only reality, but it is more of a faded reality. Heaven is not only more colorful, it exudes beauty beyond what the imagination can comprehend. And instead of the Wizard of Oz being a fake, God is real within a dream come true.

Revelation #14: Heaven is more real than this world.

The moral of the Wizard of Oz is to grab your heart's desire. But be prepared for obstacles. Plus, it helps to have reliable friends to support your quest. The reality of Heaven taught me that my heart's desire is to know God more intimately. This life is a place to express the heart of God for doing good works. To accomplish that, each of us needs to continually seek after God, get still in order to listen to God's Spirit, and surround ourselves with fellow believers to help us stay on the narrow road. Truth be told, all roads lead to Heaven, but only those who know Jesus Christ as their Lord will get to stay there. To fulfill our purpose, we are called to express the love of Christ to everyone we meet, and that can sometimes be hard in this fallen world.

A satisfying purpose in life, in a nutshell, is to glorify Christ. I understand that may seem a little too esoteric, or lofty. My wife's Christian grandmother used to say, "A person shouldn't be so heavenly minded that they are no earthly good." Her words, not mine. After hearing about others' NDEs, her faith in Heaven grew stronger. She died in absolute peace knowing that Heaven was in her future. As she fell asleep in her hospital bed, heart beating more slowly, she was more in Heaven than this world. At her last breath, she smiled as Jesus greeted her in a place surrounded by striking colors that she now calls home.

What You Can Expect to See

I used to change the subject when people would ask me to describe Heaven, because to me, the only facet of Heaven that really mattered was being with Jesus. I just wanted to talk about the awe, the amazement, the wonderment of meeting the King of kings and Lord of lords. I could have landed in a trash bin, but as long as it was with Jesus, that would have been fine with me. Only after Jesus and I walked and talked for a while did I really look around. Oh my goodness, were my eyes opened! Everything was woosoo at that point.

Towering crystal structures appeared in the distance, fronted by opalescent gates. Rows of radiant stones or crystals lined my pathway. They seemed to vibrate with brilliant colors, emitting an effervescent light. Stones in this world are lifeless, but not the ones I saw in Heaven. Everything had life, and the light of Jesus Christ illuminated everything.

From the perspective of Heaven in comparison to this life, we see colors and figures in this world through a veil that dims their true appearance. This world appears like Dorothy's black and white world before she entered Oz. And in Heaven, my colored surroundings appeared as thousands of varieties of each color in glowing luminescence. The pathways throughout Heaven were a transparent gold.

Forms appear in multidimensions, as though seeing Heaven from another aspect entirely new to me. It appeared as though I had previously viewed a flat surface in this world and then suddenly that flat surface grew into different stratums. Everything glistened in softly lit shades. Strikingly green hills and majestic mountains blended into contiguous patterns such that I could instantly climb a mountain, or run through grassy fields, and swim in the life-giving streams.

Water from the streams nourished everything they touched, even the rocks absorbed the waters. Life sprouted before my eyes. Plants of every kind budded forth new flowers over and over again in a slow, graceful motion. The illuminating light of Jesus Christ effused all of Heaven with an abundancy of life that elicited an overall feeling of profound comfort and peace.

I could soar but not like a bird or some comic book character. Travel in my spirit body proceeded from thought to thought, transporting me to places inspired through my relationship with Jesus Christ. He commanded my presence to see vistas, and for each one Jesus ascribed a meaning for being there.

Reflective colors of the flora and fauna glowed brightly in the strengthening light of God, similar to what the prophet Isaiah called the "Glory of Zion" in the biblical book of Isaiah chapter 60. My eyes drank in the grandness of sweeping valleys while simultaneously viewing the minutiae such as the veins running through leaves. Everything appeared as though looking through a magnifying glass concurrently with an aerial view, as though time and space had been reconfigured in Heaven as one magnificent assimilation of God's glory.

The context of my environment with Jesus appeared surrounded by several gates made of brilliant jewels within a holy place that evoked *"the city* [that] *does not need the sun or the moon to shine on it,"* as described by John the apostle in Revelation Chapter 21:23. My life reviews appeared within what I imagined as the "radiant glory" described during the so-called Transfiguration as explained by the disciples in three of the gospels including Matthew 17 when the face of Jesus *"shone like the sun"* and his clothes *"became white as light"* while appearing with Moses and Elijah.

The meeting with the boy from the hospital appeared against the backdrop of whispery colors overlaying an activity of figures going in and out of places indistinguishable through the mist or fog, or some other transitioning place from which they came. I saw my youthful grandmother through pleasant evocations like those elicited from the smell of her freshly baked bread, and perfumes that evoked peacefulness as though my olfactory senses elicited pleasantries from all things—and yet my blocked nasal pathways rarely smelled anything in this world.

All of the physical senses translated into perceptions or feelings rather than physiological responses. Life events appeared against backdrops of God's grace—I cannot fully explain it. It was as though God's grace served as the character of Heaven. Everything in Heaven issued the character of Christ in a heightened awareness that transcended any physical realities. Every perception reached beyond a mere cursory observation to the essence of its actuality. It was as though all of Heaven was a reflection of Christ's Love.

I DID NOT IMAGINE HEAVEN

Mind you, these were not dreams. Dreams are vague and fleeting. At the time these happened, and in my memory of these things to this day, each appears vivid, chromatic, and everlasting. I have not forgotten my time in Heaven. It stays alive in my spirit as though God packed it in a place for me to rekindle these events in Heaven again. And since my brain was clinically dead, I could not have imagined such lifelike realities, especially since I had experienced realities for which there are no parallels in this world.

Even as I share these "observations" with you, I understand that some might consider them as chemically induced, imagined, or contrived. I too felt this way about NDE stories until I experienced my own. My friend John Burke often notes a Gallup study that reported one in twenty-five claimed to have experienced an NDE. I am not alone. What strikes my reasoning, and may also impress your interpretation, is that most of the recorded NDE accounts tell of consistent stories.

If anything, the vast number of people who have experienced NDEs should speak to God's desire to confirm His reality through these accounts in paradise. Jesus healed countless people during His walk on earth to validate His authority as God. In like manner, He has returned many from death, or near death, to tell of His reality and the promise of Heaven to all who believe in Jesus Christ.

It saddens me that some choose to dismiss all NDE accounts as unscriptural, as if God's promise of Heaven is only theory. By ignoring all accounts because some claims are false, they summarily dismiss all NDE claims. Some NDE deniers—as I was before my own NDE—discard these valid testimonies of God's realities along with other falsehoods or delusions because they cannot be "proven."

If scientifically proven validations were the only way to confirm the reality of Jesus Christ, then faith would be useless. Indeed, the born-again experience that makes someone a believer in Jesus Christ by faith, and not works, would also need to be questioned. The "near-death" biblical accounts of Paul (2 Corinthians 12:2-5), John (the book of Revelation), Daniel (Daniel 12:1-4), and Stephen (Acts 7:55-60) would also need to be discounted, along with at least ten accounts of people raised from the dead as recorded in the Bible.

Writing of the ethereal poses an inevitable challenge. It would be like an infant trying to explain the law of physics. The language of Heaven has yet to be interpreted into any worldly language. What is seen in Heaven is spiritual, and yet more real than any physical experience because the spirit can see what the mind can barely comprehend.

This is why Heaven is more real to me than this world. In this world we see in part. In Heaven, we see in full. In this world we experience Jesus through spiritual impressions. In Heaven, we experience Jesus face-to-face. In this world we see people as they appear to us. In Heaven, we see them as they were fashioned in Christ. In this world we experience truth mixed with lies. In Heaven, the truth of Jesus Christ is pure and pervasive. The truth of Jesus Christ in Heaven inspires adoration.

Revelation #15: The Truth draws us closer to God.

Please allow me to pose this one distinguisher between what is false and what is true. If what I am writing draws you closer to the God of Jesus Christ, then it is the Holy Spirit doing so, and the Spirit of Jesus Christ always speaks truth. If anything I tell you draws you apart from Christ, or lessens your relationship with Christ, then I implore you to stop reading this book now. My purpose for sharing my revelations with you is single focused—to draw you closer to Jesus Christ and His Truth. The most important message is this: God loves you more than you can possibly imagine, and He cares about even the smallest matters in your life. His inspiring magnificence is reflected in the beauty of His creations that speak of God's loving attention to the littlest of things while forming the grandest of His designs.

GOD'S ARTISTRY RENDERS HEAVEN AS SUBLIME

I traveled alone along the Napali Coast on the Hawaiian island of Kauai many years ago. No one wanted to endure the strenuous hike up the narrow valleys punctuated with streams and cascading waterfalls to reach the sea cliffs. So, while everyone else sipped pineapple juice below, I endured the steep footpath lined with rocks and hibiscus flowers to reach the top. I was much younger then, and after several miles I finally reached the emerald-hued cliffs while avoiding the razor-sharp ridges to view God's extraordinary natural beauty. It was like a little bit of Heaven on earth.

As I sat to soak in the seascape, my inspiration gradually turned sullen. I was experiencing one of the most gorgeous places on earth without anyone with whom to share it. With no one to mutually experience this place, my inspiration would be isolated within my memory's vault. Have you ever felt this way? Maybe you experienced something extraordinary, but you felt disappointed because no one else could understand your experience since they were not there.

I sometimes feel that way about Heaven, and then I remember that I was never alone. My shared experience was with Jesus. Occasionally, He and I reminisce about our time together in Heaven. Tears often swell in my eyes as I recall that experience with Him. Truthfully, the only One who can empathize with us from a shared point of view in all things is Jesus Christ. What's more, only God can express to us the reality of our life. Only God can reveal His truth in all matters. Only Heaven expresses the fullness of God's creation.

That pinnacle of majesty I felt while overlooking the ocean and lush Napali Coast seems like a painted seascape in retrospect, or a scant photograph in comparison to Heaven. A photograph or painting can trigger the imagination to dream, but that mindscape cannot breathe, smell, taste, or touch what the artwork portrays. Artwork can, however, imagine things beyond what the naked eye can see. Artistry can stimulate emotions and identifiers in our mind that cause us to implicitly react.

Experiences in nature, conversely, strikes us with the reality of our current situation. When we experience something physically, our senses start interpreting our situation. Our mind evaluates each situation by using the five senses to interpret a response. Overlooking the Napali Coast struck me with a sense of awe and majesty. Later, when I viewed a tour book depicting that same coast, the photographs of Napali Coast did not nearly portray my whole experience. "You had to be there," as the saying goes.

But, when I viewed an artist's impressionistic expression of Napali Coast in a painting I later observed, something in my mind connected the physical experience of the coast with a spiritual intuition of its deeper meaning. It took me to an ethereal place apart from the stark reality of what I experienced while being there. That's because my mind combined both my physical reality of experiencing Napali Coast with the artist's emotional impression of Napali Coast to inspire a deeper appreciation of God's beautiful creation.

The beauty of this world is an expression of God's creation, while the deeper understanding of God's creation is expressed in Heaven through God's inspiration. His "artistic" impression elucidates the meaning of everything, thereby accentuating its effect. Heaven is as real as my experience while overlooking the Napali Coast, yet fully expressive of God the Artist who created it. Heaven is like a beautiful piece of artistry come to life. Heaven is like walking into a masterpiece to experience the full expression of God the Artist's intent. Heaven is both ethereal and evocative.

Heaven is as real in the spirit body as this world comes across to the physical body, with one important difference. In Heaven I could grasp the full mastery of God's creation; whereas in this world, I used to believe in my own mastery.

In Heaven, I always understood the meaning behind God's mastery. Intentionality imbued each aspect. In Heaven, there was absolutely no confusion and no happenstance. In this world we often allow things to happen to us. In Heaven, every action happens in obedience to God's will.

And everything reflects God's love. Even the rocks cried out with God's love. I understood God's will, and I felt completely understood by my Lord, Jesus Christ. Heaven is the effluence of God's unhindered inspiration.

> Revelation #16: Nature speaks of God's creation while Heaven speaks of God's inspiration.

8

TEARS IN A BOTTLE

WE CANNOT FULLY comprehend God's ways, but we can know God's way. First Corinthians 2:11 says, *"For who knows a person's thoughts except their own spirit within them?"* Romans 11:34 poses the limitation of our thoughts with a question: *"Who has known the mind of the Lord?"* These two verses tell us that only our spirit can fathom our thoughts, but that our spirit can only approximate the thoughts of God.

Our brain cannot reason God, but our spiritual connection through Jesus Christ can empathize with God. The difference between reasoning someone's thinking and empathizing with someone's thinking is that when we reason a person's thoughts, we intellectually process how they feel in relationship to how we might feel in a similar situation. When we empathize with someone's thinking, we think as they think with no need to liken it to anything familiar to us.

When we empathize with God, we feel as He feels. There is a synchronicity between God's mind and our spirit that generates an ability to know God's way without fully understanding it. Allow me to share my conversation with Jesus as we walked together, which illustrates this phenomenon:

"Do you remember when as a child you fell into the strawberry patch and your hand was pierced by the metal that was used to separate the strawberry plants from the surrounding grass?" asked Jesus.

"Yes, Lord, as an impression but not vividly like now," I responded.

"My beloved, I collected your tears in a bottle." Jesus waved His hand toward the streams that flowed from Him. "Your tears are within these waters you see."

In Heaven, what we may think of as metaphorical or figurative is actually real; however, Christ's literal words came through my impressions as God's expressions. What I saw was not metaphorical, Jesus truly did enjoin His tears with mine in the flow of life that appeared before my eyes.

"You know me like no one else," I said.

"I know everything, My beloved," Jesus said, "but you see with the eyes of your own understanding, and I see you through My eyes. You thought that you cried from the pain, but you were crying out to Me."

"The fear, Lord. You never fear…did You feel my pain?"

"My beloved, I felt your need for Me. When I walked upon the earth, I felt your pain. Here, I feel My children's need for Me."

At that moment I remember thinking how much Jesus missed me when I was apart from Him. I knew then that my emptiness always was a longing for God, and Him for me. We longed for each other. That is the empathy God feels for us.

> Revelation #17: Pain, loneliness, grief, and all kinds of sadness are rooted in our separation from God. God feels that separation and yearns to be together.

GOD'S ULTIMATE DESIRE IS TO BE TOGETHER WITH US

Soon, or in the hereafter, you will understand God's design for this world. God created our world, and then He created us. He made all of it for one important reason—fellowship. We were created in God's image to be in *koinonia* relationship with God. The word *koinonia* in the Bible is translated in four ways:

- Fellowship (twelve times)
- Sharing (three times)
- Participation (two times)
- Contribution (two times)

Foremost, God wants to experience an intimate fellowship with His children. Second, He wants His children to share in everything God experiences in Heaven and earth. Third, He wants to participate in everything we do and think, and He wants to contribute to our life as we dedicate our life to God.

Godly empathy is total immersion, one with another. Same thoughts, same experiences, same reality, same feelings. The only difference or separation between God and His children is that God is God, and we are His children. As children, we cannot entirely fathom our Father's ways.

Think of it this way: A parent knows tremendously more than his or her toddler. A parent knows that crossing the street in oncoming traffic is bad. But the young toddler is ignorant of what might happen. A parent knows the child and wants to be with the child, but the child doesn't always understand the need to obey the parent in everything. A loving parent feels lonely after parting with the toddler, either for the long term or for a day, but that toddler fears being away because he/she knows that no one loves him/her more than the parent.

Are you catching my drift as to how God feels? Everything good is magnified in the extreme with God, including His infinite wisdom and power. After all, God is Love—Love flows from Jesus. But, if that child matures in the world long enough to determine that he or she wants to go it alone without God, there is not much the parent can do at that point except to discipline the child to stay away from danger. Any parent of an adolescent knows that is not an easy job, and certainly our rebellion against God produces similar feelings for God when we run away from Him.

God is like the loving parent who stays up all night thinking about his teenager's first spin alone in the car, praying that his teen does not get hit by a demonic driver. Friend, this world is our first spin in the car—the first and only time we can drive ourselves in this world. In Heaven, we will joyfully give the controls over to God.

MOURNING FOR THE LOST

We do not need to understand God to know Him. We were created with His spiritual DNA. Some choose to run off and never look back. Mentally and spiritually, they divorce themselves from God. That saddens God. He mourns for the lost. I cannot fully express the lamentation that God feels for those who reject Him except to say that it must be like giving birth and realizing that the child is stillborn. All that promise, that life, is finally born into God's world in Heaven only to be discovered with no life.

I have known mothers and fathers who grieved the loss of an infant. When my son lived in his mother's womb, the obstetrician concluded from the ultrasound and blood tests that he suffered from spina bifida. In all likelihood he would be born either disabled, or stillborn. Renee and I cried out to God, "Save our child!"

God heard our earnest prayers and healed Ryan in the womb. We still possess the ultrasounds from the before and after, showing a clear gap in the spine initially, and the fully formed spine after prayer. God heals. He always heals either on earth or in Heaven. The true sadness occurs for those who die in the womb— in this world. They kept on speeding through this world without returning to God, their loving Parent. They decided to divorce themselves from the One who loved them more than anyone else.

If you want to know how God feels for you, think back on the river of life I saw in Heaven. Remember how God saved my tears in a bottle and then poured my tears—my cares, my concerns—into God's living streams teeming with abundant life. Your tears are also saved in Heaven within the life-giving water of Jesus Christ. He has joined your tears with Christ's atoning waters to turn your sadness into joy.

Only God can absolutely empathize with our sufferings. David recorded his own revelation of God's empathy: *"You keep track of all of my sorrows. You have collected all of my tears in your bottle. You have recorded each one in your book"* (Psalm 56:8 New Living Translation).

The following three verses explain God's river of life that contains your tears:

- Revelation 22:1: *"Then the angel showed me the **river of the water of life**, as clear as crystal, flowing from the throne of God and of the Lamb."*

- John 7:38-39: *"Whoever believes in me, as the Scripture has said, **rivers of living water** will flow from within them. By this he meant the Spirit, whom those who believed in him were later to receive. Up to that time*

> *the Spirit had not been given, since Jesus had not yet been glorified."*
- Ezekiel 47:9 (English Standard Version): *"And wherever the river goes, every living creature that swarms will live, and there will be very many fish. For this water goes there, that the waters of the sea may become fresh; so **everything will live where the river goes.**"*

God knows your pain. No one else comes close. The good news is that Jesus pours your tears into the abundant river of life. He redeems what was lost in return for a far greater gain. When my eyes first beheld Christ's river of life flowing from Him, I realized that God's love spreads forth giving life to everything it touches. I felt it. You will as well.

9

SOUL AND SPIRIT

THE FIRST TIME I entered my mother's room as she was dying, I needed to stop at the doorway because her bones shown through her skin and her eyes were deep-set within her skull, hallowed out by Alzheimer's. *This is not my mother,* I first thought.

I held her bony right hand and rarely let go for two days as she gripped me tightly. Her blue eyes looked at mine with a mother's love. On Sunday evening she began to pant. I called hospice. The nurse administered morphine. Only minutes separated her from Heaven, so I held my cell phone to my mother's ear as her favorite song, "In the Garden," played those lyrics that described her forthcoming meeting:

> I come to the garden alone
> While the dew is still on the roses
> And the voice I hear
> Falling on my ear
> The song of God discloses
> And He walks with me
> And He talks with me
> And He tells me I am His own

And the joy we share
As we tarry there
None other has ever known
He speaks and the sound
Of His voice
Is so sweet the birds hush their singing
And the melody
That He gave to me
Within my heart is ringing…

I closed my eyes and prayed that Jesus would direct the angels to sing that same song to my mother as she crossed the threshold of eternity in meeting Him face-to-face within the garden she imagined while singing that song to me as a child. A vision of Jesus appeared as He outstretched His hand toward my mother. I opened my eyes knowing that Jesus was calling her home. With tears in my eyes, I leaned over and whispered into my mother's ear, "Mom, Jesus is with you right now. He is holding His hand out to grasp you, and He will never let you go. You can let go of me now because Jesus will take you to Heaven." After speaking these words, my mother's hand relaxed. I let go and gently placed my mother's hand on the bed. She was in Heaven.

About a week later I flew to Keokuk, Iowa, with my family to attend my mother's visitation and funeral. The first time I saw my mother's neatly dressed body within the coffin, I thought, *She is not there.* Makeup had covered the paleness, her best clothes were neatly pressed, her face appeared peaceful, but there was not even a remnant of life within that mahogany casket.

I recall thinking about that time when I viewed her frail body in the skilled-nursing facility shortly before she went to Heaven. Despite her gaunt appearance, she stilled exuded life because her spirit lived within her. The essence of a person is their soul and spirit. The body is just a housing unit.

I FELT THE HOLY SPIRIT'S IMPARTATION

While Jesus and I walked together in paradise, He dipped His hand in the living stream and touched my head saying, "My beloved, you are in Me as I am within you."

I knew implicitly what Jesus meant, although as I mentioned previously, nothing in Heaven is metaphorical. While walking this earth, Jesus often spoke in parables to describe things for which no words could suffice. In the book of Matthew He used the parable of the sower to explain good works, weeds to show the effects of sin, a mustard seed to show faith, yeast to show spiritual growth, and hidden treasures to show the value of the Kingdom of Heaven.

In Heaven, Jesus did not need to use parables, because every spiritual truth manifested in Heaven is an awareness of God's truth. His ubiquitous presence was felt by everyone in Heaven. For example, when Jesus told me that I was in Him and that He was within me, I did not have to imagine the parable about the branch and the vine in the fifteenth chapter of John.

I perceived Christ's lifeblood coursing through my entire being. I felt it, sensed it, saw it within my spirit body, and I understood it as plainly as if I were actually feeling His blood coursing through my veins but in an intangible way that only my spirit could perceive.

When Jesus sprinkled the water in His cupped hand over my head. I felt refreshed by His Spirit.

"When you return, My child, this water will be My revelation to you as an impartation of Myself. Here, you know fully, but there you will know in part."

I knew that Christ's impartation in Heaven would comfort me in times of struggles. The water Jesus sprinkled over my head had a multiplying effect. It settled in my spirit like a fountain of life from which I could withdraw inspiration.

You may recall the outpouring of God's Spirit in the book of Acts. I will not go into all of the details except to explain that shortly after Jesus left this world after His resurrection and after spending forty days with the disciples, Jesus Christ sent His Holy Spirit as promised. When God's Spirit inhabited His believers, the ultimate revival happened. They felt drunk and many spoke in a foreign tongue. They were baptized with the Spirit of God as previously promised by John the Baptist when he foretold the people that Jesus Christ would baptize them with *"the Holy Spirit and fire"* (Matthew 3:11).

The "living water" referenced throughout the Bible is not just a symbol of God's presence—it *is* God's presence. Baptism with Christ's living water is God's impartation of His transcendent Love that bestows abundant life through His Spirit.

John 14:26 describes the Holy Spirit in the following ways:

- Comforter
- Advocate
- Intercessor
- Counselor
- Strengthener

For the first time in all of history, the indwelling gift of God's Spirit to each believer in Jesus Christ provided God's abiding presence following Christ's ascension. Previously, God's presence resided in a man-made temple. He spoke primarily through the prophets and the priests. Now, God's presence abides in the temple He created. God speaks intimately with each of His believers.

We hear God's voice now, while living in the flesh, mostly through inspirations or impressions or what the French translation since the 16th century termed "esprit." The language of Heaven is not only in words but in an actualization of God's truth. I have often called it a sense of knowing, but it extends far beyond just knowing to an intimate and expressive association with God in each action, thought, and impression.

EXPLAINING THE SOUL VERSUS THE HUMAN SPIRIT

Revelation #18: Christ's abiding presence refreshes our soul and gives life to our spirit.

Our senses are contained within our souls, attuned to this world. This explains why our feelings vary according to what is happening around us. Everything in this world changes, which is why a person controlled by their soul can never find rest. Persons dominated by their soul always need to interpret their views in relationship to how others view them. A soulish person lives primarily through his or her physical senses. All things of the soul are temporal.

Only our spirit can relate directly to God. Receiving the lordship of Jesus Christ reverses the relationship from a soulish disposition to a spiritual disposition. No longer are believers' thoughts exclusively controlled by the soul and flesh, they are profoundly influenced by their spirit. Being Holy Spirit-based makes us heavenly minded. This results in a spiritual foundation in place of a life governed according to our human understanding.

A spirit-led person in Christ remains at peace. A soul-led person often experiences anxiety. Spirit-led people renew their strength through Christ. Soul-led people oftentimes become discouraged from the pressures of this world. Spirit-led people are overcomers. Soul-led people are always at the effect of what life throws at them.

The soul is basically our mind, our will, and our emotions, and when these focus on the things of God we glorify God as expressed in the proverbial Mary's Song when the mother of Jesus said: *"My soul glorifies the Lord and my spirit rejoices in God my Savior* (Luke 1:46-47 NIV).

However, all too often our human tendency toward scattered and negative thinking distracts us from the things of God to the extent that the soul becomes easily preoccupied by the things of this world. Our born-again spirit, conversely, remains unblemished by the influences of this world because our spirit is always connected to God's Spirit in holy communion.

This explains why our spirit always rejoices in God, but our soul, our humanity, must be continuously disciplined to glorify God with our mind, will, and emotions. In this world our soul and spirit are contained within our flesh, but in Heaven my flesh had been replaced with a translucent spirit body that appeared as a youthful version of myself in this world, minus the flesh, and my spirit body controlled my indwelling soul.

At the risk of being too woosoo about the juxtaposition of our parts in Heaven, suffice it to say that features we identify with people in the flesh in this world will remain much the same, but the way in which we will view those features will be through the pristine eyes of how God created us in perfection. This is because the truth of God elucidates the essence of who we are in Jesus Christ. Said another way, we become in Heaven the person who God sees us as being when He formed us before we were born on this earth.

The true reality of our personhood is defined in Heaven as our spirit, and we will think, desire, and feel in accordance with God's way. You will absolutely love being free of stress, pain, and struggles of any kind within your new body in Heaven.

IN THIS WORLD OUR CHALLENGE REMAINS CONSTANT

God's truth divides the soul from the spirit:

> *For the word of God is living and powerful, and sharper than any two-edged sword, piercing even to the division of soul and spirit, and of joints and marrow, and is a discerner of the thoughts and intents of the heart* (Hebrews 4:12 NKJV).

God wants us to live by the spirit and this requires that we remain steeped in His Word through the Bible and prayer and in His presence, getting still with God. This life is so consumed by our physical and soulish realties that we often forget that our born-again personhood is mostly spirit. The physical body is mostly comprised of water and organic matter. Its primary needs are for food, water, and stimulation. The mind thinks from a soulish perspective. Its needs are for understanding, reasoning, and resolution. Our spirit can only thrive in relationship to Jesus Christ.

The human spirit's life-giving need is for intimacy with Jesus Christ. Satisfying the soul and flesh consumes most of our attention in this world; whereas in Heaven, the spirit remains the predominant influence and the soul is consumed with the prevalent presence of God in everything.

The born-again spirit abides in Christ, and the spirit without Christ is dead. The soul is eternal regardless of whether one believes in Christ or not; however, only the born-again spirit in

Christ lives eternally. The spirit needs the indwelling presence of Jesus Christ to survive, and without Christ, the spirit has no life. The physical body of course is temporal until the day our body ceases to function.

In Heaven, we receive a new spiritual body. Gone were all of the maladies I experienced within my earthly body. My spirit body in Heaven felt youthful, vibrant, and able to freely travel throughout my surroundings. I could go anywhere in Heaven from thought to thought, if I so desired. While in Heaven I only desired to be with my Lord Jesus Christ, side by side.

My spirit resided with Christ always. I could go anywhere and do anything, and His presence remained with me. The Spirit Jesus Christ was visible both in body and as omnipresent. I believe that the reason I walked with Jesus in a similar way that you might walk with a loved one on earth is that the Person of Jesus Christ is our kindred part of God's three Persons: Father, Son, and Holy Spirit. Jesus relates to us as a Friend, like us; whereas the Holy Spirit relates transcendently, and Father God relates to us as an almighty presence evoking awe and reverence. All of them relate as One, with unique characteristics.

> Revelation #19: Jesus is our Friend,
> the Holy Spirit is our Inspiration, and
> God the Father is our Creator.

In this world we often struggle with the three facets of the Godhead, but not so in Heaven. They appeared as no different from what would be the multifaceted nature of my loved ones on earth. My earthly father could be a father, son, and friend at the same time. My earthly friends could exhibit multiple characteristics within the same person. The multidimensional aspect of God is not an issue in Heaven. Each part of God relates in a symbiotic fashion with no need to understand one facet from another.

PERCEIVING MY TRANSFIGURATION HAPPENED FROM A SPIRITUAL POINT OF VIEW

Honestly, I think most would admit that we live primarily from a soul-led perspective. We try to reason everything that happens. We tend to discount or disbelieve what we do not understand. Perhaps that is why many people tend to discount the stories of NDEers. Because they cannot relate to the experience or confirm the afterlife with their own experience, they opt to dismiss NDE accounts all together.

A similar dynamic occurs between disbelievers and believers in the lordship of Jesus Christ, which I know full well having been a former agnostic. Because becoming born again is a spiritual experience, as is an NDE account, many tend to think both are imagined. Those who experience a rebirth in their spirit reorient their physical-based reality with the abiding reality of God's Holy Spirit within them, somewhat like how an inspirational thought elicits a sense of well-being. Both are equally real; however, one comes from a point of relationship by receiving Christ's Spirit, and the other comes from a point of feeling.

An even greater dichotomy exists with afterlife experiences in Heaven. In Heaven, the spirit represents the dominant aspect of a person, because a person in Heaven is spirit, minus the flesh. Therefore, all of the physical confirmations that we use to define reality in this world—reason, evaluation, sight, smell, hearing, touch, and taste—are replaced with the spiritual confirmations that are used in Heaven, which are the full realizations of one's salvation, also called glorification in Romans 8:28-30.

This transfiguration in Heaven opens the spiritual mind of those in Heaven to an awareness of all there is to know in Christ's Spirit absent being God, or Jesus Christ. Thus, in Heaven, we see what God's sees without being God, yet having the transcendent nature of God to perceive the fullness of all that God created. Explaining this phenomena is challenging given the limited nature of words.

Jesus experienced a similar problem. Jesus says in John 3:12, *"I have spoken to you of earthly things and you do not believe; how then will you believe if I speak of heavenly things?"*

Heavenly things require a spiritual assimilation—not just an assessment. The difference would be like drinking a glass of water to quench your thirst without the need to understand how H_2O physiologically metabolizes within the body to nourish cells. When we drink Christ's living waters, our spirit thrives. We need not understand God's mechanism for making this happen, we just need to trust that God knows. We need to drink of those living waters from the wellspring of God's Kingdom that is vital to our spirit.

In this world, our beliefs are primarily based on objective assessments. In Heaven, our beliefs are primarily based from God's point of view.

I cannot convince anyone to believe my insights and revelations from Heaven. Even I cannot fully comprehend them. But I know them, and I pray for God's revelation while attempting to express in words what can only be fully grasped by the spirit. Basically, I am trying to express what is good and holy and everlasting. This is not as easy as the old saying, "If it feels good it is good." No, sometimes when something feels good it is not good, like gorging or indulging our prejudices. Spiritual "goodness" pleases God. Spiritual relationship with God on earth requires a disciplined life.

Spiritual relationship with God in Heaven just happens. Living in the spirit with God is as supernatural as the natural relationships we experience with our loved ones. There is no need to further strive in Heaven. Everything is complete. The perfection for which we can only hope for on earth—and can never attain— is fully manifested in Heaven.

There is such a thing as Heaven, but it is not on earth. There is such a person as God, but He is not found in worldly things. There is such a thing as someone dying and returning to tell about God's glory in Heaven—and not only me, there are thousands of people saying the same thing, "God is real, and He loves you so very much!"

10

HELL

EVERYTHING REEKED OF mildew in the dark. Wind blew heat through the caverns as bodies lurked around listlessly, their faces dull, drawn, and vacant. Giant figures loomed over them speaking foul accusations. And then one of them looked at the man. It sneered.

"You are nothing here but a leftover," it said. Its teeth clenched as it turned away to look at its reflection from a pool of sewer water.

"Why am I here?" the man asked.

"Because there is no other place for you," the creature responded.

The man approached a moping soul who listened while perched on a rock. He looked old, haggard, and his clothes appeared as dried skins.

"Why are we here?" the man asked the lost soul.

"What do you believe?" the lost soul answered.

"I don't believe in anything but myself," the man said.

"That's why you're here," the other man said before turning his head away.

The man started walking through the mix of creatures and lost souls while maneuvering around jagged walls and stumbling over steaming rocks, looking for light. Everything was old and stale. A misty fog overlaid everything with the smell of a dirty, wet sauna.

Then the man saw a light streaming in the distance. He ran. The light grew stronger as he ran faster trying to catch up to it. He remembered others telling him about Jesus but at those times he considered them to be nuisances, and Jesus nothing more than another figment of countless other religious figures. But now he believed.

"Jesus, save me!" he cried. And then he awoke.

This experience in hell is not my story, it was told to me by a person at Teen Challenge many years ago. I used to volunteer at Teen Challenge, an organization that helps teens and adults overcome their alcohol and drug addictions. The "man from hell" as some called him back then, became a Spirit-filled believer in Jesus Christ after experiencing hell.

He still bore the teardrop tattoos from his days as a gang member signifying the number of people he had killed. If you saw this guy in town, you would be tempted to cross over to the other side of the street. Of the many men I counseled at Teen Challenge in the Chicago area, this guy was one of the most generous and joyful of the bunch. He knew the magnitude of Christ's forgiveness.

He recounted this horrifying ordeal after his heart stopped beating following a heart attack. Doctors revived him. To this day the gravity with which he shared his time in hell weighs heavily upon my soul even though at the time I disbelieved most afterlife experiences. He told me about this many years before my own clinical death.

I remember him saying, "Everything in hell was old and rotting...lifeless. The creatures I saw looked like death warmed over. And the demons spewed their words of hatred wherever they traveled."

GOD'S LOVE FOR THE LOST

First, let me emphatically state that God desires that no one experience hell, and that even those who refuse to acknowledge Jesus Christ as their Lord and Savior are infinitely loved by God. Allow me to explain Heaven and hell this way: Heaven is God's house, and hell is home to those who would rather live as their own god, or in service to another god. In this world, if a stranger showed up at your doorstep and asked to live with you, but said that he or she does not believe in you, your ways, or your reality, and that he or she just wants to use you and your place to indulge his or her desires, including violating you, your loved ones, and your rules if desired, would you allow that person to live with you? Of course not.

Now, let's take that a step further. When someone enters Heaven, God's house, they have already gone through a transformation that changes their desire from wanting to live according to their rules, to an innate desire to live according to God's rules. That believer in Jesus Christ may stray now and then, but their moral compass invariably points back to God's way. The person without this driving influence, the non-believer, will always be driven by their own psyche, good or bad. So in essence, the God of Jesus Christ requires that someone accept Him before living with Him. It really is that simple, and that necessary.

The Bible mentions hell more often than it does Heaven. If you, like me before God enlightened me with the answer, find this somewhat perplexing, consider that most people find it easier to accept Heaven than they do hell. Many spiritualists and religious doctrinaires conjure up places to avoid the concept of hell. Ideas such as reincarnation, karma, purgatory, bardos (Buddhism), levels of "heavens," Greek mythology, nirvana, svarga ioka (Hinduism), and so on and so on. I have studied them all during my life.

Many people reject Christianity because it includes hell as a place to which souls go if they are not born again through the Spirit of Jesus Christ. I must admit, having been an agnostic, that the concept of hell on the surface seems to defy the Judeo-Christian belief in a loving God. Remember how I sought to disprove all religions before becoming born again? Well, before then I considered that the gods espoused by some other religions appeared much more loving than the God of the Bible. That is—until I met Him.

Meeting God through a belief in Jesus Christ manifests through different personal experiences. Some Christians say that they were always believers in Jesus Christ, and some can remember, like me, the very hour and date when the Spirit of Jesus Christ possessed them. I was born again before I met Jesus in Heaven. However, I was not fully aware of God's infinite Love until my spirit body experienced Him in Heaven.

"I desire that no one perish," He said to me in Heaven. "If anyone loves Me then he will love My sons and daughters and he will love those who are not in Me. He will love My children as I love them, and he will love those who have rejected Me *as I desire to know them.*" I have intentionally italicized those final five words told to me, *"as I desire to know them."* That may seem puzzling, but in Heaven even the most baffling of concepts expressed by Jesus in this world revealed themselves as crystal clear within my spirit mind. My heavenly body understood from a perspective of Heaven, not from a perspective of this world.

In comparison, it would be like trying to understand math problems in class as a student in this world, in order to learn how to build a structure. In Heaven those mathematical equations were translated into a fully constructed building without any need to understand the how's or why's, because petitioning the Master Mathematician Jesus Christ was all one needed to design and create concepts.

A mathematician would calculate the square footage of a building using an equation. In Heaven, the desired outcome would no longer be a calculation, it would simply be the outcome of the equation. In this example, assimilated expressions of God's creativity would instantly appear as a majestic crystal construct made of luminescent stones. Our desires would be fulfilled by God with no need to toil. People I saw were intentionally carrying out God's will. God directed their actions. They joyfully executed God's will while enjoying His creations. They performed various duties, but joyfully as unto the Lord.

Concepts no longer existed in Heaven. They have been replaced with an appreciation for God's creations because Heaven is the perfection of all that God created. Creativity in Heaven is expanded through a divine understanding of God's will and the subsequent desire for God to construct His will in all things. In Heaven, nothing is revealed in parts, with no need to reason its existence. The sum total of understanding is the perfect outcome that we desire, and our desires are aligned with God's perfect will. We know that God's greatest creation is you and me. God's greatest gift is relationship between God and humankind.

HELL REPRESENTS THE ABSENCE OF RELATIONSHIP

I know from being with Jesus that His wholehearted desire is to love us, and for us to love others. Christ's admonition is for you and me to love the unbeliever as He desires *"to know them."* How does Christ desire to know unbelievers? He desires to know them as His children. Why would any human not know God? Because there are those unbelievers who are not related to Him as a result of them having consciously rejected Jesus Christ, or they have sought their own understanding apart from sincerely seeking the truth about God. Essentially, unbelievers become their own god. How should we love the unbeliever like Christ loves them? We should love them the same way we might love a son or daughter who has run away, or as an abandoned and abused child in need of an adopted parent.

This is an important understanding for grasping the reality of hell. God desires that no one will perish in hell (2 Peter 3:9). But He cannot relate to someone He does not know. Sure, God knows that the unbeliever exists, but there is no spiritual connection between the unbeliever and God.

For example, I cherished my daughter from the day she was born. At one period in my teenage daughter's life she said to me, "I'm leaving, you're not my parent anymore, and I don't believe in God."

I tried desperately to reconnect to no avail. Later, she returned home after visiting with friends and said, "I'm hungry."

I wrapped my arms around my daughter and said, "I love you!"

"I still hate you," she said.

Eventually my daughter learned that God really does love her, but it took my wife and I expressing that love through her anger.

This is how God loves even those who reject Him. Suffice it to say that Jesus Christ can only relate in *koinonia,* intimate fellowship, with those who acknowledge Him as their Lord and Savior. He can only accept into His perfect "household" of Heaven those who confess Christ's lordship. When Christ assumes the "throne" of someone's life, Jesus Christ makes the spirit of that person "perfect" through Christ's righteous—His spiritual blood. Please excuse my crude analogy, but becoming born again is like undergoing a spiritual cleansing. Instead of soap and water, Jesus uses His own righteous blood to perform a type of "spiritual transfusion."

The takeaway is that we must love our brothers and sisters in Christ in like fashion as to how God sees them and loves them. And we must love those who have rejected Christ as the lost children for whom God desperately wants to return home. Either way, we just need to love each other because in all cases God loves those who were made in His image. A genuine ability to return good for evil as commanded by Jesus can only happen if the righteous spiritual blood of Jesus Christ runs through our spiritual veins, and that requires confessing Jesus Christ as our Lord. Subsequently, a fulfilling life requires a daily discipline of following the leading of God's Holy Spirit.

Hell is a place without God and therefore without the love He ushers forth from His abiding presence. Heaven is the perfect place where God reigns supreme, and where Love can be found everywhere and within every child of God.

> Revelation #20: Hell is where God is not.
> Heaven is where God reigns supreme.

GRACE IS PART OF GOD'S DESIGN

Never in all of human history has God removed His presence from this world. We have no idea what that might look like on this earth, but it would be unquestionably hell on earth. It would not be a jungle, because in the jungle animals only kill for food or protection. Humans would feel free to victimize any other human being because the laws of humankind that were established largely in accordance with the Ten Commandments given to Moses by God on Mount Sinai would be abandoned if not legally, certainly in principle.

Instead of the pleasantry elicited by the sound of birds chirping in the air, ocean waves, or beautiful music, fear would maintain its constant grip on people in anticipation of some evil played out by a world gone awry. No peace. Some persecuted people in parts of this world and victims of gang violence can empathize to some extent with this type of God-forsaken world. Prayers to God would be more like futile hopes because God's presence in this world could not impart His assurances. The Bible would be banned, as it is in several places around the world now, because it teaches Jesus Christ as the only way toward salvation. In a godless society, nothing that convicts the soul could survive because the truth convicts, and there would be no truth.

If that seems horrible, then imagine that as your glimpse of hell. The only thing keeping this world from disintegrating into chaos is God's order. God does not exist in hell. Everything that is apart from God in this world serves as the accoutrements and expressions of hell. Hell quite simply is where God is not. Heaven offers everlasting life. Hell glorifies death. God gives life to the full. God is truth. Hell is full of lies. God is Love. Hell contains hatred. Adoring angels abide in Heaven. Angels/demons who hate God abide in hell. The redeemed spirits of God's children thrive in Heaven. The desperate souls who rejected Christ struggle in hell for lack of love. I imagine hell being like a zombie movie come to life; but instead of being mindless, the zombies would be hopeless.

GOD DID NOT WANT TO MAKE THINKING ZOMBIES

Perhaps the biggest challenge I receive when speaking about Heaven arises from this single question: "If God so loves people, why did He not find a way to bring everyone to Heaven since you claim that He is God, and God can do anything?" The answer is quite simple, and it arose from my interaction with Jesus. Even when I challenged Jesus in Heaven about returning to a fallen world, He responded with understanding and compassion. Jesus did not challenge me. He knew how I felt. I had disagreed with God's choice to make me return, and yet He did not argue with me, He just loved me. I knew then that God did not want to create robots or thinking zombies when He created humans—people who would obey His orders on command, unable to challenge Him or reason with Him. God wanted "free thinkers."

When I hired people in the corporate world, I did not want yes people. I wanted my hires to feel that they could challenge me, and in the process if my opinion prevailed, I felt confident that it had been the right one. Of course, God never makes a bad decision as have I on occasions; however, God still does not want to mandate, or "goddate," compliance. Relationships are not built on blind obedience. They form through respect, trust, appreciation, understanding, flexibility, shared principles, and love. All of these must be freely given. Heaven is all about relationship with God; and absent a relationship with Jesus Christ, Heaven ceases to exist.

When I voiced my anger at God two weeks before dying, I actually felt prepared to live apart from God if my then uncaring view of God proved true. I became that desperate. In my conflicted mind, I reasoned that it would be better to live in a world where I could control my actions instead of following a god who only wanted obedience but would remain unyielding toward my demands.

Friend, that was my state of mind before encountering God in Heaven. But I did not go to hell, because God also knew that I was sincere in wanting to know Him. Years before I had prayed to receive Jesus Christ as my Lord and Savior, thereby giving my life over to God. This arrangement came with a "no return policy." I could get angry with God, but my spirit was "owned" by Jesus Christ and He was not about to let me go. Anger, from Christ's point of view, was better than a deadened resolve of hopelessness. God knew my heart. My spirit belonged to Jesus Christ even if my mind had temporarily rebelled against Him.

Not only was I not condemned for my rebellion, I experienced an intimacy with Jesus that would melt even the most hardened soul. At no time in Heaven did Jesus let go of me. He held me tightly. It was not until after my return to this world that I understood how profoundly God answered my desperation. He just loved me and excepted me because I longed not just for answers to my challenges—I longed for Jesus and would not be satisfied with anything except the real deal.

If you wonder why God does not just wave a magic wand and allow everyone to go to Heaven, consider that God wants His children in Heaven to know Him as the Truth, and not just as an answer to our perception of truth. This means that we must relinquish not our mind, but our heart. It means that we must earnestly seek the Truth through a Person, not just answers. It means that we must not settle for human-made solutions; we must demand to know the one true God. Heaven is comprised of truth seekers who became Truth finders.

Beloved of the Lord, God wants you to come to Him by surrendering your all to Jesus Christ because of one reason: He loves you more than anyone in all of creation. But that must come on your terms. He will not force you to love Him, because without Jesus Christ we cannot fully love anyone, including ourselves.

THE TIME WHEN MY HEART TURNED DARK

God does not desire to send anyone to hell. But I once desired that my daughter's rapist would go to hell. This happened almost eight years after my experience in Heaven. She was only 18 and full of joy before she was drugged and raped at a Christmas party. I am not proud of my hatred for the rapist, and after much prayer and dwelling on the Lord, I now pray for his salvation. It took years for me to understand God's heart through this horrendous travesty despite my experience in Heaven. This world tends to coarsen the soul, and the violence against my daughter temporarily turned me into an uncaring soul without any grace for the victimizers of this world. Annie's attempted suicide by swallowing pills compounded my rage as I watched her heart flatline in the emergency room before God miraculously answered my prayer by restarting her beating heart.

Grace sees the broken heart of a heathen soul like my daughter's rapist. A world without grace would render judgment against every person who offends us. A world without grace is a world without God. Justice would not prevail in a world without Christ. Injustice would reign in a constant state of violence. Each person's prejudices would be acted out without any checks. Yes, there will be a judgment day for those who do not know Christ, but it will be the rejection of Christ that condemns unbelievers, not God's rejection. God gives grace to all who seek Him, the Truth.

JUDGE NOT

I remember going to a church one time while on a business trip after the 1989 earthquake struck the San Francisco Bay Area. I lived in the Bay Area at the time. Phone lines were not working shortly after the earthquake. News of the quake's devastation monopolized media reports. Fires burned. Houses and freeways collapsed leaving many dead. I had just gotten off my flight in Dallas, Texas, after taking off from Oakland Airport minutes before the earthquake. I feared that some of my loved ones left behind had been hurt with no way to reach them.

The following day I attended a church service to join my brothers and sisters in prayer for the victims of the devastation. The pastor pounded his fist on the pulpit and said, "This earthquake is God's judgment on the sinful San Francisco Bay Area. He is rendering His judgment against homosexuality and the ungodly ways of that place."

My jaw dropped thinking, *And did God forget those of us living there? What if that was your family killed in the quake?*

I walked out of that church not wanting to hear any further from the pastor's self-righteous condemnation. I was sure that none of his loved ones died during the earthquake, and if any of his loved ones lived there, he surely showed no concern for them.

I know that God sees the devastation of this world and cares for both His children and the lost victims of this world. Jesus uniquely cares for us because He walked this earth. He does not desire judgment—He suffered to redeem the lost, not to judge them.

People judge themselves when they reject Love. They think that sin automatically disqualifies someone from God's love, confusing God's love with God's redemption through Jesus Christ. They condemn the lost, rather than showing them the light of Christ through love. They are like someone who sees a sick person and blames the person instead of the disease. They are like the person who sees an abused child and says, "He/she got what he deserved because he/she is a bad person."

When that self-righteous person appears before God on the day he or she dies, they may hear these words, *"I never knew you; depart from Me, you who practice lawlessness!"* (Matthew 7:23 NKJV). Their condemnation of others serves only to condemn their own failures. Part of my life review in Heaven showed me the times when I condemned others without showing them love. It was only because of God's grace that He forgave me because I had earnestly regretted my own self-righteousness.

Lawlessness happens in souls without God's Spirit to direct them. Lawlessness corrupts the soul of those who believe they are always right without any need to understand the heart of God. The only way to obey God's law is to surrender to the One who fulfilled God's law, Jesus Christ.

If you are feeling judged right now, please understand that it is not God condemning you, it is God revealing your need to draw closer to Jesus Christ, and to repent of your self-righteousness, as did I before meeting Jesus in Heaven. That takes humility. Humility says something like this: "God, I am so lost without You. I cannot do this alone. I have done things that are wrong, and it seems like the right things I want to do are not within my control. That is why I need Jesus Christ to take full control of me. Dear Lord, forgive me."

Brother or sister in Christ, I did not give this prayer just for those who do not believe in Jesus Christ as their Savior. I wrote it for us—the believers.

> Revelation #21: The farthest we will ever be from Christ is the closest we will be to thinking we no longer need God's influence.

ONE LAST CHANCE FOR ALL

Just after I died, when my heart stopped, a "nanosecond" of feeling space-less consumed me. Scientists tell us that the brain cannot be fully restored after ceasing to function while the body exists at room temperature. My heart had stopped for almost thirty minutes. Hospital monitors can record a patient's vital signs. Shortly after the heart stops, blood flow ceases. Certainly, my NDE was not the result of brain activity. There is a period of time between when the heart stops beating and the brain's continued survival, which amounts to about six minutes.

After that time, the brain begins to die. After about three to four minutes the brain becomes damaged.[1] A lot can happen during those few minutes of brain survival, including a deathbed call-out to Jesus Christ. As someone who maintained a brief consciousness after my heart stopped before my consciousness transitioned to a spiritual awareness strikingly different from any state of mindfulness previously known, I can testify that during those final seconds or minutes of brain activity, the first inclination is to either "get right" with God or just hang on for that final "roller coaster dive." I had lost consciousness for a while, but not my ability to think.

After a few minutes post my heart's cessation, my brain ceased functioning as well. My spirit mind took over at that point.

One of the observations in Heaven that surprised me was the sheer numbers of people there—countless numbers of people. I now believe that even those who had rejected Jesus Christ all of their lives may have accepted Him up until that last moment of their brain's function.

The soul is the supreme animating principle by which we think and feel, independent of the body. My first thought after dying was, *I'm going to be okay.* The spirit is the channel between God and His children. At the moment we die, our body ceases to exert dominion over the soul. The born-again spirit immediately reigns over the soul since the body is dead. After death, my spirit was freed to be wholly dedicated to my Lord Jesus Christ in communion with God's Spirit.

My next recollection after dying was a beaming light from above that soothed me like a warm blanket on a cold night. It shined above me as my body ascended, and I could initially see my lifeless body below. As I was rising, the light permeated the darkness, illuminating everything around me. At this point I could only faintly see rolling green hills and lakes. In the valley I saw warring creatures. On the left side were gangly and grey giants lifting swords. On the right side were giants covered in a thick garment, also lifting swords that reflected the light from above. On the ground were fallen giants from both sides.

I knew something ominous was happening, and that there appeared to be a battle either for the lost souls in this world, or for my life in this world. If it were for the latter, I thought, I had better start praying that the righteous warriors on my right would win. So I shouted out the name of Jesus Christ. I said something like, "My

Lord, my Savior Jesus Christ. I give You all glory. I am Yours, my Lord. Jesus, take me!"

In that next moment I was side to side with Jesus Christ. As I mentioned previously, that moment was the best moment of my life! And it happened after what most think of as the worst moment—death. Today, I do not suffer from any brain damage. At least, I do not think I suffered any damage (ha ha). One night at a dinner someone from my high school days told the others around the table that I was "very smart" in school, to which I replied, "That was before my accident in the hospital."

Yes, God does have a sense of humor, but not like a stand-up comedian's way of joking. It is more like Jesus showing me some of the cute creatures that forced a smile, like a long-nosed proboscis monkey or the bug-eyed tarsier. Jesus outstretched His hand to show me the wonders of His creation saying, "See, beloved, I give you the desires of your heart."

I next saw a vision of my boyhood dog, Casey, a rat terrier twirling like a ballerina causing me to laugh. As an overweight and sickly boy, I was oftentimes bullied in school. No one outside of school knew about the times when a pack of bullies called me "Lard Boy," dumped my school papers in the garbage, and spread malicious gossip about me—no one knew except Jesus and Casey. That little dog could sense my depression after returning home, immediately jumping up to lick my face and wagging his tail as though I were a steak bone. Seeing him in Heaven reminded me that Jesus understood my troubled childhood even if others could not. I now fully expect to see and hold my little Casey in Heaven next time I take a permanent trip there.

FIGHTING THE GOOD FIGHT

The other ominous vision of the fighting warrior angels during my ascension speaks to the fact that right now, angels and spiritual influences are battling for our souls. If you are a believer, they cannot invade your spirit. Jesus Christ has protected your spirit from evil influences. But they can infiltrate our souls.

Ephesians 6:12 states: *"For our struggle is not against flesh and blood, but against the rulers, against the authorities, against the powers of this dark world and against the spiritual forces of evil in the heavenly realms."*

When Christ said, *"For what will it profit a man if he gains the whole world, and loses his own soul?"* (Mark 8:36 NKJV), He spoke of the battle for our soul. Not only do God's angels fight on our behalf, we also must enjoin the fight. This translates into a daily discipline of prayer, study, and fellowship. It requires humility. A good fight does not require that we be perfect; rather as warriors in the spiritual realms, we must declare Jesus Christ's authority over everything.

We cannot relinquish God's authority over any territory. We should not believe that satan owns certain places, like territories that are controlled by terrorist forces. We must claim God's Kingdom authority over every place controlled by the powers of darkness. Satan is not omnipresent. He is only one of millions of fallen angels, demons, who seek to take control of souls.

There exists a dynamic in Heaven that I realized in witnessing God's influence over this world. God's authority must be nourished by the prayers of His children to bring into being His sovereignty. I liken prayers to watering a seed so that a plant may grow. When we rain down prayers, petitions to God, we bring the seed of God's habitation in that place to fruition.

Right now we need to claim Christ's authority over our minds, our thoughts, and desires. We should claim Christ's authority over our loved ones. We should claim Christ's authority over our works. We must claim Christ's authority over government officials, schools, and over the media. We must claim Christ's authority over our households and our finances. I know from being in Heaven that God receives our claims as a transference of binding "ownership deeds" in the spirit realm that will shift back to us what the enemy has stolen.

But first we must stop fearing. Demons thrive on fear. Fear to demons is like the smell of a wounded prey to wild and hungry animals. People thrive on hope, and hope comes from Jesus Christ. Believers in Jesus Christ should not fear hell. If you are unsure about your position in Heaven today, pray the prayer I offered to you earlier in Chapter 6. Give your life to Jesus Christ. Once you do that, you will never see hell—NEVER.

NOTE

1. https://science.howstuffworks.com/life/inside-the-mind/human
    -brain/braindeath1.htm; accessed January 25, 2021.

11

THE KINGDOM OF GOD

MANY EXPERIENCES IN Heaven defy explanation. Jesus often related spiritual things in relationship to earthly things for a good reason. The reverence for God as evidenced in Heaven exceeds the mind's ability to assimilate the magnitude of the Almighty. All of Heaven speaks to the glory of God in one grand consonance between His creation and His Word. There exists no parallel, no exact explanation in this world to describe Heaven. We cannot fathom perfection.

Those of us who experienced glimpses of it in Heaven are left with just a lingering memory of what the fullness of God's glory used to be while we sojourned there for a brief time. Every once in a while I find myself stopping, remembering, and thinking about the incomprehensible as if I could once again slightly grasp its splendor with my unencumbered spirit while basking in the fullness of relationship with God as my closest Companion. My heart aches to share in words what can only be shared in Heaven.

Heaven is impossible for any human in this world to fully comprehend. Jesus did not spend much of His time in this world talking about Heaven. He did speak on numerous occasions about the Kingdom of God, and synonymously, the Kingdom of Heaven.

Jesus said that the Kingdom of God is within His children (Luke 17:20-21).

Throughout the Bible we can find several references to *"the kingdom of God."* John the Baptist often used this term as he said, *"Repent, for the kingdom of God is near"* (Matthew 3:2). Jesus taught the disciples how to pray saying, *"Your kingdom come"* (Matthew 6:10); and at the Last Supper He said, *"I will not drink again of the fruit of the vine until that day when I drink it new in the kingdom of God"* (Mark 14:25).

The NIV, NKJV, and KJV versions of the Bible use the phrase "kingdom of heaven," whereas the "kingdom of God" is used in Matthew 12:28 and Matthew 19:24. Several theologians define these terms as being synonymous, and for the sake of discussion, I will henceforth use their opinion with the coda being that for me, God's Kingdom is plainly spoken of as wherever He resides, and God's presence is not bound by any common vernacular.

Herein lies perhaps the most telling truth about the Kingdom of God as explained by Jesus in Matthew 6:33 (NKJV), *"But seek first the kingdom of God and His righteousness, and all these things shall be added to you."* In Luke 17:20-21 Jesus says that *"the kingdom of God is within you."* The Greek phrase *entos humon* is translated "within you."

Seeking after God, as in spending time with Him, ushers us into God's presence, and being in God's presence reveals the Kingdom of God to us in direct communication from God's Spirit to our spirit. A spiritual transformation must occur in order to reveal God's Kingdom. Paul wrote in First Corinthians 15:50 (NKJV) that *"flesh and blood cannot inherit the kingdom of God; nor does corruption inherit incorruption."* Only through the spirit can one enter the gates of God's kingdom.

When my body died, my spirit was pulled toward Heaven, but I had already been familiar with the Kingdom of God in my spirit because my spirit communed with God's Spirit in this world. Jesus said to the believers that His Kingdom was "within" them, as a spiritual connection. Today, as believers in Jesus Christ, our spirits are in communion with God. Seeking after God reveals that spiritual connection making us aware of God's presence. God's Spirit dwells with His children.

> Revelation #22: Our communion with God is our spiritual connection to God, and on the day our body dies, that connection ushers us into a full awareness of God's Kingdom.

It disturbs me that some define the Kingdom of God, or the Kingdom of Heaven, as a "process." God's Kingdom is a place. The very definition of a kingdom is a territory ruled by a king or queen. The Pharisees, during the time when Jesus Christ walked in the flesh, expected the Messiah as prophesied by Isaiah to be like a king in this world. They expected a preeminent ruler. They expected the Messiah to be a deliverer of the Jews. Imagine their shock in seeing Jesus riding on a donkey.

The Pharisees' expectation was worldly, not heavenly. Jesus spoke of spiritual truths. He often used parables to explain these truths. So when He spoke of the Kingdom of God, or the Kingdom of Heaven, He was speaking of that dwelling place where He communes with His children.

In this world, that place is sequestered within us, isolated from the effects of this world; similar to how an unborn child—in this case the born-again spirit—is protected from the effects of this world within its mother's womb; in the case with the spirit, protected by the "blood" of Jesus Christ. We hear God's voice mostly through inspirations and through the words expressed by God within the Bible. On the day our bodies die, we will no longer perceive the Kingdom of God faintly, we will perceive the Kingdom of Heaven more strikingly than we perceive people and places in this world.

What my spiritual eyes perceived in Heaven was beyond the imagination's ability to comprehend, and clearer than what the physical eyes could process. I assimilated God's Kingdom with my spirit unencumbered by my body. My spirit had been birthed into a new macrocosm.

THE BLOOD OF JESUS CHRIST

Let's stay with the analogy of our spirit being protected in the "womb" being fed through the blood of Jesus Christ. I am going to get woosoo with you now. Please be patient. It is hard for me to translate spiritual impressions using physical words. For Jesus, it was easy. But for me, it is taxing my physical brain, like trying to write sentences using the air. I will start with this Scripture in Ephesians 2:13: *"But now in Christ Jesus you who once were far away have been brought near by the blood of Christ."*

The blood of Christ connects our spirit to God. A mother's lifeblood to her infant is transported through an umbilical cord. The spiritual blood of Jesus Christ nourishes our spirit in like manner. Without that life-giving connection from Jesus, we would figuratively die in the womb, our spirit would have no life.

Jesus shed His blood on the cross, but that blood was not just physical blood, He shed His spiritual blood to give spiritual life to everyone who receives Jesus Christ as his or her Savior and Lord.

Before that "infusion" from Christ, our spirits were lifeless. What I call The Age of Grace following Christ's sacrifice was a shift in the way God communicated with His children. Before Christ's redemption, believers heard God's words mostly from the prophets and priests, and occasionally directly through visions, angels, and even through a donkey at one point. Now we can hear the voice of God directly within our spirit. Moreover, God was able to infuse His lifeblood and abiding presence into each believer as a means of establishing a *koinonia,* an intimate relationship.

I do not intend to get into a full theological discussion. I have read the Bible several times, studied it, learned from some masterful theologians, and completed an ordination, but I am not an expert. The good news is that neither were the disciples. None of them were theologians. Please know that I am not adding or changing what is in the Bible.

My words are not to be compared in any way to the historical recordings of God's words in the Bible. The Bible is essentially a containment of God's "love letters" to the world. The Bible is God's Word. This book of mine is basically about my observations and interpretations. When you read the Bible, you are literally reading God's expressions. As you read *Revelations From Heaven,* you are reading my interpretations.

That said, the spiritual blood of Jesus Christ will *"reconcile all things to Himself"* (Colossians 1:20 NKJV), and it *"cleanses us from all sin"* (1 John 1:7 NKJV). This means that the spiritual blood of God was imparted to us through Jesus Christ so that we could have life and communion through God's Holy Spirit. Friend, that is an awesome gift from God. With my spiritual eyes in Heaven, I could see that spiritual blood infusing life throughout all of Heaven and earth. It was somewhat analogous to the flow of red blood cells within our physical blood, although in the spirit it felt like the wind.

I FELT THE WIND OF GOD

When I stood overlooking the expanse of Heaven that seemed a composite of everything good that I had experienced on earth, only better and within a dimensional space both ethereal and relatable, a warm wind blew refreshment into my body. The wind rolled throughout Heaven, making a long, soft whispering sound, as when those soft linens fluttered in a rolling motion. It was both comforting and awesome, soothing and inspiring.

Only weeks later after recovering from my physical damages after leaving the hospital and studying about the wind as recorded in the Bible did I fully understand this experience. In Acts 2:2 (NKJV), there were 120 disciples gathered in the Upper Room, waiting for the presence of God that Jesus had promised them. While they waited, *"Suddenly there came a sound…."* The word "sound" in this verse is the Greek word *echos*, which was also used in Luke 21:5 to describe the deafening roar of the sea. The verse in Acts explains this Holy Spirit whisper as *"a sound from heaven."* Luke compared this sound from Heaven to a *"rushing, mighty wind"* (Acts 2:2 NKJV).

Now I believe that I heard and felt that wind in Heaven as God's abiding presence. In Heaven, it felt and resonated to me like a soft summer breeze, but I can imagine that in this world it would sound more like a roar because in Heaven we are spirits consumed with God's comforting presence, whereby in this world our bodies only perceive God's Spirit dimly, such that the presence of God might sound more intimidating, because what appears unfamiliar to us can seem more daunting.

To highlight the difference between the soothing voice of Father God in Heaven in comparison to the intensity of God's voice in this world, allow me to attempt a meager comparison. My boyhood friend's father was a police officer. To me his father seemed like an intimidating giant, but from my friend's account his father was like a "big teddy bear." Familiarity and closeness can soften even the most intimidating presence. Being entirely familiar with God in Heaven served to make Him seem more congenial than how I perceived Him in this world. In Heaven, God is not quite like a big teddy bear, but His embrace made me feel protected and thoroughly adored. And His presence infused me with refreshing winds that I knew emitted from God Almighty, Maker of Heaven and earth.

Jesus referenced the wind to explain to Nicodemus how the Holy Spirit gives birth to the spirit. Jesus says in John 3:3, *"no one can see the kingdom of God unless they are born again."* The wind I felt in Heaven was not like the wind we think of on earth. It was a living presence. We know how the wind can cool us on a warm day, or it can refresh us when it hits our face through an ocean breeze. I absolutely love to go the beach and soak in the ocean air. The wind in Heaven breathes life, much like the air we breathe on earth.

Consider it this way: Now, hold your breath. You feel just like I felt when I suffered from blood clots blocking my airway. Keep holding your breath. Panic will start to set in. Every fiber in your being will want to inhale some air. Now breathe and exhale. You feel relaxed. What we take for granted, in this case breathing, in that moment becomes the most welcome reprieve. We can breathe. Only when air is deprived can we fully appreciate the oxygen that air provides.

That oxygen is required to keep our blood cells alive. It is transported by red blood cells to the entire body to produce energy. As I painfully experienced with pulmonary embolism, without oxygen our cells cannot survive. They die.

The blood of Jesus Christ carries spiritual "oxygen" to the "body of Christ" to keep alive our spirits. As with our physical blood, we cannot feel Christ's blood coursing within our spiritual bodies, but we can feel the air we breathe, which intakes the oxygen we need to survive. The blood of Jesus Christ provides us with spiritual air, and its effect is ushered throughout Heaven as the very breath or wind of God.

IS IT PARADISE OR HEAVEN?

My friend Ray used to talk about going to Heaven a lot. He loved the Bible. He loved God. He loved people. He died in his nineties. My wife and I attended his memorial service. I enjoyed seeing images of Ray in his youth. He was always dapper, hair neatly combed, meticulous and impeccably dressed. Ray had previously owned several high-end clothing stores. His enunciation reflected his flair for perfection, so I was not surprised that Ray would desire the perfection of God in Heaven.

When the pastor began speaking, he talked about the fact that few messages from the pulpit explain Heaven, and the afterlife. Perhaps that is because the Bible speaks mostly about the Kingdom of Heaven and not Heaven itself. Heaven is ethereal. The Kingdom is innately understood by the believer.

What bothered me was the pastor's opening statement: "Ray is not in Heaven today." My spirit nearly leapt out of my skin. *What!?* I thought, *The person who talked about Heaven the most in my lifetime is not in Heaven?* The pastor proceeded to explain that Ray was in paradise, not Heaven. He used some biblical references to teach about the heavens (Paul used the plural form when speaking about his revelations in Heaven) and about God's restoration of His perfect kingdom on earth using several verses from the book of Revelation.

I wanted to shout to the pastor, I HAVE BEEN THERE, AND HE IS NOT JUST IN PARADISE, RAY IS WITH JESUS RIGHT NOW IN HEAVEN! I know that Jesus said to the thief on the cross who acknowledged Jesus as Lord that the thief would be in "paradise" that day, but my own experience and the experience of thousands of NDEers expressed something beyond a restoration of the Garden of Eden—we witnessed Heaven.

I wrote about the Bible's references to Heaven in my book, *Dying to Meet Jesus*. In a nutshell, Heaven is the manifestation of God's Kingdom. Whether there are multiple heavens, or layers of God's kingdoms like some planetary spheres, I do not know. Certainly during my ascent to Heaven I viewed what appeared to be a myriad of galaxies the likes of which cannot be ascribed to any comparison in this world. All I can tell you is that Heaven is a spiritual place and that it is spectacularly amazing and that it is real. The purpose of my writing to you is not to cajole you with the wonderment of Heaven. My purpose is to bring you closer to God, as the ultimate best Friend.

Is Ray in Heaven today? Yes! I cannot talk with him in Heaven because Heaven is insulated from this world for a reason. Because Heaven is perfect and this world is imperfect; to usher anyone back from Heaven would be to expose that person to the same sadness, regrets, and so forth that spoiled their joy on earth. To bring any part of this world into Heaven would be like placing a drop of contamination into a pool. Think of it like the poopoo babies sometimes deposit in a swimming pool. That one contamination would necessitate the entire pool be drained and refilled. This would be the spiritual effect of any impurity in Heaven.

The purity of Heaven cannot be spoiled by anything of this world. None of your loved ones in Heaven want to reexperience their worldly failures that sucked out their joy in Christ. When I awoke from my time in Heaven to experience my life in this world again, I closed my eyes wanting just a little more of Heaven. I even tear up thinking about it. Even today I am reminded of Jesus' parting words to me, "I am returning you to fulfill your purpose, My beloved. Remember that I am always with you and that I will never forsake you. You need only trust Me."

And that made all the difference in my ability to carry on. My purpose, friend, is you.

LYING IN THE CAVE WHERE JOHN SAW HIS REVELATION

Jesus first appeared on this earth as the Lamb of God, prepared for the ultimate sacrifice. His atonement was once and for all time. His second coming to this earth will be as the Lion of Judah:

> *I saw heaven standing open and there before me was a white horse, whose rider is called Faithful and True. With justice he judges and wages war. His eyes are like blazing fire, and on his head are many crowns. He has a name written on him that no one knows but he himself. He is dressed in a robe dipped in blood, and his name is the Word of God* (Revelation 19:11-13).

Years ago I visited the island of Patmos where the imprisoned apostle John experienced his Revelation. After that he wrote the final book of the Bible. John was imprisoned in a cave. I rested my head in the hole about one foot from the floor of the cave where traditional accounts state that John rested his head while experiencing the revelation of God's second coming.

While lying there, I looked up to an indentation in the ceiling that appeared as if a 10-foot-long wrecking ball had punched the ceiling to make a lasting indentation. My guide said that generations believe the indentation on the ceiling was the force of God's Spirit pressing in, as if that little cave could not contain the fullness of God's presence.

I understand the power of God's Spirit as you might encounter when looking up at the starry sky while imagining the Almighty's greatness. I would be honored to behold the greatness of my Lord Jesus Christ parting the sky while riding in His full glory from Heaven. I have never seen His full glory on earth. I have witnessed it in Heaven with my spirit, but not on earth. In Heaven, with Jesus, I first caved to my knees in adoration. His glory echoed through Heaven with a pleasant roar causing everything to submit to His authority. My guess is that only my spirit could encounter the glory of God with familiarity whereas my physical brain would have been overwhelmed.

"My Lord and my God!" I cried out. "How majestic is Your glory. Holy be the Lamb, the King of kings, my Lord and my Savior. Glory be Your name!"

Jesus gently lifted me from my knees to experience His gentle embrace. Jesus is both awesome and familiar, both God and Friend, both fearful and comforting. He is, after all, I AM. Though my spiritual eyes could perceive Christ's glory with warmth, I am sure that my physical body would perceive God's glory with giant goosebumps if He were to return to this world.

The book of Revelation tells us that the Kingdom of Heaven will be ushered into this world at Christ's second coming. He came as a humble servant during His first coming, but His second appearance will be more like what the Jews in the time Christ walked on this earth expected. We discover in Revelation that Jesus Christ will rule in this world for a thousand years on the throne of God the Father.

Jesus Christ is currently situated at the right hand of the Father, meaning that Jesus reigns with the Trinity of God in power and community. At some point in the future, Christ will bring His rule to earth from Heaven. In this way the power and authority behind the reign of Christ can be "of God" and "of Heaven." Whereas now we see Christ dimly, then you and I will see Him face-to-face (1 Corinthians 13:12).

Seeing Christ face-to-face is looking into the face of divinity. He showed no guile. His skin glowed and His body emanated a gentle light. The wind of Christ's Spirit wafted through His dark brown hair. His smile gracefully parted His lips exposing perfectly formed teeth. His hands felt like pillows, and His embrace felt like a refreshing bath. Oh...and those greenish-brown eyes of His glistened in a pool of love that soothed over my soul.

I witnessed Christ with my spiritual eyes and mind. But that was in my spirit. I cannot comprehend how God would rule this earth through Christ. I can barely comprehend how this world would function under the rule of Jesus Christ because it certainly is not under His full authority now. Though confounding, I know that God's glory will elicit adoration from His followers.

I LEARNED ABOUT PAUL'S THIRD HEAVEN

Having visited the celestial nature of Heaven that combines both earthly and transcendental characteristics, I can more easily theorize how the perfected earthly qualities of Heaven could be established in this world in exception to the supernatural qualities of Heaven. Said another way, a perfected earth would allow us to enjoy unfiltered *koinonia* with God even if the ineffable qualities in Heaven remained a mystery.

As for me, I wholeheartedly believe that I experienced both. I sometimes imagine in childlike abandonment how God might one day load His "moving truck" with the earthly qualities of Heaven and substitute them for the fallen earth we view today.

One fact is that Heaven is never boring! People often talk about being "intentional" without fully understanding the meaning of that word. The dictionary term for that word is "done on purpose." In this world, our focus rarely stays on purpose. As a teacher, I often mention the human mind's tendency toward scattered thinking. At any given moment, we typically are thinking about several things other than the topic at hand. For example, while speaking to a friend about something, like an important event, a myriad of other thoughts circle within our brain, such as, *I've got to go to the store,* or, *What am I going to say next?* This explains why life in this world can be exhausting, requiring that we take a break and just get still.

In Heaven, I was 100 percent focused on everything. If I saw a flower, I comprehended everything about that flower, but everything was in the context of God's intention for me while regarding that flower. What I am saying is that in Heaven, we will always be in the process of discovery and intentionality.

Did I work with my hands? Yes, I moved landscapes much like an artist would position a tree in a painting. Did I influence people? Yes, I influenced others with truth and love. Did I accomplish works? Yes, I felt more accomplished in Heaven than at any other time before and after being in this world. However, here is the caveat: I lived intentionally according to my Lord's intention for all that I could influence in Heaven. In other words, God's will served as my motivating force.

Often I have prayed for wisdom as to why God allowed me to view Heaven, a place far greater than my mind could fathom. Indeed, the apostle Paul described himself as being caught up in the *"third heaven"* (2 Corinthians 12:2). Does this mean there are multiple heavens? The Bible describes the heavens, plural. The first would be the earth's atmosphere in Deuteronomy 28:12. The second would be the galaxy including the stars, sun, and moon in Psalm 19:4,6. The third heaven is explained as the dwelling place of God in Matthew 5:16.

My experience taught me that Heaven is one entity with multiple facets. What is more, God the Father is unfathomable, Jesus is relatable, and the Holy Spirit is inspirational. Heaven reflects those differences. There was a place in Heaven that defied understanding, which I presumed to be the throne of God because it appeared gleaming in white with majestic figures about it and saints walking to and fro along a crystalline flow of waters, with God's brilliance all about—awesome to say the least. There was a place in Heaven that was familiar and relatable during my time walking with Jesus. And there was a place that bridged relationship with God and us, His most beloved creation, so as to impute God's presence from Heaven to earth, which I assumed to be the Holy Spirit's domain.

So in my estimation, Paul was speaking about Heaven in these three parts, or places. My third heaven would be the place I perceived while walking with Jesus. Jesus illuminated my understanding such that my body literally glowed with the Spirit of God who was in total control of my spirit body that looked and felt much like my body in this world, except that my fleshly longings in this world had been replaced with only two longings—to love God with all my heart, and to love others with God's heart.

For me, I think that God was opening a window through which others could peer in order to confirm not only God's reality, but to express the most important aspect of Heaven—the omnipresent and abiding presence of God, everywhere and in everything. I have heard "spiritualists" speak of the universe as though it were a thinking presence. Perhaps they mistake God for some extraterrestrial being or some cosmic force. The universe is God's creation. Relationship with God can only be imparted through the Spirit of Jesus Christ, and that can happen anywhere and anytime, but it can only happen without barriers in the place we call Heaven.

Revelation 11:15 says:

> *The seventh angel sounded his trumpet, and there were loud voices in heaven, which said: "The kingdom of the world has become the kingdom of our Lord and of his Messiah, and he will reign for ever and ever."*

I cannot imagine all of the disparate groups in this world—Democrats, Republicans, Socialists, Libertarians, Dictators, etc.—submitting in unison to the authority of Jesus Christ, but my guess is that either they acquiesce to the King of kings and Lord of lords, or else! Whew, I would not want to be the person who rejects Jesus Christ on that day.

Without getting too much into the weeds of John's revelation, Christ is going to reign on earth until handing over the Kingdom to the Father (1 Corinthians 15:22-26). When all of this has been accomplished, God will reestablish His authority from Heaven to earth (Revelation 21:1-4).

That is a lot to digest. Before writing this, I prayed that God's wisdom (remember the butterfly?) would illuminate my ability to interpret a spiritual language into this world's dialect, so that I could help you understand, primarily, the Love of God.

There are a several theories about the end times. Most of them detail a final battle between good and evil before the Day of Judgment. After God renders His final decree, or judgment, the glorious sounds of angelic trumpets I heard in Heaven will sound the return of Jesus Christ. Some think that the Garden of Eden will be restored, and I cannot definitely say one way or another. I do know this: no one exists in a state of slumber in perpetuity after their body dies while in Christ. God's Spirit expressed in First Thessalonians 4:16-17 says:

> *For the Lord himself will come down from heaven, with a loud command, with the voice of the archangel and with the trumpet call of God, and the dead in Christ will rise first. After that, we who are still alive and are left will be caught up together with them in the clouds to meet the Lord in the air. And so we will be with the Lord forever.*

In First Corinthians 15:51 (NKJV) Paul writes, *"Behold, I show you a mystery: we shall not all sleep, but we shall all be changed."* The word "sleep" in the Bible is a metaphor for death. Simply put, some will never die physically. Will our physical bodies rise and again be inhabited by our spirit and soul? A study of the Scriptures suggests that phenomenon. Only God knows the means by which He will reestablish His full Kingdom authority. Does that mean that God cannot take our spirits to Heaven after our bodies die? Of course not. God is God. All things are possible through Christ (Philippians 4:13). Thousands of verified cases like mine attest to the actuality of encountering Jesus after physically dying.

A word of caution to my beloved brothers and sisters in Christ, please. Although God promises a blessing to those who study the book of Revelation in the Bible, many have been so intrigued by end-times prophecy that they miss the essential message of God's plan. Since the beginning of time on earth when human-kind rejected the authority of God, our loving Father, Son, and Holy Spirit have been planning a way to reestablish the perfect bond between God and humankind that God fashioned in Heaven before all of creation. The end of this world as we know it will be the "re-beginning" of life as God knew from the time He formed flesh from ashes. The point of all this, my friend, is that God so loved the world that He has always been creating a way for com-plete and unobstructed *koinonia* with the ones He created in His image—you and me and the rest of our believing families. The only difference between the first beginning and this new forth-coming beginning is that the latter will create a union with God that can never be broken, because as believers we have already willed ourselves to Jesus Christ.

You may be asking at this point whether I inquired of Jesus when and how He would return to this world. For the sake of my loved ones and future generations, this question could be impor-tant. I know that Jesus' disciples asked Him that question. But they were in the flesh. Being transparent with Jesus in His glorified state answered all of my questions with this one simple answer: God's timing is perfect. I felt no need to know the time or day of Jesus' return, or anything else for that matter, because I did not question God's decisions. In this world, most people question God, as I did when insisting that God "show up" during my suffering just two weeks before physically dying. After I died and actually saw Him, no doubts remained.

Jesus knew my thoughts though, and He knew that I desired that my loved ones who refused to acknowledge Jesus Christ as their Lord would someday come to their senses. So He responded to that desire with this answer: "My beloved are not My slaves, they are My children," He said. "On the day I return to claim what is Mine, those who seek the freedom of My Spirit will have already been made free."

For a long time after recording this in my journal, I did not understand its meaning. Did Jesus tell me that only the slaves of this world would be remaining when Jesus returns in His glory to this world? Did Jesus tell me that His children would have been raptured before His return? I prayed for wisdom to know the answer. Only years later did I understand my Lord's prophetic words. I believe now that God is waiting for the captive souls in this world to receive the freedom that Jesus Christ offers before He reclaims this damaged world. He will restore this world spiritually in a similar way that restoration experts physically restore damaged homes and automobiles; only instead of repairing plumbing or engines, He will restore the hearts of His beloved human creations.

Of this I am confident—no one will be denied the truth who earnestly seeks the truth, and the Truth (capital T) is Jesus Christ. Knowing Jesus Christ as both Lord and Savior sets souls free, as explained in John 8:32. I discovered this intellectually at Northwestern University. I discovered this spiritually when I became born again decades ago; and, I discovered this in person while communing with Jesus in Heaven as an elucidation that my home, *our* home—Heaven—is for those who bow down to Jesus Christ and not to the false images in this world.

It seems silly now to doubt Heaven is our eventual home. Regardless of how God ultimately develops His final formations, I will be satisfied living wherever Jesus lives. A reporter once asked Billy Graham:

> "When people ask if Heaven is a literal place and where it is, what will you tell them?" Looking through the window that framed the beautiful Carolina mountains surrounding his home he proclaimed, "Of course Heaven is real because Jesus is real—He is the way, the truth, and the life—and Heaven is where Jesus is—and I am going to Him soon."[1]

Who can argue with the sage wisdom of Reverend Billy Graham?

One of the reasons I did not share my NDE for several years was that I did not want some theologians to summarily discount my experience as "unscriptural." One denominational distributor of books has even prohibited any of their stores from carrying books about NDEs. As I noted previously, several persons in the Bible experienced something similar to what we call a near-death experience. I am not special, and neither is my NDE account.

I do not want anyone to miss the point of this book and about my experience. I met the Person of Love in Heaven. I hope you know the Person of Love in your heart. Someday you will meet Him face-to-face in Heaven or on earth when God reclaims this world. Until then, I want you to know that your faith is entirely merited. Even if you cannot grasp the concept of a real God who always fellowships with His children whether they know it or not, I want to testify that He is with you now. Even though we cannot understand all of His ways, we should know that God's way is perfect.

THY WILL BE DONE

Jesus explained Himself as the only way, so our quest in life translates into following the way of Jesus Christ. When Jesus began preaching in this world around AD 27-29 as the only sinless human being, He had sacrificed His heavenly glory (as explained in Philippians 2:5-11) to become a servant to humankind for the purpose of bringing a new covenant in fulfillment of the law as Jesus explains in Matthew 5:17. Jesus ushered in a new period of grace where all that is required for salvation is to believe in and trust Jesus Christ (Acts 16:31).

At the moment of a believer's confession, the compelling nature of the believer begins to transition from an egocentric fixation to a Jesus-centric desire. Our heart changes such that we can only be truly satisfied by following after Jesus, and frustration happens when we drift away from Jesus. The preeminent position of the conscience is replaced with the indwelling influence of the Holy Spirit. This explains why joy for the believer can never be fully realized through temporal affairs; it can only be fulfilled through a closeness to Jesus.

Staying close to Jesus is a challenge in this world fraught with pitfalls, as the apostle Paul notes when he wrote, *"For I do not understand my own action. For I do not do what I want, but I do the very thing I hate. ...For I have the desire to do what is right, but not the ability to carry it out"* (Romans 7:15,18 English Standard Version). The back and forth experienced by Paul as a common human struggle reminds me of a game I used to play for hours on end, The Labyrinth Wooden Maze. The top of the box is a tilting wooden platform. On two sides of the box there are dials to tilt the platform up and down, or side to side. On top of the platform there are raised walls that make a maze and one solid, snaking black line that runs throughout. Underneath the platform is a hollow area so that when a marble falls through one of the twenty-four holes, it rolls through the exit so that the player can start over.

The goal of this game is to use only the dials to tilt the maze up and down and left and right, send the marble through the maze, following each number in order (or the black line), and get all the way to the bottom right corner of the platform without letting the marble fall through any of the holes. Getting to the corner end-game (the final hole) sometimes took hours because of all the other holes along the path. Playing this game sometimes felt like an exercise in masochism. Such is life. As we move through the labyrinth of life, a myriad of pitfalls lie in wait, and some of them force us to start the game all over again. The game requires skillful perseverance to win, not unlike our walk of life.

For Paul and many of us, we seek God's direction and strength to persevere. We pray, but sometimes our prayers seem unanswered. We may read the Bible, but the words may appear empty. We seek elusive answers. The walk with Christ is fraught with obstacles that can cause us to fall. Why does prayer sometimes feel useless? Perhaps it is because prayer is not simply a petition. Indeed, in Heaven I discovered that God-inspired prayer reaches beyond our wants to reveal God's wants; and when that happens, we can know exactly for what we should ask. Once that happens, we can avoid the pitfalls that arise when we ask for things apart from God's will.

In Heaven, I observed that Jesus continually prayed because I understood that prayer is not only a request for help from God or giving thankfulness to God. Sincere prayer is an expression of the Holy Spirit to us and the influence of the Holy Spirit that inspires us to conjoin with God in an alignment of wills.

When Jesus prays, He imparts His heart's desire so that His beloved would desire the same. Prayer for me in Heaven consisted of a conversation from my heart toward God and God's heart toward me that was translated not just into words, but also into shared desires. We were on the same proverbial page since all I wanted was to please Jesus and Jesus always wanted what was best for me. In Heaven, I knew explicitly God's will for me; whereas here, in this world, I sometimes struggle trying to understand God's ways.

Regrettably, the perfect heavenly communion I enjoyed while walking with Jesus in the afterlife has been broken by millenniums of transgressions in this world. Not until we experience God's perfect heavenly Kingdom can we experience a melding of our will with God's will. The only way of reestablishing perfect communion with God is to be reunited with Jesus Christ in Heaven within a marriage of wills. When that happens to the full, the trajectory of our path perfectly aligns with God's way to reach our final destination without fail.

This only happens in Heaven when the will of God for us is the same will, or desire, we have for ourselves. Until then, we just need to work through the labyrinth of life knowing that we may occasionally fall through the cracks in this fractured world. For now, our goal should be to renew our mind, by steeping ourselves in the Truth of Jesus Christ, and by testing our assumptions so that we can discern the will of God as explained in Romans 12:2. We need to stop trying to be perfect and instead grow our personal average to be better, not the best.

When Jesus first looked into my heart in Heaven, I knew that He understood my sincerest desire to please Him despite my inabilities—and all I felt was God's acceptance. He loved me in spite of myself. Too often I tried to please God when my striving should have been to seek an understanding of God's will for me and then to expect the Holy Spirit's empowerment as the result of a personal sacrifice of my will in adoption of God's will for me. My prayer became simply wanting less of me and more of God.

Friend, I can testify from my own stubborn inclination that God is exceptionally patient with us. He waits for us to give up so that we can give in to His will, even if that place of following after God's heart is only temporary. If not for Jesus' infinite patience, I would have been burnt toast, as they say. Now I am just crusty in this world, but not burnt.

Adopting the will of God is harder than any game, which might explain why God does not judge our scars, and this applies doubly to those who have been severely abused and broken in this world. Of course assimilating and acting upon God's will is furthered through personal devotion, but it is ultimately and only consummated in Heaven. Earnest and honest communication with God in this world, as in Heaven, proves essential. Jesus modeled this for us on earth. On numerous occasions in this world Jesus prayed to His Father in seeking power (John 11:41-42) and wisdom (Mark 1:35, 6:46).

As spelled out in John 17, Jesus had temporarily relinquished the full glory of God while in the flesh. While walking upon this earth, Jesus had sacrificed the radiance of that glory as explained in Hebrews 1:3 to be a humble servant to humankind. At no time did Jesus sacrifice His divinity on earth; however, in the flesh He became a servant to enact God's will on earth.

When I met Jesus in Heaven, He was in a glorified state appearing as both human and transcendent. The glory of God within and about Jesus cannot be translated into a physical appearance except to crudely explain that in Heaven God's glory shined like a burst of sun shattering through a formless prism that scattered into radiant rainbow colors, and that brilliance infused adoration into every creation from the flowers that waved in attention, to God's children who basked in His glory.

The glory of God saturated every fiber of existence that seemed to cut from a depth that glistened like sweetly kissed light. Everything was bathed and impregnated with God's presence—stronger, deeper, truer, richer than life, a permeating influence that became the beauty it emitted. I remember thinking that God's light could settle into every dark place such that only God's love was real, a glory and connection that swept me out of my cares, out of my consciousness, so that only a comforting afterglow remained. It felt like a fusion of everything that was good. Thus explains my meager attempt at explaining the full glory of God Almighty.

Glorification in Heaven as described by Paul in First Corinthians can best be described as being fully consumed with the presence of God; and since Jesus was and is God, and I was not, the mere presence of Jesus imparted a form of like-mindedness. I did not become like God; rather, I was possessed by God's Spirit in a similar way that a born-again believer in this world is transformed by the renewing of his or her mind through the Holy Spirit, except that in Heaven this transformation had become all-consuming.

I mention this as a precursor in attempting to help you conceptualize a profound dynamic in Heaven between God the Father and God the Son, and the Holy Spirit. An inner sanctum appeared in a space entirely dedicated to Father and Son (Jesus) in which the two appeared together in shared holiness. They appeared as one, but distinct, in a way that cannot be compared to anything in this world, and the Holy Spirit was a relatable essence who existed as a symbiotic being that related as both nondescript and intensely felt.

In this world the dynamic between the Father God and the Son of God confounded me, but in Heaven it made perfect sense. Now, with my "earthly" mind I cannot fully explain in words this woosoo experience. Suffice it to say that in Heaven there appeared a Father/Son relationship between the two unlike any comparison in this life such that the two could only be complete with each other.

I also perceived that there remained something "unfinished" in Heaven, like a word from the Father that would consummate the marriage between Jesus the Son and His beloved in this world. I felt it as an impending impartation. I knew it as a cloak of secrecy as with that hunch we get when someone withholding information gives off an indescribable impression, an intuition. It was wonderful—a forthcoming union of God's will with the will or desires of His children in a place yet to be formed.

Now in hindsight, *"Thy will be done on earth as it is in heaven"* no longer seems like just the common "Lord's Prayer" some of us learned in childhood; it was, as I realized in Heaven, an actual prayer from Heaven from the Father to establish God's will on earth through Jesus Christ as a process of completion. The Greeks used the word *telios,* meaning having reached its end, a word that fits in describing the final consummation of God's will on earth. Jesus instructed His disciples to pray for the Kingdom of Heaven to be established on earth so that God's will would be instilled within those living on earth.

My mother taught me the Lord's Prayer that Jesus gave to the disciples after they asked Him how they should pray. It goes like this:

Our Father which art in heaven,

Hallowed be thy name.

Thy kingdom come,

Thy will be done in earth,

as it is in heaven.

Give us this day our daily bread.

And forgive us our debts,

as we forgive our debtors.

And lead us not into temptation,

but deliver us from evil:

For thine is the kingdom, and the power,

and the glory, for ever.

Amen

(Matthew 6:9-13 KJV).

I used to pray this prayer not fully understanding its meaning. Now I realize that when we earnestly pray something like this prayer, by…

- first revering God and
- asking that God's will be established on earth as it is in Heaven, and
- praying for the Father's "bread" (all provisions needed for our spiritual and physical sustenance), and
- asking for God's forgiveness and likewise forgiving others, and
- requesting God's protection from temptation and evil…we are being made holy and acceptable before God. When expressed with sincerity, those invocations prepare our heart before God.

The Lord's Prayer might be compared to a spiritual cleansing that prepares our heart to adopt the will of God into our life. The words need not be the same, rather the sentiment behind the words matters most. I prayed this prayer with my dad in the hospital, and at "Amen," he breathed his last breath. I know that my father prayed something like the Lord's Prayer in preparation for his forthcoming union with Jesus in Heaven.

Jesus gave the Lord's Prayer as a model for preparing ourselves to unite with God's will on earth. I know that my dad felt ready to meet Jesus after preparing his heart one last time; and shortly after he passed to Heaven, I smelled the aroma of Heaven in the room. It was the same exact fragrance I smelled in Heaven—and it smelled glorious. I believe this fragrance was sent by my Lord as an assurance that my dad, my hero, was with God, and that someday I would be with Jesus and my dad again. Death is no more than the darkness we experience before the dawn.

Death has almost always ushered believers into the presence of Jesus Christ in Heaven, but not Enoch and Elijah. They were taken into Heaven while still being alive on earth. In the blink of an eye God may do the same for those living on this earth before the second coming of Jesus Christ to this world. An expectancy remains in my heart to this day that God is waiting to birth His will on this earth.

I felt it in Heaven, and I feel it now after returning from Heaven. It feels like a rolling thunder in my spirit that portends the final climax of God's restoration of His perfect plan on earth. Friend, it will be glorious beyond your grandest imagination times one thousand. That burgeoning outflow of God's glory I witnessed in Heaven will be poured forth unto this world. Wow oh wow—I have "holy goosebumps" just thinking about it.

Most of us get consumed with the political dynamics in this world. Many have speculated as to a world order that will usher in the antichrist, which seems to be playing out as I write this section. But no one knows the day or the hour as Jesus said within the passage of Matthew 24:36 (NKJV):

> *But of that day and hour no one knows, not even the angels of heaven, but My Father only.*

There remains only one secret yet to be revealed by the Father to the Son within the final hour of this world as we know it. My friend, I encourage you to not get so bogged down by the governmental happenings in this world that you lose sight of what is most important—drawing closer to Jesus Christ in order to align your will with God's will. Take a "walk" with Jesus each day in prayer and devotion, and some day you will walk with Jesus in Heaven as did I. Neither religion nor politics must ever obfuscate that one vital goal of every human being on this earth—to know and desire the will of God.

In retrospect, I believe that sanctum I viewed in Heaven was indeed a place where Jesus awaited the final call from the Father to make complete His Kingdom authority on earth. We may very well be living in the last days, but it matters not in comparison to God's desire for us to prepare our hearts and minds with an urgency to understand and follow the will of God. If we make that our goal, there is no need to worry about becoming perfect, which is an elusive and unattainable goal. Being perfected by Jesus, on the other hand, is a growth process that is entirely attainable.

In the ancient times of Jesus on earth, to prepare for her wedding, each day the bride had to get ready as if it were her wedding day, although she had no idea as to the time or day when the wedding would occur. The parable of the Wedding Feast describes

Christ's body of believers in this world as His "bride." Jesus the "Bridegroom" awaits the hour for His return to claim His bride, the believers in this world (Matthew 25:1-13). Our challenge must be to grow toward God each and every moment of every day in preparation for this stupendous event.

We cannot earn God's acceptance. We will not meet Jesus, on the day we die or are raptured, as a perfect person. Being incrementally perfected happens from an alignment of God's will with our will through daily preparation in prayer, worship, and by knowing and following God's Word. We can unite our will with God's will by seeking after an intimacy with Jesus in word, deed, devotion, and faith. Each time you or I pray something like the Lord's Prayer, we are preparing ourselves for Christ's return. We do not need to ramble on with "vain repetitions" as Jesus forewarned about in describing how the pagans prayed in Matthew 6:7. God already knows our thoughts as stated in Psalm 94:11. We just need to keep our "light burning" through a constant state of readiness in anticipation of being reunited with Jesus.

One day that expectancy I witnessed in Heaven within the inner sanctum of the Father and the Son will be effectuated and followed by a marriage feast as explained in the parable of the Wedding Feast in Luke 14:7-14. I did not experience that wedding feast in Heaven because, of course, that feast is intended to be shared with all believers upon completion of God's final restoration plan. What I perceived in Heaven was a glimpse, a marvelous revelation of Heaven and what Heaven models for each of us for our lives today.

With the culmination of God's Kingdom plan, the marriage of God's will with the will of His creation will be completed. I expect that the perfect will of God will happen when Jesus Christ returns to establish the Kingdom of God on earth. For now, all we need to concern ourselves about is doing the will of God which is in Heaven. Let God take care of the other stuff.

IT IS TIME FOR A BREAK

Now I want to give you a break. Stop. Get still. Invite Jesus Christ to reveal Himself to you. Then wait. Waiting is hard in this world, is it not? But not in Heaven. In this world, God often brings us to the eleventh hour of our desperation before meeting our needs. Why? Because God must burn through the shackles of our dependence on this world so that we can be freed to depend solely on Him. Indeed, just before my heart stopped, I felt as though God had abandoned me at the sunset of my life.

In the flesh, survival represents our most fundamental need. But not in Heaven. In my heavenly body, reliance on God served as my most fundamental need. This began with waiting on God to direct my steps. It strengthened me and I realized as it says in Isaiah 40:31 that I could soar throughout Heaven. Waiting on God does not produce idleness. It refuels our soul to do what matters most. I accomplished more while in Heaven for thirty minutes than during thirty hours of my most productive time in this world, because all that I accomplished mattered to God.

In Heaven, I prayed for those left behind in this world—I may have even prayed for you. Certainly my prayer for you now is that you and I live more intentionally for Jesus Christ in this world by getting still with Him now. Our greatest time wasters arise from trying to get ahead of God's plan. We accomplish more on bended knees than we do while running after misguided intentions.

So now I implore you to put down this book, close your eyes, and pray. Your loving Father is waiting for you. Today is the "Eleventh Hour" of human existence as we have known it since humankind first sinned against God. I felt the urgency of God to restore His perfection to a fallen world while I sojourned in Heaven. It felt as explained in Romans 8:22, *"that the whole creation has been groaning as in the pains of childbirth right up to the present time."* The time of Jesus Christ's return is approaching, and it will happen in less than a second within the scheme of eternity.

NOTE

1. Donna Lee Toney, "Billy Graham's Thoughts on the Promise of Heaven," *Decision Magazine,* September 18, 2015; https://decisionmagazine.com/billy-grahams-thoughts-on-the-promise-of-heaven/; accessed January 25, 2021.

12

ALL ABOUT RELATIONSHIP

I COULD SEE FIGURES not in form but in expressions. The equivalency of their characteristics flowed out of them like we might smell a flower, only that fragrance emitted characteristics. They emitted varying degrees of boldness, gentleness, curiosity, fondness, compassion, delight, and other attributes.

Each one spoke in a language I could understand and yet I also sensed that many came from different nationalities while living on earth. Perhaps they spoke their native tongue and I understood *"them in their own native language"* as explained in Acts 2 after the Holy Spirit came upon the apostles and they began to speak in tongues to the crowd of Jews from all over the world.

More likely, I now believe that everyone spoke in a shared language because I noticed no accents, and my own comfort in speaking with Jesus seemed to be spiritually infused with an ease of expressing all that I intended to speak; whereas, in this world I often struggled with the right words to express my meaning. Words in Heaven expressed each other's intended meaning while also expressing an empathy for the other person. I could also understand the essence of those I viewed in Heaven.

"You see them as I see them, My beloved," Jesus said. "In the world you understand people by their outward appearance, but I see their hearts. I know them as they are, not as they appear."

"I can realize people here as I never knew them before, my Lord, and each one reflects Your light in some way," I said.

"You see the reflection of My presence in each one. Here, My beloved, you see not with your eyes but with your heart."

Now, in attempting to write what I beheld, I was caught in my own woosoo moment. I saw things in Heaven just as I could see them in this world in combination with a plethora of other perceptions within an environment that was both physical and impalpable at the same time. Each part of Heaven evoked God's love. And each person in Heaven presented his or her essence as their main signifier. I saw people in Heaven as they truly were, not simply as they appeared to be outwardly.

In Heaven, immersive relationships form through an extended reality that overlays the essence of a person onto another person's observation. People in Heaven perceive the true attributes of a person by completely immersing themselves within the soul of the other person. The closest analogy in this world from my perspective happens when two people fit together like a hand in glove. They know everything about the other person and can read each other's thoughts.

Identical twins who share the same genes tend to think more alike than unrelated people, because of their shared genetics. In Heaven, every soul shares the spiritual genetic make-up of our Creator, Abba, which is the most common term for the Creator within Christianity because it was the title used by Jesus for God the Father. Here, in this world, we reflect the image of God even though the deleterious effects of this world have altered our genetic makeup in a similar way that radiation causes genetic mutations. There, in Heaven, our new bodies will be made genetically perfect, and identically shared with other believers, so that we can relate to each other as one body in Jesus Christ.

As I observed the interactions of people and with Jesus in Heaven, an epiphany struck me as to what life was all about. God created everything for the purpose of loving His children. God formed substance from thought to abide within us. Our life on earth is to love God, just as it is in Heaven.

LIVING THROUGH THE SCARS

That revelation of God's love and how He sees us, changed the way I view other people. I now try to understand the essence of a person. Rather than make a cursory observation, I more so perceive their vulnerabilities and their importance to God.

> Revelation #23: God knows the totality of a person, but we see in part. The objective should be to try to view people through the eyes of God's Spirit, not through our own eyes.

One inescapable fact tops every other conclusion—God loves us more than we love Him. I understood this dynamic after my children were born. As parents our worlds revolved around our children. Renee and I pampered them. We tried to teach them about the important things. Our love for our children would cause us to sacrifice anything for them. That love caused God to sacrifice His own Son for us.

Everything in Heaven reflects God's love. And God's presence spoke of love in every possible way. When our children started rebelling during their adolescence, we still loved them, but sometimes we did not want to be around them. They tested us. Blamed us. Accused us. Afterward, we hugged them knowing that they were simply trying to figure out life as an emerging adult. We do the same to God as would an adolescent to his or her parents. We often seek independence from God to do life our way.

God understands that we are trying to figure out life. He shows mercy when we might deserve to be disciplined; and sometimes He disciplines us, but always with love. The very foundation of our relationship with God and each other requires love; and when people are deprived of love in this world, they sometimes get stuck in "adolescence."

LIVING THROUGH THE ABUSE

I used to be an emergency foster care parent. Abused children would sometimes show up at my doorstep in the late evenings after being pulled from their homes because of horrific beatings. One night, a case worker called me saying, "Randy, I know it's late, but we have a young teenager who needs a home, and if we can't place him with you, the only place left is the jailhouse until we find a place for him."

Later after opening the door, I almost fell back from shock. Very little skin remained on the boy's face. After making a hot chocolate for the boy, the case worker explained. "His mother's boyfriend told him to take a shower, and he refused. So the boyfriend grabbed a Brillo pad and started scrubbing his face with it until it was raw."

Soon after, the case worker left the house. I had been trained for these situations—what to say, what questions to ask. Most abused children blame themselves. Many want to return to their parent in a futile attempt to find the love they desperately need. As a counselor, my objective was to help this child to be open about his anger and emotions. The end goal would be to introduce him to God's love. Otherwise, his feelings would settle into his soul causing him to lash out with aberrant behaviors.

"Jerry (not his real name), I don't know you, but I have no doubt that you are an amazing young man," I said at the kitchen table while he munched on cookies.

"No I'm not," he replied. He kept chewing his cookie while staring at the table.

"I'm a pretty good judge of people, Jerry, and my first impression is usually pretty correct. I see you as a very strong person to get through what you just experienced."

"Right," he said. His head remained downturned.

"Jerry, let me first tell you that what happened to you was very wrong. It is okay to be angry...in fact you should be angry."

"I'm not angry," he quickly replied.

"It was not your fault, Jerry," I said. Jerry pushed his plate of cookies away.

"It was my fault. I should have just taken a shower." He looked up at me with fists clenched.

The boy's open wounds on his face were beginning to scab over. I thought about school, and how anyplace this boy went for weeks thereafter, kids would stare at his scabbed-over face and some would ask what happened.

"Jerry, you refusing to take a shower does not justify what happened to you. Your mom's boyfriend is being charged and he will be judged for committing a crime against you. I'm here to protect you, but I want you to know without any doubt that you did not deserve what happened to you and that you should be angry about it. Right now, I'm furious even thinking about it."

The boy teared. "Can I go to bed now?" he said. The boy smelled of sweat, but no way would I ask him to bathe before going to bed.

"Sure, you're safe now," I said. "Your bed is made in the guest room. Get some sleep."

It took weeks for Jerry to open up about being abused. Eventually he shared his dreams with me. He wanted to be a truck driver. His eyes lit up each time he spoke about driving a semi across the country. His face healed, but the scars underneath remained.

After aging out of foster care, Jerry learned how to be a professional truck driver. He hauls tractor trailers far away from the place of fear where he grew up.

My experiences with abused children revealed that they always carry with them the scars of their abuse. Many of them succumb to alcohol and drug abuse. Some become promiscuous. Sadly, only a few grab on to a purpose like Jerry that allows them to escape their past.

My reason for telling Jerry's story lies at the center of how Jesus saw me in Heaven, and how God sees each of us. I never knew how much harm this world had inflicted on me until experiencing my new body, which felt free of any damage. I felt in Heaven as though I had traded in a junkyard jalopy for a brand-new sports car. Though I could not see my old scars, Jesus saw them. I knew in my spirit that He saw my scars because Jesus carried the scars in His palms as a result of Jesus taking upon Himself all of the scars this world had inflicted upon us. Even in Heaven, Jesus continues to bear our burdens because only He can heal our inner wounds.

Friend, this world and the subtle abuses of others can inflict a similar effect on us. Even the most well-adjusted people carry some scars, either from rejection, failure, or self-judgment. The good news is that God sees our scars but not our faults. Others' rejection is God's redirection. Those broken by this world represent our Lord's most magnificent works. They are like the broken Venus de Milos of the world, the famed Greek statue whose missing arms only serve to accentuate its influence. God chose some grossly damaged people to bring His words to the world. God chose murderers (David and Paul), a prostitute (Mary Magdalene), a burnout (Elijah), a quitter (John Mark), and a denier (Peter) to tell His story.

I started a ministry after receiving many messages from people struggling with thoughts of suicide and other travails. God had taken me on a journey I never thought possible, or even wanted. I started becoming like a pastor to the broken people of this world, which is just about all of us, but my ministry was to those caught in the midst of severe struggles. Some shared their grief through a loved one's suicide. "Will he/she still be able to get to Heaven even after committing suicide?" they commonly asked. One mother noted that her church considered suicide as the "unforgivable sin." My answer? "If suicide is an unforgivable sin, then I would have to assume that physical death is worse than spiritual death; and the Bible in James 1:14-15 states that the full manifestation of sin leads to death, but it is referring to a deadening of the soul…"

"Huh?" she said.

I quickly realized that I was getting too much into the weeds. God does not confuse people. His truths are simple, and our tendency oftentimes is to overcomplicate them. "No," I finally answered. "Suicide is a sin, but the Bible only lists one sin that is unforgivable, and that is rejecting Christ." (See John 3:18.) I could hear her sigh of relief.

"Did you see that in Heaven?" she followed.

Thoughts drifted to my daughter who once attempted suicide.

"I saw the infinite grace of Jesus," I answered. "I have absolutely no doubt that some of the people I saw in Heaven had committed suicide. But here is what I do know. That period between the heart beating and the brain dying is very brief, but if anyone still rejects the love of Jesus after that happens, I suppose they were more foolish than a ballerina on thin ice. Was your son a thinking person?"

"Yes," she said.

It was then that I heard the familiar whisper of my Lord within my heart. "Then imagine him in Heaven, because my spirit tells me it's so, and more importantly I hear the voice of my Lord telling me that your son is with Him now."

Tears ensued.

When I looked into the eyes of Jesus, I saw consummate love. His tight hug impressed upon me Christ's desire to stay close to me through each journey. He knew everything. He sensed each scar inflicted upon my soul, and yet His righteousness perceived only what was right with me. Most of all, Jesus knew that I loved Him. He smiled in response to my love, and I delighted in giving joy to my Lord through my love for Him, because He loved me all the more. Guess what...God even loves your loved ones more than you.

WHAT MAKES GOOD RELIGION?

The Bible is all about God establishing and then reestablishing love with His most treasured creation—you and me. It started with Adam and Eve and ends with John telling about God's reunion with His children. Everything in between speaks of God's love for His children and His attempts to bond with His children. God originally communed in Eden with His children, and subsequently He used judges like Deborah, and kings like David, and prophets like Isaiah, and finally God poured His Spirit into flesh to tell us about Himself through the Spirit of Jesus Christ.

Sometimes God expressed righteous anger, as with conquering the Egyptian persecutors of the Jews, and sometimes He performed miracles and healings to reveal His truth to others. Throughout the Bible a lineage of people was recorded to confirm the prophecies of Christ's birth. The Bible reveals the authenticity of God's love to His people.

Conversely, people have always tried to fit God's love into manmade practices, liturgies, and doctrines. In God's Word, He describes acceptable religion: *"Religion that God our Father accepts as pure and faultless is this: to look after orphans and widows in their distress and to keep oneself from being polluted by the world"* (James 1:27).

In this Scripture, God records both an expression of His love and the discipline required to receive His love. Serving others is the foundation of our purpose in life. Abstaining from the abusive effects of this world results from a disciplined life. Do these things, and God's love will be freed within our souls to motivate us toward doing good works. You and I do not need to be perfect. I repeat—perfection is neither a requirement for salvation nor a requirement to serve God. We need only be obedient, giving, and sensitive to the Spirit's leading.

True joy in life happens in relationship to God. The gist of fifty years of research confirms that relationship, more than any other factor, causes joy. Human relationships will occasionally fail. God will never fail us. When we remain steeped in God's presence, seeking after His truth, and repentant of every wrongdoing that sullies our relationship with God, then we will experience joy regardless of our situation because only then can God relate to us through the hardness of our heart.

God desires relationship with us. Romans 8:26 says that the Spirit of God *"groans"* in intercession for us. The word "groan" means a "deep inarticulate sound made in pain or despair." In Heaven, I heard the groans of my Lord in remembrance of the lost souls here on earth. His countenance changed and He groaned for those whose rejection of Him might eventually lead to hell. The only time I saw the sadness of God was in recognition of those with whom He could not relate because they knew Him not.

> Revelation #24: God's inability to relate to those who do not know Christ saddens God.

In God's paradise, *koinonia* became the modus operandi. Heaven was the first place where social relationships with strangers felt kindred. Families were not comprised by ancestry. There were no marriages and no clans because everyone belonged to the same family. The only family member from this world that I met in Heaven was my grandmother, and although seeing her evoked a familiar affection, a similar fondness resulted from the myriad of saints around me who elicited similar relatedness in Christ. This Christ-centered bond dispelled all of the conflicts we normally experience in this world.

Psychologists reason that hatred stems from a fear of things that are different from us. Everyone in Heaven is of the same mind and familiarity. Hatred ceased in Heaven. Historians claim that the most revolutionary concept that Jesus brought to this world was the idea of returning love for hate, and "turning the other cheek" (see Matthew 5:39; Luke 6:29). Prior to Jesus, the acceptable response to offenses was *"an eye for eye"* (Matthew 5:38).

How can we model Heaven on earth? We can be the face of God in this world. Return hate with love. We can represent a loving God to an unloving world. If people see the love of Christ through us, they will be drawn to know Him. And that, my friend, makes God joyful.

RELATIONSHIP WITH GOD BRINGS JOY

Joy is not the same as happiness. Happiness is situational. We can see a great movie, visit Disneyland, experience a beautiful landscape while on vacation, or enjoy a celebration party, but each of these will eventually end, as will our happiness while enjoying them, especially after we get the bill to pay for those excursions. Joy, on the other hand, is a condition of the heart. Although it is just one of the fruits of the Holy Spirit listed in the book of Galatians, it ranks as probably the most sought-after state of mind among all the people in this world.

The depth and breadth of healthy relationships in a person's life best determines the level of joy in that person. We also know that relationship with Jesus Christ produces the most lasting joy. In John 15:11 (NKJV) Jesus says, *"These things have I spoken to you, that My joy may remain in you, and that your joy may be full."* The fullness of our joy can be found in Heaven. There, everyone exuded abundant joy.

In Heaven my awareness was multiplied to the extent of knowing truths intuitively. One of those truths was that treasures in Heaven do not relate to any material things in this world. Consider what Jesus says in Matthew 6:19-21:

*Do not store up for yourselves treasures on earth, where moths and vermin destroy, and where thieves break in and steal. But store up for yourselves treasures in heaven, where moths and vermin do not destroy, and where thieves do not break in and steal. **For where your treasure is, there your heart will be also.***

Jesus stated that our lasting treasures emerge from the heart. That treasure is the fullness of joy. Our joy can be spoiled by the cares of this world. Only in Heaven did I experience the fullness of joy. I felt it. Others radiated joy. Joy is the ethos of Heaven.

That joy can only be made full through our closeness to God. If you want to experience more joy, then you will need to draw closer to God. But only in Heaven will we experience the fullness of that joy. In Heaven, God is not only close to His children, He is an infusive Companion to those whose spirits come home to Heaven.

> Revelation #25: Joy is directly proportional to a person's closeness to God.

The doors to Heaven open through the restoration of our souls to finally place our spirits as the foremost part of our being. No longer will we walk by faith in Heaven but in close relationship with God. Then, like Moses and Elijah when meeting with Christ on the Mount of Transfiguration with their new bodies, and as I experienced in Heaven, our soul and spirit will reside within our new bodies to fellowship with Christ in a constant state of pure joy.

13

THE MEANING OF LIFE

I GREW UP ON Covered Bridge Road in Cherry Hill, New Jersey, living in a $17,000 house eight blocks from an old covered bridge painted in peeling red. The bridge crossed over a creek below. After school I road my bicycle to go down to the creek looking for tadpoles and box turtles. Sitting on the pebbly ground I would sometimes close my eyes and listen to the trickling waters. Dad worked long hours as a sales manager for a dry ice company, and Mom sold Avon products door to door, and occasionally she served as a census taker.

I heard Mom's voice calling from the roadside above the creek one day. "Randy, I need you to come with me," she said.

Suddenly my attention turned from tadpoles and turtles to Mom's venture going door to door asking people questions about their lives. As a census taker she asked people at their doorways about the number of inhabitants, occupations, age, and interests. Initially I was bored stiff. Being nine years old I hardly wanted to tag along with Mom while she asked people about their lives. Tadpoles and turtles were much more interesting.

One lady answered the door of her apartment and invited us into her living room. Back then in the mid-sixties, furniture was streamlined as were lifestyles. Homes were modest except for the wealthy people I saw on TV, or so I thought. This white-haired lady motioned us to her olive-colored sofa while all I could think about was the musty smell coming at me throughout that place.

"Do you live alone?" my mom asked as she ran down the list of questions on her census form.

"Yes, dear, I lost my husband to cancer. Would you like some cookies, young man?" she asked of me.

"No thank you," I responded. The sooner we got out of that place the sooner I could return to the creek.

"Do you have any children?" Mom asked.

"Oh my. We wanted children, but, no. Are you sure you don't want any cookies?" the old lady insisted.

"No thank you," I said.

"I haven't lived an exceptionally interesting life," the woman continued. "I live alone. I've always been mostly alone except for some people here and there."

The lady continued talking about things other than the census questions my mother asked. It was obvious that she wanted to talk to any listening ear so she could recount her rather mundane life while living here and there and doing this and that. It mattered nothing to me then. But it means a lot to me now.

This incidental meeting only now comes to mind because it speaks to the ordinariness of most lives. Most people do their chores, meet with people occasionally, work, play, etc. Some will be memorialized at the end of their lives and some will be buried in unmarked graves leaving no vestige of their past. Years, maybe decades later, someone may come across a photo, but most lives become relegated to the past with no thought given to people in the present.

Sound depressing? Aha. I am about to "un-depress" you, my friend, because God remembers every detail of our lives, and nothing goes to waste. God knows the number of hairs on our head—or were on our head (Luke 12:7). In fact, the only person who can establish value to our life is God. Our loved ones may validate our worth during their lifetimes, but in time their lives will also be relegated to the past. All of those daily activities will be as nothing to those left behind. But not to God. Even the mundane things in life are important to God. He remembers them all.

My father-in-law, Ron Vanderbilt, has built several houses in the past. He is the only person I know who, in his contractor days, could build an entire house with just a few helping hands. He knows how to install the foundation, utilities, cabinetry, walls, custom designs, and every other component of a house. I have been amazed watching him build constructs that would confound most of us. He calls his houses "living monuments."

Indeed, most of those houses will outlive their occupants. But the sad reality is that most of the occupants in the future will give little or no thought to who built their house. But God knows. He remembers every nail pounded by Ron. He even remembers every drop of sweat in creating them. And it is not the result of Ron's handiwork that God has memorialized, it is the character of the man that finds its imprint in Heaven.

GOD BUILDS MEMORIALS IN HEAVEN

The measure of our life in Heaven happens not just through results. Rather, God evaluates our intentions. While in Heaven God revealed to me impressions of my expressions. He revealed not only what I did, but why I did it. I saw a vision of myself driving in the car and praising God. These visions appeared like a three-dimensional movie with me as one of the actors. God brought to mind some of our conversations.

Jesus exposed my reason for my activities, whether to honor God or to increase my status or to simply kill time. Nothing was considered unimportant. They all formed impressions on my soul, both good and bad. Time spent with God strengthened my soul and counted as "good" to Jesus. Time spent trying to impress others weakened my soul. God did not condemn me for any of my actions, but revealing my life's moments did cause me to wish that I had spent more time with God.

In this world we measure success by the accomplishment of a goal. In Heaven, God measures the value of a person in relationship to Himself. Remember how I referenced God's Word that whatever we do, we should do it as unto the Lord (Colossians 3:23)? Now I know that every time Ron put up a wall or when that old lady offered me cookies when I was a boy, they probably were not mindfully committing all of their works to God in the moments of their activities. But my point is that God knew their hearts, and their hearts compelled them to do good works. Ron did not just build stuff to make money. He wanted to do a great job. That lady did not offer me cookies to just keep us in her apartment so that she could talk on and on. She wanted to make a little boy happy. When I brush my teeth in the morning, I am not just fighting cavities, I am maintaining the temple of God's Holy Spirit. Everything in Heaven is intentional as it should be in this world. Nothing goes to waste in God's Kingdom.

"Beloved," Jesus said to me while we walked the soft and translucent pathway, "you toiled in the world, but tell Me what you are thinking now."

"I am at peace," I responded.

"Yes, you are at peace because I am in you, and you in Me. In the world you toiled for the sake of pleasing others. Here, you find peace because your life is consumed by Me."

"So it's about the being part and not the doing," I said.

Jesus smiled. "My Spirit has told you this, My beloved." That revelation changed me forever.

"So everything I do should be in trusting that You will make it right," I said.

Jesus smiled again.

"Who made you?" he asked.

"You, of course."

"Be at peace in the world, My beloved, for I will turn everything for good, and I will turn your ways toward Me. But you must turn to Me. Stop striving, My beloved. Turn your heart to Me and I will make your paths straight."

At that moment our current path ended, and before me appeared endless ways to any destination of my choice. I knew then that Jesus was showing me a thousand journeys that would always lead to His destination. A thousand roads in Heaven all lead to God.

Revelation #26: Stop striving to do something; rather, trust in God to do a good work through you.

That seemingly fortuitous day with the little old lady while my mother was taking census would have otherwise appeared inconsequential in the scheme of my life. But now it has been memorialized not just in this book, but also in Heaven, as a pivotal lesson that all things work for good to those who are in Jesus Christ (Romans 8:28), even the minutia. The little things in life really do matter to God. That woman positively influenced my life on earth as it was established in Heaven.

WRITING YOUR OBITUARY

My father breathed his final breath following the "Amen" after a few of us recited the Lord's Prayer while holding hands at his bedside. Later that day, I began to recite his obituary: World War II Navy hero, started with nothing and rose the corporate ladder, father of three, married 63 years to my mother; and, then the final sentence for the obituary: "A more virtuous man we have never known." How does that last sentence strike you about my father, Robert William Kay? It expresses not the accomplishments of my father, rather it tells of the character of the man.

How do you want your character to be remembered? I spent almost an hour thinking about the right "character word" for my father before noting the word, virtuous. Virtuous is defined as "having or showing high moral standards." My father had his faults. He was not a saint. However, my lingering memory of him is that he was always trying to do the right thing, and if he failed, he tried to make it right. I think that both he and my mother esteemed integrity above all other characteristics of a person.

What character words do you want someone to use in writing your obituary? Kind? Giving? Loving? Industrious? There are dozens of words that you could use. Think of just one. It is hard, isn't it? Yet thinking of one word to describe our character forces us to sift through all of the other attributes and accomplishments that cloud our ability to determine what is most important. It also prevents us from noting the people and things in our life that, albeit are vital to a life well lived, do not constitute our quintessence—the most typical example of our nature.

The importance of thinking about that one thing is that our goal should be to live as that person. It may not represent the ideal, but it is your ideal. And generally speaking, your ideal is God's ideal for you. Nobody chooses character words like "hateful," "spiteful," or "grumpy." I bet you can think of a few people whose character words might fit that description. Thankfully God does not view the outward appearance of a person. He looks upon the heart. Our heart's desire is to be good. Even the most wicked people often confess that they wish that they could have been better. Only the true reprobates of this world settle for being bad.

Our problem lies with our inability to be good. In speaking to the rich young ruler, Jesus said that *"No one is good—except God alone"* (Mark 10:18). Despite our most noble efforts, we all fall short. The good news is that Jesus makes up for our shortcomings. He fills the gaps of a broken life. He sees the abuses and neglect that damaged a person's soul. He sees the fallen nature of our soul (our thoughts) and our body (our physical desires). Jesus imparts to the believer the heart of God to overlay the effects of a broken heart.

That is why, despite the believer's occasional evil doings, God makes a way to reestablish a heart after God's own heart. But that requires brokenness. It also requires discipline. Most importantly, it requires the humility to ask Jesus Christ for forgiveness.

If you were to write your own obituary, try writing it from the perspective of God's heart toward you. What would you want inscribed on your headstone or memorial plaque? Mine would be something like this: "Loved by Jesus." That is all anyone needs to know about me. Because I was loved by Jesus, I could love others.

My ideal character word would be "Devoted." Devoted means very loving or loyal. No matter how far I stray from my Lord, my heart of hearts desire is to be with Him. I love Jesus, because He first loved me, and His abiding Spirit compels me to love others.

Because my heart is with Christ, and His with mine, I could remember that lady in her living room while my mother was taking census several decades after it happened. I remembered her because God's Spirit reminded me of her. That woman always remains top-of-mind to God. And what I remember most was the Bible sitting on her side table all those years ago. She belonged to Christ.

"But I Did Terrible Things"

Did I see criminals, gang members, or deviants in Heaven? No, I did not. There are only redeemed souls in Heaven, with spirits born through the spiritual blood of Jesus Christ. If I saw a formerly notorious killer in Heaven, I would probably not recognize him because he no longer carried any remnant of his former corruption.

That, my friend, is the incredible irony in Heaven. We can justify people who lived honorable lives being in Heaven, but sinners, rapists, even child molesters? I am about to share with you a very personal story that I have never shared with any stranger previously.

My only brother died of Parkinson's disease a couple of years ago. He served seventeen years in prison. I remember the day my father called me in tears at my office in South San Francisco asking me to leave my work to travel across the Bay so that I could visit him in Walnut Creek. I had never heard my father cry before that time. He would not even fathom interrupting me at work. So his phone call alarmed me.

"Did Mom die?"

"No," he replied. "It's about Doug, he's been arrested."

"What did he do?" I asked.

"Just please come here," he replied.

"Did he murder someone?" My older brother had been the "wild child" growing up. *Maybe he got messed up in some drug deal*, I thought.

"Worse," he replied.

Worse than murder?

My father would not tell me what happened until I got to his house. My mother had already taken a flight to Florida to be with my brother. I felt terrible for my father. He lived a virtuous life. He raised my older sister and his two sons to be honest and hardworking.

"So tell me, what happened?"

"He raped a child," my father said. I could not believe it.

"A child?"

My father continued to explain as much as he had understood about the situation.

A few years later I drove to where my brother was in prison in Florida after I flew to Orlando for a business meeting. My brother was ten years older, and we had never been close because of our age difference, and my brother's teasing as I was growing up.

When I saw him walk through the prison door to enter the meeting area, I was taken aback. My once slender and athletic brother had gained what appeared to be about a hundred pounds. His hair had turned white.

I hugged him and gave him the sealed foods I had purchased from a few of the vending machines lining the back walls. As he sat down, my brother piled the snacks together as if he had not eaten for days. I do not recall our specific words, but most of our conversation focused on his Parkinson's and the inmate assigned to be his caretaker.

And then I mentioned the unmentionable.

"I don't understand why," I said to my brother.

"I don't either," he replied. "It was wrong, and I deserve to be here."

"And God?"

"I believe in God..."

"Jesus Christ?"

"Yes."

"You've asked for His forgiveness?"

"I have."

That was the end of our conversation about the incident. I could tell that my brother did not want to talk about it further. He told me that the other inmates did not know the reason for his imprisonment. Otherwise, he said. "I would probably not be alive."

He wanted to talk about funeral plans. His greatest fear seemed to be the possibility of his dying in that prison.

"I don't want to be buried in the prison yard, please," he said while his hands started shaking and his body began twitching from the Parkinson's.

More than a decade later my brother was released after serving his full term. Two weeks later he died in a hospice facility under the care of the staff and after visiting several times with his daughter as a free man. He was cremated and his service was combined with my mother's service following her death two weeks prior to my brother's passing.

Where is my brother today? Only God knows. I can in no way justify the act of child rape. It is abhorrent to the extreme. Still, I loved my brother despite our lack of closeness throughout his lifetime.

My reason for writing about this painful chapter is not to suggest that God can forgive anyone. I know that is true. My brother believed that Jesus Christ had forgiven him, though he could not forgive himself. God loved my brother and God loved his victim and the victim's family. Just as my father wept after hearing the dreadful news of his son's arrest, I am confident that God wept as well.

As I have said time and time again, God weeps for the lost and for the victims of this world. The evils of this world affect all of us. No sin is beyond Christ's ability to forgive, as painful as that may seem to its victims. In Heaven I saw no victims or perpetrators. People in Heaven reflected the nature of Christ within them.

As an emergency counselor for troubled teens in the past, I know that abused children often grow up to be abusers. To my knowledge, my father never abused my brother, but it is possible that someone else may have abused him. If not sexual abuse, certainly there were times when people silently or verbally called him a "loser," either implicitly or outright. This does not excuse my brother's violent behavior, but it does tend to soften the otherwise unthinkable alternative that he was a monster.

My friend, when God weeps, all Heaven shakes with weeping. And when one sinner repents and is adopted through Christ, all Heaven reverberates thunderous joy. God sees the wounded soul. His forgiveness blots out even the most vile of sins. The blood of Christ purifies each of us if only we ask Christ to forgive us.

Revelation #27: God weeps for the wounded soul and spreads His cleansing righteousness to all who call upon the name of Jesus Christ with pleading hearts. No earthly being is beyond God's ability to forgive.

When I came face-to-face with the Author of Love, the words that sunk into my soul and spirit were beyond any common explanation of love. For me to try to explain that love in worldly terms would be like Michelangelo trying to paint the ceiling of the Sistine Chapel using only stick figures.

All I can say is that the Word, Love, became flesh and lived among the people in the time of Christ, and His name is Jesus Christ. And He loves you beyond your capacity to understand true Love. This I know.

14

THE FINAL JUDGMENT

A ROLLING WIND HOWLED, causing Heaven to tremble. Jesus stilled me with His embrace as airy figures swooped in unison chanting, "Worthy is the Lamb. Holy is the Lord of Hosts. Let all of Heaven and earth rejoice." The light emblazing all of Heaven turned into a penetrating glow through an oncoming storm. It lingered as a roar causing all of creation to look above.

I turned my head to see His blazing face spreading fires like the sun, His arms outspread with the brilliancy of a starry galaxy glistening in light. The light engulfed my Lord so that only one figure appeared in a single stream, glorious and brilliant as a conflagration to things below, and calm to everything in Heaven and to those bathed in the shimmering light of Elohim, the Almighty. Heaven quaked.

This vision appeared to me as a glimpse so intense that it still causes my muscles to tense. It was the only time in Heaven that I actually feared being in Heaven despite the awe of God's majesty—I feared the outcome of those who were lost should they continued to ignore God. It happened at the end of my time with Jesus, just before waking. Now I tend to believe that this appearance came from Theos, the Greek name given for God the Father in the New Testament, as I witnessed the full glory of God ushering forth His appearance from God's throne in another dimension within Heaven. His figure appeared like a marble statue come to life, and His throne was comprised of gems I had only seen in museums. Flames around the throne were topped by misty auras. Angelic figures surrounded God in His glory and a glassy promenade stood before the throne. All this time Jesus remained by my side in oneness with Theos.

Despite being gobsmacked by this spectacle, I still felt comforted and reassured. However, I imagine that if someone did not know the Love of God, he or she would be struck with fear and not the awe with which I beheld this turn of events. In that moment I sensed the absolute power of God Almighty. I also felt judged and approved. I recalled words I had spoken, both those that were empty and those that were full of intention. My life spun before me reminding me of the good and the bad and yet all of it was made good through Christ. Nothing condemned me. Every expression spoke of the grace of Jesus Christ.

My final recollection of Heaven was with the familiar touch of my Friend, Jesus Christ. The glory of God's fullness settled into a pleasant *koinonia* with the One who knew me and believed in me. I left there knowing the overwhelming power of God as well as the tender grace of God. No longer would I think of Him as some distant figure. No longer would I take Him for granted. He is Elohim, El Shaddai, Jehovah—God—the great "I AM."

HOW GOD JUDGES US

My personal opinion is that the two extremes of spiritual teaching—the "fire and brimstone" or the "all roads lead to god" beliefs—portray a misconception of God and creation. God is just.

God is merciful. None of us can fully comprehend how a perfect God can tolerate injustice while allowing the innocent to suffer, because the truth is that God does not tolerate injustice. Our misunderstanding stems from our inability to reason the means through which God executes judgment.

Think of it this way, when a criminal in the world's court system goes before a judge, he or she pleads innocent or guilty. If the plea is "not guilty," the accused must prove his innocence. In the court of the United States of America, the accused is considered innocent of the crime until proven guilty. If the accused admits guilt for the crime, he is normally sent to prison, but not always. Sometimes the guilty person pays a fine or some other form of judgment outside of prison.

Unlike the judge in a human court, God already knows that each of us has committed "crimes." We have lied. We have thought about or acted upon destructive impulses. We have deceived, misrepresented, stolen ideas or things, falsely accused others, rebelled against authority, lusted, and thought about if not acted upon a desire to kill, abuse, or commit other forms of malice. That person who looks like a saint to us is far from being a saint. The person reflected in our mirror is sometimes the accuser of the same offense levied against another person. I, Randy Kay, am guilty of all the above.

"Guilty," a judge would say in court. I have previously discussed Christ's revelation of His forgiveness to me. Those fires I witnessed scorched both Heaven and earth. In Heaven, they evoked awe in conveying God's authority and power. On earth, they consumed all the sins of those forgiven by Jesus Christ, whereas they convicted those without Christ.

Some of those who were convicted went about their lives unaware that they are fugitives from God's judgment. They think that they will not be caught, but they are fools in thinking that they can evade justice. There are those who feel guilty, and all they need to do is turn their lives over to Jesus Christ. Once that happens, the "proxy" judge, Jesus Christ, will exonerate that person.

Acknowledging guilt and asking Jesus Christ for forgiveness may seem like a no-brainer in the scheme of things. As such, why do so many people deny the truth? People look inwardly for grace. They look toward some "enlightened guru" for absolution and peace. They adopt a religion founded on people. Many ignore the fact that one day they will die, and then what? Ignorance is not a justification for absolution. Denial of one's culpability is an avoidance of reality. Failing to seek after the one Person capable of absolution is...well...grievous.

As an agnostic who denied the truth of Jesus Christ, I made this simple prayer to an unknown God, "God, if You are real, show Yourself to me. Open my heart and mind to know You as real as I know anyone in my life." God honored that sincere prayer. He revealed His truth to me. I stepped over the foundation of my own disbeliefs and walked across the bridge of faith to meet an unknown God. Once I got to the other side, I could see Jesus Christ with my spiritual eyes wide open because Jesus breathed new life into my spirit. I was forgiven.

ETERNITY IS REAL

Even those who believe that after this life they will exist in a state of nothingness must come to terms with the fact that no one can slide into an abyss of nonexistence. Nonexistence is the absence of existence, by definition. Nonexistence does not exist as a conclusion in accordance with our language or vernacular. The ontological principle of eternal existence crosses all religions and physics.

The documented testimonies of people who physically walked, talked with, or heard Jesus during His sojourns on earth testify of Christ's reality. The testimonies of hundreds of persons in the most validated documents in all of history—the Bible—represent a collective testimony of Christ's divinity. Their testimonies are corroborated by millions or billions of people who claim to have met Jesus Christ in their spirit. And their testimonies are substantiated by countless near-death experiences from those of us who claimed to have met Jesus Christ in Heaven, or paradise, as spirit to Spirit.

Not only are the probabilities of eternity spoken about by Jesus Christ exponentially confirmed, they are further validated by the documented fact that Jesus Christ reappeared for forty days following His resurrection from an empty tomb that remains empty to this very day. The existence of nonexistence cannot be validated by anyone; however, the existence of eternity has been validated by countless sources including the Originator of those sources, the God of Abraham and the same God who is Jesus Christ.

Jesus claimed to be God. He called Himself by the commonly understood name for God, "I AM," and was found guilty by the Pharisees for claiming to be God in the flesh. Jesus criticized Philip for doubting that Jesus was the Father saying that *"Anyone who has seen me* [Jesus] *has seen the Father"* (John 14:9) If we accept Jesus as God, and we except eternity as fact, and that God has dominion over eternity, then we also must apply God's rules to our existence.

Rule #1 as stated by Jesus: *"Love the Lord your God with all your heart and with all your soul and with all your mind"* (Matthew 22:37).

Rule #2 as stated by Jesus: *"Love your neighbor as yourself"* (Matthew 22:39).

To accomplish rules one and two, we need a power beyond our own capacity. How can anyone possibly abide by either of these two rules all of the time? Through the compelling Spirit of Jesus Christ, we can abide by these rules sometimes, but our mind and body oftentimes get in the way of fulfilling these commandments. It would be like a judge saying to the criminal, "You cannot tell anymore lies. You need to be perfect or else you go to jail."

The grace of Jesus Christ makes up for our imperfection. However, a perfect Kingdom of Heaven cannot include anyone who is imperfect, or else by definition Heaven would become imperfect. An eternity with God requires the controlling influence of Christ's Spirit to become the person we have always wanted to be.

My new body in Heaven appeared in the youthful form of my body on earth, yet what I call "purelescent." Purelescent by my definition combines a luminescence and opaque appearance without any blemishes, and a feeling of being lightweight yet strong. It seemed perfect to me. We cannot be perfect in this world, but we can be made perfect through Christ.

> Revelation #28: We are made perfect
> through Christ and Christ alone.

THE APOCALYPSE FULFILLED

Many believe the Apocalypse to be God's final judgment. The book of Revelation speaks of several judgments rendered by God at the end of our world as we know it. A period of Tribulation will ensue before or after believers in Christ are raptured, according to many scholars. War, plagues, famine, and general lawlessness will prevail during a period when God lifts His protection from this earth and renders final judgment in a world that by and large has rejected Jesus Christ.

This represents a tough pill for many to swallow. Why would a loving God do this? The answer is that a loving God did not do this. People did this to our world. Famines around the world today were caused by warlords and unscrupulous mercenaries who destroyed natural habitats. Wars are initiated by tyrants and terrorists. Disease ravages those exposed to toxins caused by human-infected foods, environmental contagions, genetic flaws, and anxieties.

As an agnostic, I used to cite stories in the Old Testament as evidence of the harshness of the biblical God, like God's order to Joshua in Deuteronomy 20:17 to *"completely destroy"* the tribes of Hittites, Amorites, and Canaanites. What I failed to understand was that many of these tribes were akin to the Nazis, and other terrorist groups. Archeologists are still excavating bones of their victims, some of whom were impaled, beheaded, and tortured alive. The fact remains that all people will eventually die, both those who do good works and those who do evil.

God's mercy is to remove the devourers of this world in order to save the innocent, and sadly, to sometimes remove the innocents to save them from the devourers of this world.

One afternoon I rushed to the hospital surgical area after hearing of an urgent trauma case. When I entered the Operating Room (OR), surgical instruments littered the floor and lying on the operating table was the body of a small boy with long stringy hair. A nurse informed me that a surgeon threw the instrument tray after noticing that there were too many "bleeders," meaning that several of the boy's blood vessels had ruptured in his brain and body.

I later learned that earlier that day the boy had been thrown repeatedly against his apartment's walls by the boy's abusive father.

The boy had died within two minutes after entering the OR suite to repair the massive bleeding caused by severe head trauma. The nurse turned to me knowing I was a Christian and asked, "Why didn't God save that boy?" I answered: "God did save that boy. He rescued him in Heaven, and now he will have the loving Father that this boy always wanted and could never find in this world."

God will always right injustices, even if they must be settled in Heaven or hell. God has protected this world from a massive implosion by virtue of the good works inspired by God's love.

At the end of this era, God will remove His protective covering. Why? Because His plan is to establish His Kingdom both in Heaven and on earth. What that looks like nobody knows for sure. Many of God's final redemptive plans remain a mystery. Some have speculated as to how this will appear. A new Garden of Eden? A connection between Heaven and earth? A transference of Heaven to earth? A transference of earth to Heaven?

TIME IS IRRELEVANT IN HEAVEN

Here is what I know: God will do what is best for His children. It will be perfect. It will be paradise. There will be lots to do in Heaven. In Heaven, I was in a constant state of purposefulness, and others were intentional in accomplishing God's goals. Did they work? You may have heard the old adage: "If you love what you do, you will never work a day in your life." In Heaven, you will accomplish more than you have accomplished in this world through an abundance of joy. Everything done in Heaven is in service to God. There exists no further need to toil in futility because of the corrupted nature of this world. There will be no more beginning and no more ending, and no more time.

Time is a human-made construct. It became a "concept" when Egyptians around 1500 BC used a sundial to measure the period of daylight. In Heaven, time was irrelevant. When time is removed from our environment, an array of opportunities opens for us to live unrestricted by a schedule. In Heaven, the nanoscopic aspects assumed a preeminent position. In this world we strive to comprehend the totality of something—the "10,000-foot perspective." In the process we miss enjoying the moments. In heaven, moments are consuming and relevant. God cares about all of the details from the 10,000-foot perspective as well as caring for the microscopic aspects of life, thus relieving us of the burden to "figure out life." Consequently, time is no longer a factor. Schedules are replaced by doing only what is worthwhile from God's perspective, and that frees us from the burdens of this world.

The judgment of God releases us of the shackles of this world. Imagine waking up to find that there will be no more cause to sleep because life will present endless possibilities that are good. Being compelled to eat at certain times of the day in order to avoid a sugar or energy slump will be unnecessary. All of our desires will be satiated by the Love of Jesus Christ within the immersion of God's presence. Nothing will escape our notice since everything is worthwhile and vital and perfected in Christ. We will be driven through the pleasantly compelling influence of God in all things. This is the Heaven I know.

For the believer in Jesus Christ, judgment is good because our judge is righteous and loving. God wants us to taste only of those experiences that are best; and conversely, God protects us from destructive influences. Apart from love, judgment turns entirely selfish. The God with whom I walked in Heaven was anything but selfish. I learned that God does not desirously condemn unbelievers to hell; rather, God frees all of those made in His image to accept Christ's benevolent authority or to reject that authority. The consequence of rejecting Love as the Person of Jesus Christ is to accept the authority of the rulers in this world who have likewise rejected Jesus. The good news is that there is still time left in this world to choose the only guiltless authority, Jesus Christ.

THE JUDGMENT OF GOD IS SWEET

Here is the flip side: After we are judged in Heaven or on earth, it will be sealed, done, and irrevocable. There are no second chances after God renders His final judgment. Second chances are for those who live and breathe in this world. But beware, there is no promise of another minute or day in this life. The Bible references this life as a mist, it comes and then it goes. From the perspective of Heaven, it is like the blink of an eye.

In Heaven, I had no sense of time, but everything existed in a perpetual state of hope fulfilled. Nothing remained undone. There was no passing of time because time became irrelevant. There was no boredom because God's direction purposed God's design for all of His children. The only time I felt something missing was during the heavenly storm I explained at the beginning of this chapter.

The missing persons were those who have rejected the lordship of Jesus Christ. Perhaps that is you. If so, do not delay. One day you will not have a second chance. One day your body will die. The eternity that awaits you is entirely dependent on your relationship with Jesus Christ.

Now to my brothers and sisters in Christ. We are commissioned by Christ to represent God to a lost world. We are not here simply because of our own volition. We are here because we are sojourners in this world with a divinely appointed job—to become more

Christlike, to become the person God designed us to be through an earnest devotion to Him. By consistently surrendering our will to the overriding will of God's Holy Spirit, we become the person God wants us to be so that we can fulfill the purpose God established for us in this world.

Our job here is similar to our job in Heaven. To stay close to God so that the harkening of God's voice becomes innate, allowing the works of His Spirit to just pour out of us. What an awesome honor to serve the One who loves us the most with our spirit, soul, and body. Bottom line—our primary responsibility is to get closer to God.

God's judgment is sweet to those who know Jesus Christ because His judgment is grace. God's judgment appears harsh to those who only love this world because they know not grace. Eternity is in our future either way.

15

NO MORE DEATH

A FTER ATTENDING THE gravesite of my mother and father at the National Cemetery in Keokuk, Iowa, my eyes sighted a butterfly flitting about. My thoughts turned to my time with Jesus, and the butterfly in Heaven that rested on my shoulder as a lesson in stilling myself with my Lord, listening to His voice of wisdom, and of learning my purpose moment by moment instead of seeking after some grandiose plan.

Uniformly ordered rows of white headstones stood at attention as far as the eyes could see along fields of neatly trimmed grass on rolling hills. I took one last glance at the final marker of my parents' lives, before departing for the airport to return home. A butterfly had rested atop their headstone, gently opening and closing its sloping wings. I rested my eyes on the butterfly while thoughts drifted to the place my parents now lived. In the stillness of my spirit, moments turned to lifetimes, seconds passed timelessly, endlessly. I was still.

In that hallowed place Jesus whispered to my spirit, in silence not with words as before, "My beloved, I am with you always." Impressions expressed God's voice in this place, in this world. A cooling wind whooshed through the warm and humid air and off flew the butterfly. It was time to leave.

As the poet Langston Hughes wrote: "Life is for the living. Death is for the dead. Let life be the music. And death a note unsaid." Before that final note, we can express the love of Jesus Christ in everything we do, before it is too late.

LESSONS FROM THE BUTTERFLY

I no longer believe in coincidences. Heaven impressed this upon me. We are taught to think that randomness must be ordered to avoid chaos, so we plan some busyness to avoid disarray. We feel compelled to talk when faced with awkward pauses in conversation. We strive too often after peoples' expectations to please those who could not care less about us. It is so hard to remain still, even for a few moments, and dwell with God.

The amazing butterfly intrigues me. It thrives in gentle atmospheres. I was surprised to learn that the vivid and bright colors of the butterfly's wings are caused by complex reflections of light called iridescence. A close-up observation of a butterfly will reveal that the wings seem to be covered in dust. Their dust-like scales are angled in place to determine how much light reflects off of them. Various colors and shades depend on how far apart the scales are placed. Different shades and colors appear, depending on how far apart the scales are located. Butterfly wings display colors by the way they reflect light. Even the slightest change in the angle of their scales changes their colors.

Two epiphanies came to mind after learning of God's fascinating design for the butterfly, and how Jesus used the butterfly to teach me about life. First, God always creates a more sublime design than what a cursory observation by our minds can reveal.

And second, the light of Jesus Christ shines brightly over His creations to reveal their beauty.

> Revelation #29: The light of Jesus Christ
> reflects the beauty of His design in
> turning ashes to beauty, death to life.

Jesus sees us like the beautiful butterfly. He does not see the ashes underneath of our flesh. Jesus views us from the light of His Love to reflect Christ's heart in illuminating our wondrous expressions that are beautiful to God's eyes.

The most common recollection from those who passed through an NDE is a bright light. That light stems from the brilliance of Jesus Christ. Such brilliancy would blind the physical eyes and burn the flesh; however, spiritual eyes can behold that light and sense its warmth. The light of Jesus Christ is the way, the life, and the truth (John 14:6). That light illuminates our pathways, gives everlasting life, and guides us with the truth. The key for us is to stay immersed in God's Light so that we can reflect His beauty to others.

BIRTHING LIFE THROUGH DEATH

There is no coincidence in God's Kingdom. And there is no anguishing experience that cannot be redeemed by God. The butterfly I mentioned flew over that cemetery in Keokuk, which interred veterans and their spouses. One of my forefathers is buried there after losing his arm in the Civil War. Trees cast their shadows over gravesites and beautifully manicured lawns covered over buried caskets. Life sprung from the ashes beneath. God always ushers forth life through the ashes.

Death was not in God's original plan. As I have said, this world is God's Plan B. Plan A was to live within an idyllic world called the Garden of Eden. Obedience to God was paramount to abiding in a perfect world, because, as one of my favorite 1950s television shows was titled, *Father Knows Best*. We cannot always make the right decisions. We strive, we struggle, and we oftentimes move beyond God's will to impose our will, thinking we know better. Corruption enters in place of God's will. Perfection cannot survive in the midst of imperfection.

Plan B as chronicled within the Bible was always about atonement. Removing the stain of imperfection caused by rebellion against God's perfect will required someone to assume the imperfections of humankind, and the only One capable of doing this was the embodiment of perfection in Jesus Christ. We struggle on this earth because God's perfect plan has yet to be fully established. Our bodies crave the things of this world. Our soul strays toward the enticements of this temporary home. Our revived spirits fight against the influences of the body and corrupted soul. Whereas now we struggle, in Heaven my spirit body was completely beholden to Jesus Christ such that doing good felt effortless.

In this world, the only way to free us of our defiled body is death. But the good news is that Jesus Christ has overcome death. On the day that our spirits are freed to reunite with Christ, we will be reestablished on God's Plan A, which is uninterrupted communion with the King of kings and Lord of lords.

Many in this world only give a cursory acknowledgment to God. "God is good," "God is in control," "God loves people," and other flippant clichés can mask over our spirit's desperate need to be wholly engaged with our heavenly Father. God requires our all, and in return God gave us His all on the cross. Heaven is the only place where I was capable of giving Christ my all.

Now, God wants our attention. This world distracts us from God. By devoting ourselves to God, we are preparing ourselves for Heaven. My greatest reward in Heaven was complete intimacy with Jesus, but my fondest memories in this world were times when my soul was surrendered to God's will by trusting Him implicitly.

HEAVEN IS OUR DELIVERANCE FROM PERSECUTION

I traveled to a missionary conference in South Carolina several years ago. Many of the missionaries came from the Middle East, where the penalty for proselytizing—sharing the good news of Jesus Christ—is death. I became fascinated with their stories. They told of other missionaries tortured for months and some were even buried alive.

"Your chances of dying in the Middle East must be greater than your chances of living," I said to one young man who dressed modestly. I had noticed from afar that this man rarely deviated from his steady emotional state. When someone joked, he just listened. When someone spoke of the greatness of God, this man never returned the comment with a cliché. He roamed the room with the same placid look.

"Yes, I expect to die there," he said without emotion.

"And that doesn't worry you?" I asked.

"No, this is my calling. I am prepared to die. It's a small price to pay." The man was offered a drink by someone and he politely refused while keeping his eyes squarely focused on mine.

"May I pray for you?" I asked.

"That is the one thing I desire the most from here," he responded. *"Yes."* The man said that final yes with more emotion than I had previously noticed from him.

We prayed in the corner of the room. Mind you, when I pray post my time in Heaven, I can sometimes alarm people with my fervency. I pray not with just a request, I pray with an expectation; and sometimes I pray like a commander barking the general's orders to the troops because now I know the out-and-out authority of God in Heaven and on earth.

The man soaked in my prayers with hands raised in the air. Of course I prayed for his protection, but mostly I prayed that this man would be so consumed with God's presence such that his mind would be inspired to think like the mind of Christ, and that God's Spirit would comfort him during his greatest trials.

Later I learned that this man became lost somewhere in the Middle East. No one was able to retrieve his body, and no one could confirm his death. He simply faded into anonymity until forgotten by most. My spirit told me that he was in Heaven.

Meeting this man reminded me of the Shekinah glory of God that I viewed in Heaven. Shekinah is the Hebrew word for God's dwelling that reflects the brilliance of the Almighty's light from His throne. I witnessed in Heaven figures dressed in gleaming white robes that I knew reflected God's light from His throne. They appeared closest to the throne along with a number of immense angels.

Their lustrous white colored robes were bathed in the spiritual blood of Jesus as explained in the book of Revelation chapter 7:13-17. Now I believe that those figures around the throne were like the young man I met at the mission conference. The saints closest to God gave their all for the sake of Jesus Christ's mission to save the lost, and because they were closest to God's glory they received the ultimate reward in Heaven.

STUDYING SCIENCE AND THE SPIRIT

Friend, although my body clinically died, I never experienced a loss of consciousness. Some scientists have tried to attribute NDEs to physiological responses. They discount the spiritual aspect of human beings as speculation. The spirit cannot be weighed, dissected, or measured. It cannot be reasoned. Neither could scientists in the first century reason electrophysiology or the chemical reactions used by all aerobic organisms. Science will always be trying to catch up to God.

I was a science major at Northwestern University. I have worked in the field of science and healthcare almost my entire career. I have completed graduate courses in physiology, biology, chemistry, cardiology, neurology, epidemiology, anatomy, electrophysiology, and surgery. Nothing in my training explains my NDE because all of these sciences detail characteristics of the physical body. Hence, a scientist is no more qualified to explain the spiritual domain than would be an atheist trying to explain the parables spoken by Jesus Christ.

Certainly, I do not condemn anyone who doubts NDE stories. I was a bona fide skeptic of NDEs before I had my own NDE. Neither do I profess to be exceptional in anyway. My point in establishing the credibility of many NDE accounts is that God is doing something special through them. As mentioned, nothing in God's Kingdom is coincidental. There is a reason Dr. Jeffrey Long, Dr. Mary C. Neal, Dr. Eben Alexander, Dr. John Burke, and numerous other credible clinicians and doctoral PhDs believe in NDEs and the afterlife. John Burke spent more than thirty years researching this topic before completing his book, *Imagine Heaven.*

Near-death experiences (NDEs) are reported by an estimated 200,000 Americans a year, and studies around the world suggest NDEs are a common human experience as confirmed with Dr. Jeffrey Long, radiation oncologist and founder of NDERF, the largest NDE website in the world. Dr. Long stated in his ground-breaking book, *Evidence of the Afterlife,* that "there is currently more scientific evidence to the reality of near death experience (NDE) than there is for how to effectively treat certain forms of cancer."

In a 2005 survey of doctors in the United States, it was shown that 59 percent believe in some form of afterlife. The most notable finding was that doctors, those closest to dying or recently deceased patients, believed in afterlife experiences more than almost all other professions where dying was not an observable part of the job. Many of those trained clinicians who are most discerning of whether afterlife experiences are real have deemed NDEs as a valid experiential outcome.

I believe that God's intention in returning people like me is to testify of His reality, and of His Kingdom. Moreover, I believe that God wants you to know how much He loves you. Who better to validate the reality of God and of Heaven than the people who have been there?

You and I are students of the Spirit of God. Instead of earning an MD or a PhD, we are earning treasures in Heaven. Our joy on earth does not even compare to the joy you will experience in Heaven. Our moments of peace on this earth will be the constant state of our spirit mind in Heaven. Our faint relationship to Christ in this world will be face-to-face in Heaven.

One of my favorite songs is "I Can Only Imagine," composed by Bart Millard. The lyrics begin with these words:

> I can only imagine what it will be like
> When I walk, by Your side
> I can only imagine what my eyes will see
> When Your face is before me
> I can only imagine
> I can only imagine
> Surrounded by Your glory
> What will my heart feel
> Will I dance for You Jesus
> Or in awe of You be still
> Will I stand in Your presence
> Or to my knees will I fall
> Will I sing hallelujah
> Will I be able to speak at all
> I can only imagine
> I can only imagine

I do not need to imagine that moment, because I have been there. When I met Jesus, I cried and dropped to my knees. To this day, whenever anyone asks me to talk about that first meeting, tears well up within my eyes. Sometimes I sob, just like I did in Heaven. Sometimes I do not want to go there, just because that first meeting far exceeds my ability to explain the most profound encounter in my life.

It interested me to learn that Bart Millard faced abuse during his childhood. He grew up mostly without a father's love. It makes perfect sense to me that God would choose to inspire Bart with one of the most beautiful songs ever written because he could fathom the wonderment of being in God's presence having been deprived of that love on earth at a very impressionable age. The brilliance of God's Spirit shines most brightly through the broken lenses of our soul made whole through Jesus.

Friend, we have all been abused in some way, even if that abuse came from some incidental accusation like someone telling us that we are stupid, or treating us like a failure, or dismissing us at a gathering as though we are unimportant. God heals the wounded hearts. He is close to the brokenhearted (Psalm 34:18).

Jesus Christ loves you enough to be spat upon, pierced in the flesh, and hung on a cross. He even went to hell to redeem those of us who were lost for a price that could never be repaid. I only wish that I could even remotely express the love of God for you. No song, no book, no poem, and no message can ever fully express that Love. Please allow me to simply state these words:

The light of Jesus Christ shines His light upon your spiritual wings so that you can express the majestic colors of His love to a broken world, and so that one day, you can fly away to Heaven.

Oh my God...

16

GOD'S LOVE

A WOMAN EMAILED ME after reading my book about bro-kenness. She informed me that she had been contemplating suicide. I was surprised to learn earlier that the number-one audience for this book was people thinking about suicide. I will not note the email verbatim to protect this woman's confidentiality. Here is the gist of what she wrote:

> Randy, I have been saving my pills to take my life. I have been studying about how much would be needed to stop my heart from beating. I had set the date and was ready to end the pain that I have had for years. When I read your book [*Dying to Meet Jesus*] I heard you say that God loves me. Nobody has ever shown me love and I never really believed in God. I asked him to be real like you said. Earlier today he showed up. For the first time in my life I felt loved. I dumped the pills down the toilet and flushed them. Thank you.

I just had one thought after reading this moving account— *I was saved from death so that Christ could save that woman.* In Heaven, I heard the rejoicing over just one person saved by Christ. Jesus pointed below and said, "Your joy is complete in Heaven,

My beloved, but My joy is complete through the saving of one lost soul."

I never thought that God's joy would be incomplete. Would not Christ's joy be more complete than any other person's? After all, Jesus was the personification of joy, or so I thought. Now I understand that God can never be fully satisfied until all who would be saved will be saved. What I mean by that is that God is withholding the final closing of His Kingdom until every person is given the chance to decide whether to follow Jesus Christ or not.

Our joy will not be complete until we arrive where our spirit began, understanding Heaven as though it were the first time, having sojourned in this world undaunted by the past, at the feet of Jesus being refreshed with His river of life, and rediscovered through faith that is realized in Heaven as actuality. Heaven is home.

> Revelation #30: God's joy is not complete until every soul who would possibly give his or her heart to Christ has been reached with the Truth.

THE GOAL IS TO REACH THE UNREACHED

Before the turn of the 21st century, I was a small part of what was called the AD 2000 Movement. The largest church in the world, based in Seoul, South Korea, led this movement and was joined by the Billy Graham Association and some of the largest churches and Christian organizations in the world. The objective of AD 2000 was to reach the "unchurched" with missionaries carrying Bibles translated into their native tongue. The focus was primarily to reach what was called the "Two-Thirds Window," which included most of the Middle East.

The core of AD 2000's mission was based on what is commonly referenced as The Great Commission:

> *Then Jesus came to them and said, "All authority in heaven and on earth has been given to me. Therefore, go and make disciples of all nations, baptizing them in the name of the Father and of the Son and of the Holy Spirit, and teaching them to obey everything I have commanded you. And surely I am with you always, to the very end of the age"* (Matthew 28:18-20).

This movement was the most concerted Christian outreach in my lifetime. It included the mobilization of thousands of Christian organizations and it enlisted more missionaries than at any time in known history up to that period. By the year 2000, the goal would be to reach the ends of the earth with the truth of Jesus Christ. Some believed this to be an end-times mission, whereby once all people around the globe had been given the opportunity to accept or reject Jesus Christ, God's church body would be complete, triggering God's completion of the prophecies in the book of Revelation.

This goal was not fully completed, and it continues to this day under the revised name: AD 2000 and Beyond. Of the more than 17,000 people groups in the world today, it is estimated that there remains slighted more than 7,000 unreached groups.[1] Even if there existed one unreached person, I am confident that God would make available the keys to His Kingdom until that one person decided to accept or reject Jesus Christ.

One of those "unreached" in the jungles of Africa had never heard the name of Jesus Christ. Her gods were manmade wooden figures with whom she could not relate. Her heart yearned for a relationship with One greater than herself. One day she looked into the sky asking for the one true God to reveal Himself to her. The clouds formed a cross. This meant nothing to the woman at the time. She went to a watering hole one morning and explained the odd cloud formation to a friend. Her friend made a cross with her fingers.

"You saw this?" the friend asked while placing her right index finger slightly above the joint of her other index finger.

"Yes," answered the woman. "That is exactly what I saw."

"That is the Christian symbol of the cross where Jesus Christ died," the woman explained. "He claimed to be God."

The woman dropped to her knees. "Jesus, You are the one true God. I give myself to You. Take me."

That woman had sincerely sought the truth, and God honored her sincerity.

I similarly searched for the one true God many years ago. *All Christians are hypocrites*, I thought. A neighbor moved in who modeled the character of Christ more than any other person I had ever met. Witnessing someone who modeled her faith testified to me of the one true God.

Friend, we are Christ's emissaries in this world. God is waiting for us to reach the unreached, and to model the character of Christ.

DOES GOD EVER GET LONELY?

That God is waiting for the proverbial "prodigal children" of this world to return to Him by tarrying before closing the window of opportunity to enter Heaven speaks to God's sense of family. A healthy family unit in life provides support, love, and fellowship. A strong family life is, according to many experts, the most important determinant for a well-adjusted life.

Isolation and loneliness on the other hand can produce depression and illness. A 2010 meta-analysis of 148 studies involving more than 300,000 Americans confirmed this finding: the lonelier someone is, the higher that person's risk of death. Some psychologists equate loneliness to cigarette smoking or eating junk food 24/7, citing inflammation, depression, and higher incidences of suicide as evidence that loneliness can actually kill.

Heaven exuded a familial relationship of everyone to each other. In the beginning, before God created humans, I wondered if God was ever lonely. Then I deduced that God is in three Persons—Father, Son, and Holy Spirit—in a constant state of relationship to each other. A sort of me, myself, and I type of relationship. God is an island to Himself, incomprehensible, and never fully understood. Only God can completely relate to Himself. However, He is not egocentric, or "godcentric"; rather, God is centered on His creation. He is like a benevolent parent whose interest in his children exceeds even his own interest. God's relationship to us remains foremost.

This attitude of "family first" shifts God's focus on keeping His family together. There is an adage that says, "You are only as happy as your least happy child." I can certainly attest to this as a parent. When my daughter began taking drugs, our family was torpedoed. After she was raped at the age of 17, we struggled with mixed emotions, all of them dark. She started cutting her wrists after suffering from mini-strokes. Our once happy family always seemed to live under an oppressive cloud with occasional breaks of sunshine. To say it was hell on earth would be a compliment to hell. This despite living in an upscale neighborhood, blocks from the beach, and making enough money to live in comfort. I would have preferred living in the ghetto if only my family could be made whole.

In similar fashion, a cloud reigns over this world and God sees the pain, the devastation, and those who have run away from Him as a wrenching impediment to His fulfillment. Heaven groans for the lost. A vacuum exists. The names of those who have run away are missing from God's Book of Life, leaving it unfinished. Today my beautiful daughter is our family's most impactful evangelist because she can most empathize with the lost. She bears the scars of redemption within her tender heart.

I came away from Heaven realizing this undeniable fact—we have grossly underestimated God's love. As hard as we may try, the depth and breadth of that love is beyond any other relationship on earth. No loving parent can perfectly emulate God's love. The most loving soulmate can only attain a mere fraction of God's love. God is entirely alone in expressing the magnitude of His love for His children.

Is God alone? Yes. He alone knows love. We only catch glimpses of that love. Even when I was face-to-face with Jesus, I desperately tried in vain to return Christ's love, but I could not. Nothing I could do would even approximate the love Jesus has for me. And that was okay to Jesus.

"My love is sufficient for you, My child," Jesus said.

All I could do was hug Him as tightly as possible. I so enjoyed His smile in knowing that I loved Him as much as I could possibly love anyone.

That final revelation pretty much sums up how Heaven changed me. As hard as I try to please God, I always seem to fail. I can never be found worthy of God's love despite my most earnest attempts. Still, if I can elicit just one more smile on the face of Jesus, I am contented.

Before leaving Heaven, Jesus held my hand and looked at me with the eyes of love.

"I love You," I said to Him.

He smiled, kissed me on the cheek, and that was enough to carry me through a lifetime.

Revelation #31: Pleasing God is the most fulfilling feeling known to humankind.

As we conclude our journey together, I consider our lives as destined to be memories to those we leave behind after we depart this world. Such is the passing nature of this life. Our wonderful hope and our future are to be reunited with those who have passed before us upon entering Heaven. Much grander will be our constant friendship with God face-to-face in Heaven. No matter the state of affairs in this world, our future is destined to be the best part of our lives.

Fear not the inevitability of death, beloved of the Lord Jesus Christ. The truth is that you and I will really never die. Our journey will never end. You and I will remain as friends forever. This life is a temporary mission to serve each other with love. In Heaven, we will be united with Love forever. For that we can be eternally grateful to Jesus Christ.

In the way of righteousness there is life; along that path is immortality (Proverbs 12:28).

Hallelujah!

ONE FINAL LOOK INTO THE EYES OF LOVE

When I first looked into the eyes of Love I knew that Jesus was my home, my friend, my God, and my refuge. So as Jesus held my right hand and cupped my left forearm with his other hand, I knew that my sojourn with Him had ended. *Do I dare look into those eyes knowing that I will miss His gaze when I awake?* I turned my wet eyes toward Jesus for one last look into the eyes of Love. Jesus took His left hand and gently pressed his index finger to the tip of my eye. One teardrop turned into a drip drip drip from His fingertip as I listened to what sounded like a dripping faucet into the well-spring of Christ's rustling river below. But I could not take my eyes away from the eyes of Jesus, and neither would He turn from me. Instead. He rested His forehead onto mine and whispered these words: "Well done my good and faithful servant."

I will always remember His parting words as the ones I most longed to hear upon my arrival into Heaven. He knew they spoke of the promise of my return.

I never told Him that I loved Him in Heaven. He knew. But still, for the record…

"I love you Jesus."

Friend, our time together within these pages has ended. Now having declared my love for Jesus, I leave you with these parting words: Jesus has been with you all this time, and all this time He has been declaring His love for you. Will you turn to Him now, and praise Him with all your heart?

NOTE

1. https://www.quora.com/What-are-the-countries-where-people-have-never-heard-of-Jesus-and-the-gospel-of-Christianity; accessed January 26, 2021.

Conclusion

THIRTY-ONE REVELATIONS

THROUGHOUT THIS BOOK sharing my near-death experience and impressions of Heaven, I cited thirty-one revelations that left a lasting impact on me. May they positively influence you as well:

1. You are like the only person in the world to God.
2. God does not value His children by their actions. Rather, He values their hearts.
3. We can only see God through the eyes of our heart.
4. The flip side of a worldly point of view is that our hearts will determine the merit of our contributions in Heaven.
5. The extent of our love for God determines our Kingdom success.
6. The *doing* part of pleasing God cannot be achieved before the *being* part of wanting to please God is achieved.
7. What we pray on earth is enjoined in Heaven such that God can pour forth His will on earth.

8. On the day we die, what matters most is how we lived our life for God.

9. The only adoration that gains God's approval is our adoration toward Him.

10. The longing we have for something greater is the hope of Heaven, our everlasting home, for which God ultimately designed us.

11. Wisdom is the voice of God telling us what to do.

12. God records all of your life, but failures will not be condemning for the believer—they will only reveal God's grace in a redeeming fashion; and the positive things in this life will overlay everything with God's loving influence so that they will all appear as good and pleasant.

13. A life is never wasted. Even the young in Heaven leave a lasting legacy that lingers in this world.

14. Heaven is more real than this world.

15. The Truth draws us closer to God.

16. Nature speaks of God's creation while Heaven speaks of God's inspiration.

17. Pain, loneliness, grief, and all kinds of sadness are rooted in our separation from God. God feels that separation and yearns to be together.

18. Christ's abiding presence refreshes our soul and gives life to our spirit.

19. Jesus is our Friend, the Holy Spirit is our Inspiration, and God the Father is our Creator.

20. Hell is where God is not. Heaven is where God reigns supreme.

21. The farthest we will ever be from Christ is the closest we will be to thinking we no longer need God's influence.

22. Our communion with God is our spiritual connection to God, and on the day our body dies, that connection ushers us into a full awareness of God's Kingdom.

23. God knows the totality of a person, but we see in part. The objective should be to try to view people through the eyes of God's Spirit, not through our own eyes.

24. God's inability to relate to those who do not know Christ saddens God.

25. Joy is directly proportional to a person's closeness to God.

26. Stop striving to do something; rather, trust in God to do a good work through you.

27. God weeps for the wounded soul and spreads His cleansing righteousness to all who call upon the name of Jesus Christ with pleading hearts. No earthly being is beyond God's ability to forgive.

28. We are made perfect through Christ and Christ alone.

29. The light of Jesus Christ reflects the beauty of His design in turning ashes to beauty, death to life.

30. God's joy is not complete until every soul who would possibly give his or her heart to Christ has been reached with the Truth.

31. Pleasing God is the most fulfilling feeling known to humankind.

ABOUT THE AUTHOR

Randy Kay has founded four companies including a biotech company and media company, served as an executive for Fortune 100 companies such as Johnson & Johnson, and was the corporate operations director for the fastest growing pharmaceutical company in the world. He has served as chairman and board member for numerous nonprofit philanthropies and Christian ministries.

Randy graduated from Northwestern University having completed undergraduate and graduate degrees in science and business with additional advanced certifications and degrees from numerous other organizations and universities including clinical training in cardiovascular minimally invasive surgery, cardiology, neurology, emergency medical services, Christian ministry ordination, and over 200 human-development programs.

Kay has authored seven books. His newest book, *Dying to Meet Jesus*, became an Amazon best seller. He has written more than 1,000 articles that have been read in publications including the *Wall Street Journal* and *Forbes* magazine.

As an ordained minister, Randy Kay is a sought-after Christian speaker and podcaster who can be found at randykay.org. He is also chief learning officer of Pacesetters, a human-development firm, CEO of TenorCorp, a strategic development firm, and founder of Abundant Life, an online Christian personal development site.

Kay has trained and coached more than one million people worldwide. His breakthrough research on thriving in life spans several decades, as he has uncovered practical ways to overcome trials. Kay's near-death experience after his heart stopped for thirty minutes gave him exceptional insight into the afterlife with Jesus Christ.

Randy Kay has appeared on many television programs, podcasts, and blogs such as GodTV, Cornerstone Television, Charisma Media, K-Love radio, and NBC, reaching more than 300 million people worldwide while sharing messages of encouragement. He lives in Carlsbad, California.